A Practical Approach to

EIGHTEENTH-
CENTURY
COUNTERPOINT

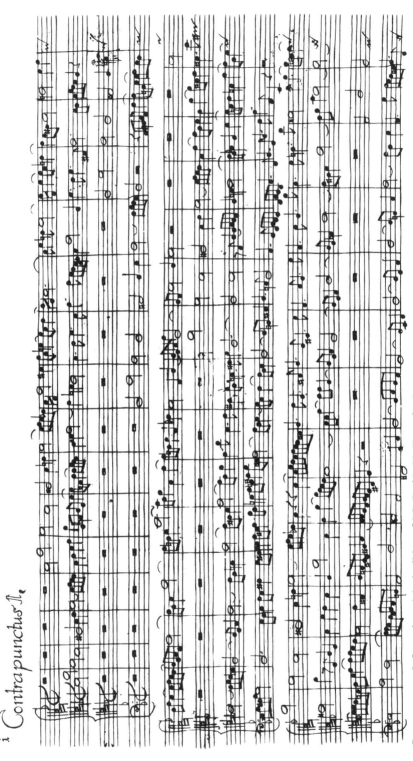

Contrapunctus I, from the original edition of J.S. Bach's *Die Kunst der Fuge*.
Reproduced with permission of the Sibley Music Library, Rochester, New York.

A Practical Approach to

EIGHTEENTH-CENTURY COUNTERPOINT

Robert Gauldin

Eastman School of Music

WAVELAND
PRESS, INC.

Long Grove, Illinois

For information about this book, contact:
Waveland Press, Inc.
4180 IL Route 83, Suite 101
Long Grove, IL 60047-9580
(847) 634-0081
info@waveland.com
www.waveland.com

10-digit ISBN 0-88133-853-2
13-digit ISBN 978-0-88133-853-9

Printed in the United States of America

17   16   15   14

For the moon child

Contents

3

GENERAL CHARACTERISTICS OF COUNTERPOINT; PEDAGOGICAL FOUNDATIONS 33

Pedagogical Foundations of Baroque Polyphony, 35

4

TWO-VOICE NOTE-AGAINST-NOTE COUNTERPOINT 41

Typical Melodic Problems in the Counterpointing Voice, 42
Harmonic Intervals, 43
Melodic Motion between Consecutive Harmonic Intervals, 45
Harmonic Implications, 47
Voice-Leading Reduction, 51
Chordal Dissonance, 53
Tonicization and Modulation within the Phrase, 54

5

SIMPLE DIMINUTION; 2:1 ELABORATION OF THE COUNTERPOINTING VOICE 57

Diminution with Consonant Intervals, 58
Diminution with Dissonant Intervals, 61
Suspensions in Simple Diminution, 66
Chordal Dissonance in Simple Diminution, 67

6

FURTHER RHYTHMIC DIMINUTION; TWO-VOICE CHORALE PRELUDES 69

Further Contrapuntal Diminution, 69
The Two-Voice Chorale Prelude, 75
Compositional Unification in the Chorale Prelude, 75

7

FREE COUNTERPOINT; SIMPLE TWO-REPRISE FORM 83

Simple Two-Reprise Form, 85

8

FURTHER DIMINUTION TECHNIQUES IN TWO-VOICE TEXTURE 96

Figuration Preludes, 102

9

REAL IMITATION AND DOUBLE COUNTERPOINT 107

Real Imitation at the Octave and Fifth, 107
Double Counterpoint at the Octave, 113

10

THE TWO-PART CANON AND INVENTION 117

Two-Part Canon, 117
The Two-Part Invention, 122

11

INTRODUCTION TO THREE-VOICE TEXTURE; NOTE-AGAINST-NOTE AND SIMPLE DIMINUTION 131

Note-Against-Note with Consonance only, 131
Note-Against-Note with Chordal Dissonance, 135
Simple 2:1 Elaboration in Three Voices, 137

12

FURTHER RHYTHMIC DIMINUTION; THREE-VOICE CHORALE PRELUDES 141

Further Rhythmic Diminution, 141
Three-Voice Chorale Preludes, 144

13

CHROMATICISM 155

Non-Structural Chromaticism in the Major Mode, 157
Non-Structural Chromaticism in the Minor Mode, 159
Structural Chromaticism, 162

14

FREE COUNTERPOINT IN THREE VOICES; EXTENDED TWO-REPRISE FORMS 167

Free Counterpoint in Three-Voice Texture, 167
The Baroque Suite, 170
Extended Two-Reprise Forms, 174

15

TONAL IMITATION; FURTHER STUDIES IN INVERTIBLE COUNTERPOINT 177

16

ADDITIONAL CONTRAPUNTAL DEVICES; FURTHER STUDY OF CANON 194

17

THE THREE-VOICE FUGUE 209

18

INTRODUCTION TO FOUR-VOICE TEXTURE; FURTHER STUDY IN CHORALE PRELUDE 229

19

VARIATIONS 244

20

FURTHER STUDIES IN FUGUE 260

21

CHORAL WRITING 276

22

THE PEDAGOGICAL FOUNDATIONS OF COUNTERPOINT
IN THE CLASSICAL PERIOD 289

23

EXAMPLES OF COUNTERPOINT IN THE CLASSICAL PERIOD 298

APPENDIX: CHARACTERISTICS OF DANCE MOVEMENTS 310

BIBLIOGRAPHY 313

INDEX OF NAMES AND WORKS 325

INDEX OF TERMS 331

✕✕

Preface

The purpose of this text is to equip the student with analytical and writing skills in the contrapuntal technique of the eighteenth century. Its orientation is strongly stylistic, dealing basically with the polyphony of the late Baroque period, although the two final chapters explore counterpoint in the Classical era. Three aspects of counterpoint are stressed: history, to establish the origins of different forms[1]; analysis of music literature, often in voice-leading reductions; and practical work in writing counterpoint utilizing various textures, devices, and genre of the period.

The opening chapter reviews some general features of the late Baroque. After a brief survey of melodic characteristics, the study of counterpoint ensues with procedures associated with two, three, and four voices. Each texture is studied in three ways, which become more complex. We will start with note-against-note settings employing *cantus firmus* (usually chorale tunes), then go on to diminution techniques, and finally the chorale prelude. The fixed cantus is dropped in favor of free counterpoint, which is reinforced by the use of dance movements and their two-reprise structure. Finally the topics of imitation and invertible counterpoint are introduced, culminating in the study of canon, invention, and fugue. Chapters

---

[1]For examples, see Chapters 3 and 22.

on chromaticism, contrapuntal devices, variation, and choral writing are also included.

Most musical examples are taken from instrumental works or theoretical treatises of the eighteenth century. A wide sampling of various composers is included, although a majority of the compositions are by J. S. Bach.[2] With the exception of two student pieces, unlabeled music was composed by the author. Almost all of the compositions cited are available in practical editions. It is imperative that the student either purchase or have access to Bach's Two- and Three-Part Inventions and the *Well-Tempered Clavier* (Vol. I and II).[3]

Student assignments consist of analytical problems, error detection, fill-in or completion drills, and original writing projects. In the case of *cantus firmus* exercises, most of the melodies are drawn from the Lutheran chorale literature of the period.[4] Further assignments may be added at the discretion of the instructor. Note, however, that spending too much time polishing the skills of any one chapter may not allow study of later material.

Prerequisite for this manual is a standard two-year course in harmony. It should include some skill in four-voice part-writing with figured bass (triads, seventh chords, and suspensions), chord function with Roman numerals (including secondary dominants, simple mixture chords, and the Neapolitan and augmented-sixth chords), non-harmonic tones, and modulation to closely-related keys. All of these are briefly reviewed in Chapter 1. It would also be helpful if the student has had a survey course dealing with eighteenth century music history, but this is not absolutely necessary.

The ideal time span for covering the material of this text is one year; however, many tonal counterpoint courses last only one semester or quarter. Although it is doubtful that everything can be covered in that time, it was felt that too much information is better than not enough. The teacher should therefore feel free to include or omit material. Indeed, the basic emphasis may be varied — in one situation historical/analytical aspects may be stressed, while in another the acquisition of writing skills may be the basic goal.

Following an appendix on dance movements, there is an extensive bibliography on counterpoint texts, treatises, related books, articles, and analyses, with some annotations in the first two sections. Indices on composers/works and terms are included.

The author wishes to acknowledge the assistance of Alfred Mann, who kindly offered suggestions for many of the historical and bibliographical portions of the text. The staffs of the Sibley Music Library

---

[2]For the less well-known Bach compositions, *Bach Werke Verzeichnis* (or BWV) numbers will be included.

[3]Reprints of these from the *Bach Gesellschaft* edition are available from Dover Publications, Inc. The Peters editions are also reliable.

[4]An attempt has been made to include the more important and familiar chorale tunes.

(Rochester, New York) and the Music Faculty and Bodleian Libraries (Oxford University) were particularly helpful in securing scores, theoretical treatises, and reference sources. Finally a special token of appreciation goes to the author's wife, whose hours of proofing and typing provided a special encouragement.

1

⚹⚹⚹

Introduction

This chapter highlights some characteristics of the late Baroque period, approximately 1685–1750 (the dates of its greatest master, Johann Sebastian Bach). We will review general aesthetics, texture, aspects of formal construction, performance practice, thoroughbass, the major-minor tonal system, cadence formulas, and sequence patterns. Much of this material may be familiar to students who have studied harmony. Nevertheless it should be a useful review prior to studying polyphony.

The late Baroque period was one of intense musical activity. Among its more renowned composers were, in Germany, J. S. Bach and his son Karl Philipp Emanuel (1714–1788), Dietrich Buxtehude (1637–1707), Johann Pachelbel (1653–1706), Johann Kuhnau (1660–1722), Johann Gottfried Walther (1684–1748), Georg Phillipp Telemann (1681–1767), and Georg Böhm (1661–1733); in Italy and Spain Arcangelo Corelli (1653–1713), Antonio Vivaldi (1678–1741), and Domenico Scarlatti (1685–1757); in France François Couperin (1668–1733), and Jean-Philippe Rameau (1683–1764); and in England George Frederick Handel (1685–1759) during the latter part of his career. Important theorists include Friedrich Erhardt Niedt (1674–1708), Johann Mattheson (1681–1764), Johann Fux (1660–1741), Johann David Heinichen (1683–1729), Friedrich Wilhelm Marpurg (1718–1795), Jean-Philippe Rameau (1683–

1764), and somewhat later Johann Kirnberger (1721–1783) and K. P. E. Bach (1714–1788).[1]

DOCTRINE OF THE AFFECTIONS

This term, *Affektenlehre*, coined by musicologists of the last century, refers to how the Baroque composer was expected to move the affections of his audience. Discussions of this principle in treatises of the period involved many analogies between rhetoric and music. In vocal works the text should be given an appropriate musical setting to effectively reinforce specific emotions it might convey: joy, love, hate, or sadness.[2] From this marriage of words and tone (or *text painting*) evolved a number of stereotyped musical figures (such as the "half-step sigh"), which often surfaced in purely instrumental compositions—hence the expression *Doctrine of Musical Figures*. Individual movements, both vocal and instrumental, tended to express one affection. This "affective unity" controlled the musical material and its subsequent development to such an extent that contrasts of mood or ideas were minimalized.

TEXTURE

The texture of this music is contrapuntal. The concept of "melody and chordal accompaniment", with the possible exception of the recitative, is foreign to this style. Even a well defined melodic foreground is supported by voice parts that are linearly rather than harmonically derived. The polyphony of the late Baroque may be relegated to four general categories:

1. A preexistent or original *cantus firmus* (fixed melody) could be set in a contrapuntal environment. Such pieces may incorporate a chorale tune (chorale preludes) or a recurring bass theme, as in some continuous variations. Even chorale "harmonizations" arise from counterpoint.

2. *Continuo* polyphony may occur in solo arias (often with an instrumental obbligato) and solo and trio sonatas. In this case, the *basso continuo* and one or more of the upper voices determine the piece.

3. Many dance movements and keyboard genre (preludes, fantasias) dispense with both the cantus and continuo, thereby permitting an independent interaction between the voices. The term *free counterpoint* seems appropriate, although, as we shall see, polyphony is never completely "free."

4. Finally, *imitative* pieces (such as fugue), which are based on one or

---

[1]See under Treatises in the Bibliography.
[2]The relation of text to music will be explored further in chapter 21.

more subjects and their contrapuntal associates exhibit greater equality of the separate voices. Their entry and exit is strictly accounted for through the use of rests.

ASPECTS OF FORMAL CONSTRUCTION

Compositional structure is determined more by tonal centers than by thematic contrast. The initial idea forms the material basis for the remainder of the piece. There is a great economy of means; a few motivic figures undergo intensive development through repetition, modulation, sequence, or melodic mirror. With the exception of some smaller dance forms, there is little sense of periodic phrasing.

Once a new key is reached and confirmed cadentially, the music will frequently veer off immediately toward some new tonal goal. The resultant tonal hierarchy in relation to the original tonic is crucial in defining the formal scheme of a composition.

PERFORMANCE PRACTICE AND MUSICAL EDITIONS

Our knowledge of the performance practice (*Aufführungpraxis*) of the late Baroque has expanded enormously in the last fifty years.[3] Even volunteer church choirs performing the *Messiah* have not been exempt from this progress. Most historians point out the different mannerisms of the Italian versus the French school, and the occasional interaction of both in such composers as J. S. Bach. The responsibilities of the keyboard player in regard to thoroughbass realization and accompaniment are treated in great detail by some contemporary treatises.[4] The question of ornamentation, either notated or improvised, is vast and sometimes confusing.[5] The application of certain rhythmic conventions (such as dotted values and *notes inégales*), with revised notions of tempi and dynamics have often transformed the character of familiar pieces. A concerted attempt to perform works on either restored instruments of the era or accurate reproductions has had repercussions on our perception of Baroque timbre.

The C clefs (soprano, alto, and tenor) were traditionally used in vocal and keyboard pieces for notating the upper voices. In this text the G or

---

[3]For a good survey of Baroque performance practice see Robert Donington, *A Performer's Guide to Baroque Music* (London: Faber and Faber, 1973).

[4]In particular Johann Heinichen and K. P. E. Bach; see under Treatises in the Bibliography.

[5]For a comprehensive treatment of this subject see Frederich Neumann, *Ornamentation in Baroque and Post-Baroque Music* (Princeton: Princeton University Press, 1978). Less ambitious is Walter Emery, *Bach's Ornaments* (London: Novello, 1953).

treble, along with the familiar bass clef, has been substituted. The accidentals in key signatures were sometimes on different lines or spaces from those to which we are accustomed (see Ex. 17-7); these have also been modified. Dynamic markings were used quite sparingly, more usually in ensemble music. They consist solely of a written out *forte* or *piano* (echo effects are a typical example); no crescendo/diminuendo markings exist. Contrasts of loudness levels were achieved through the sudden addition or subtraction of voice parts (or organ stops), a device termed *terraced dynamics.*

Scholarly editions of Baroque music attempt to arrive at the most accurate possible version of the music through a careful comparison of various autographs, copies, and early printed editions. They contain no markings other than those authentic with the composer's intents. Complete works of composers or reprints from these are typical examples.[6] *Practical* editions are slanted more toward the immediate needs of the performer. They may include fingerings, pedaling, articulations and phrase markings, dynamics, and tempo suggestions inserted at the discretion of the editor. A note of caution is advised, since some older practical editions reflect the performance practice of the Romantic rather than the Baroque period. Some editions happily combine both scholarly and practical aspects; any editorial additions can be distinguished from the composer's original markings.[7]

THOROUGHBASS

The Baroque has been called the era of the *thoroughbass.* It served as the textural/harmonic foundation for most choral pieces, ensembles, arias, and instrumental sonatas of the period. Other equivalent terms are *basso continuo* (Italian), *basse continue* (French), and *Generalbass* (German). It consisted of a bass instrument (usually cello or bassoon) and a *Klavier* or keyboard instrument (usually harpsichord or organ). The bass line of the keyboard, which is doubled by the cello, was *figured* with intervallic numerals, so that the player *realized* chords above it by filling in the gap between the lowest voice and the upper parts of the score—hence the expression *figured bass.*[8] Since this text will make continual use of figured bass notation, it is imperative that you are thoroughly familiar with the symbols and their realization.

---

[6]The Dover reprints, for instance.

[7]Bischoff's editions of some of Bach's keyboard works published by Kalmus are good examples of this latter category.

[8]*Unfigured bass* was also prevalent. Here the performer had to rely on his knowledge of *implied* harmonies to realize the accompaniment.

Although figured (or unfigured) bass served an eminently practical purpose in the *continuo* of the Baroque, it was later utilized for more theoretical reasons. The figures became a kind of musical "shorthand", inserted to denote specific or implied intervals and chords above the bass, and could even indicate the linear voice leading of the upper parts. In two-and three-voice excerpts in this text where added figured bass symbols are employed, they will be inclosed in parentheses.

Figured bass numbers refer to *intervals above the bass,* not to chord members. In ⁵₃, the 3 may be the third of the triad, but in ⁶₄ it is the fifth. In modern practice compound intervals are normally reduced within the octave (12 = 5, 10 = 3). Although the notational procedure of that period was to denote the figures *above* the bass, they will be placed in their customary position beneath the bass clef. A review of the bass symbols for triads, nonharmonic tones, suspensions, and chordal dissonance follows. All employ four-voice texture, either in close or open structure.

The thoroughbass treatises in the Baroque speak of "chords of the 5th" and "chords of the 6th". In modern terminology this means root position (⁵₃) and first inversion (⁶₃) respectively. Common abbreviations omitted the ⁵₃ altogether and shortened the ⁶₃ to simply 6 (see Ex. 1-1A). A change of inversion over a common bass note is denoted by 5–6 (Ex. 1-1B). Unusual chordal doublings are rarely indicated in figured bass practice. It is important to remember that the intervals above the bass are always realized in accordance with the prevailing *key signature* of the composition. Any accidental above the bass (but not the bass itself) must be indicated. In the case of the third (3) a single accidental suffices (Ex. 1-1C). For others consult Ex. 1-1D, noting the use of the slash (𝟨̸) to raise a note one half step.

EXAMPLE 1-1 Figured bass symbols for triads

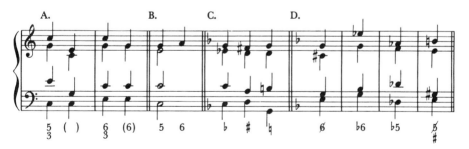

Figured bass does *not* normally denote the sometimes intricate non-harmonic activity in the upper voices. This is usually of little concern to the performer in realizing his basically chordal accompaniment. In those instances where they might appear, the resultant intervallic relations above the bass are written out in a linear fashion. Some typical illustrations of unaccented dissonance, shown in Example 1-2A, are the passing tone (P), neighboring tone (N), anticipation (A), escape tone (E), and leaping tone (L). The last three are sometimes called *incomplete neighbors* (IN). Several *appoggiaturas* (or accented dissonance which resolves by step) arc cited in Ex. 1-2B.

EXAMPLE 1-2 Non-harmonic activity above the bass

Suspensions may occur above the bass or in the lowest voice itself. The former category consists of the $\binom{5\text{-}5}{4\text{-}3}$ (see Ex. 1-3A), the $\binom{9\text{-}8}{3\text{-}3}$, and the $\binom{7\text{-}6}{3\text{-}3}$; the numbers in parenthesis are usually understood. The 4–3 and 9–8 normally resolve to root-position chords. Observe the common cadential formula $\frac{6\text{-}5}{4\text{-}3}$, which is in reality a suspended "dominant" (Ex. 1-3B). The 9–8 sometimes features a *change of bass* upon the resolution of the suspension (Ex. 1-3C). The 2–1 is actually the 9–8 by octave displacement (Ex. 1-3D); it is somewhat rare. While the dissonant or suspended note is usually tied over from the preceding consonance, it can also be reiterated: compare Ex. 1-3A and 3C. In general, 4–3s occur over scale degrees $\hat{1}$, $\hat{3}$ and $\hat{5}$ in the bass, while the 9–8 favors $\hat{1}$, $\hat{6}$, and $\hat{4}$. The 7–6 suspension, resolving into a first inversion, can be found on any scale step, quite often in succession (Ex. 1-3E). Bass suspensions are customarily limited to the $\frac{5\text{-}6}{2\text{-}3}$ (Ex. 1-3F).

Chordal dissonance or chords of the 7, $\frac{6}{5}$, $\frac{4}{3}$, and $\frac{4}{2}$ are what we call seventh chords today. The dissonance arising from the seventh originates in the voice leading practice of the earlier Renaissance. In the Baroque period they continue to be approached (prepared) and left (resolved) like some non-harmonic tones, in particular the suspension, and passing,

EXAMPLE 1-3 Figured bass symbols for suspensions

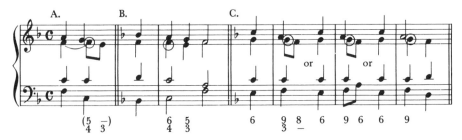

neighboring and leaping tones. Some typical examples of the various seventh-chord "inversions" are listed in Ex. 1-4A through D, with the relation of the chordal seventh to a specific non-harmonic idiom indicated. Note the common "passing $\frac{6}{4}$" device in Ex. 1-4B, which bridges the 6 and $\frac{6}{5}$. The $\frac{4}{3}$ chord is infrequent, again usually relegated to a passing function. The subjects of non-harmonic tones, suspensions, and chordal dissonance in regard to two-voice contrapuntal settings will be discussed in greater detail in Chapters 4 and 5.

EXAMPLE 1-4 Figured bass symbols for seventh chords

THE MAJOR-MINOR MODES AND THEIR DIATONIC SCALE DEGREES

By around 1700 the familiar major-minor tonal system was well established. Example 1-5 illustrates these scales. In the major mode (Ex. 1-5A) scale degrees $\hat{1}$, $\hat{3}$, and $\hat{5}$ are relatively stable, with the remainder (noted in black) assuming a more "active" status. The 5th degree (or dominant) can be either, depending on its harmonic association. The minor mode (Ex. 1-5B) is somewhat more complex. Although the more passive degrees ($\hat{1}$, $\hat{3}$, and $\hat{5}$) remain, the number of diatonic scale steps is increased by the use of both lowered *and* raised 6th and 7th tones. This produces a potential nine-tone system, which may be divided into a diatonic pentachord ($\hat{1}$ up to $\hat{5}$) and a chromatic tetrachord ($\hat{5}$ up to $\hat{8}$). When ascending from $\hat{5}$ to $\hat{8}$ the raised degrees are employed ($\hat{5}$ #$\hat{6}$ #$\hat{7}$ $\hat{8}$), while falling motion uses the lowered degrees ($\hat{8}$ ♭$\hat{7}$ ♭$\hat{6}$ $\hat{5}$); see Ex. 1-5C. The raised mediant in minor (or so-called *Picardy third*) is occasionally encountered in the final chord of compositions in the minor mode (Ex. 1-5D).

EXAMPLE 1-5 Diatonic scale degrees in the major and minor modes

The few vestiges of the Renaissance modal system that remain occur mostly in chorale tunes which may have originated during that period. Purely "modal" settings of such melodies are rare, since the phrases are almost always harmonized in terms of major or minor keys. The opening phrases of two of these are cited in Ex. 1-6. Aside from the chorales the use of modal key signatures is infrequent, although one may be found for no apparent reason.[9]

EXAMPLE 1-6 Harmonizations of modal chorale melodies   *Aus tiefer Not* (Phrygian)

[9]For example, the first version of Bach's C minor Prelude (*WTC* I) appears in his *Klavierbüchlein* with a key signature of two flats (see Example 8-18).

Der du bist drei in Einigkeit (Mixolydian)

DIATONIC CHORDS AND THEIR HARMONIC FUNCTION

Viewing the settings of Ex. 1-6 you might assume that the various "triads and seventh chords" would form progressions conforming to functional harmony. But this would be viewing the music through contemporary glasses colored by analytical procedures of the present century. Obviously the musical style and practice of the late Baroque does share common characteristics with concepts of tonal harmony. But how did the theorists of that period (excepting Rameau) treat this question of functional tonal progression? There were two ways. The first deals with possible chords implied above a given bass note. Gasparini (1708) states the Rule of the Octave (*Regola dell' ottava*), in which the diatonic scale degrees in the bass may support either a chord of the 5th or the 6th ($\frac{5}{3}$ or $\frac{6}{3}$).[10] In his discussion on unfigured bass, Heinichen (1728) refines this with eight special rules.[11] The results of these are summarized (with some slight additions) in Ex. 1-7. The initial figures under each scale step denote the most common possibility, those to the right indicate less frequent usage, while the ones in parentheses are somewhat rare. Chords of the 7, $\frac{6}{5}$, and $\frac{4}{2}$ might also be appended; in general those bass notes carrying a 7 resolve a fifth lower, $\frac{6}{5}$ a step higher, and $\frac{4}{2}$ a step lower. Thus we have the spectrum of possible diatonic chords available in the major-minor modes of this period.

EXAMPLE 1-7 Possible diatonic chords on the bass scale degrees

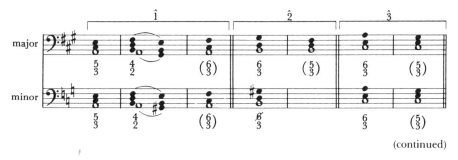

(continued)

[10]Francesco Gasparini, *L'armonico pratico al cimbalo* (1708).
[11]Johann David Heinichen, *Der Generalbass in der Komposition* (1728).

EXAMPLE 1-7 (cont'd)

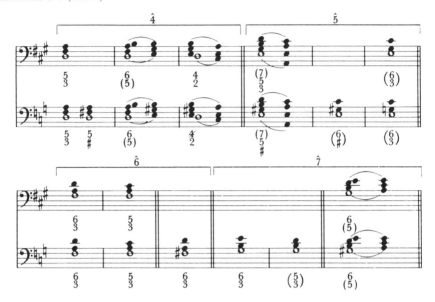

For the most part, this chart does not tell us the *tendency* of a bass note, with its supporting chord, to move to another bass note and chord. It does not establish the probability of chordal succession. Heinichen suggests eight rules for this. For instance, if the bass descends a half-step, the second note will carry a 6. From such lists of "expectations" may be deduced a general theory of harmonic function in this period. This was Rameau's great contribution, although he explained it in terms of a hypothetical *fundamental bass* (*basse fondamentale*) consisting of the roots of the chords in descending fifth progression, rather than by the more linear concepts of pure thoroughbass.

Using present day terminology, harmonic function can be confined to three basic "classifications" of chords (see Fig. 1-1). The *pre-dominant* category tends to progress in either direct or indirect fashion to the *dominant* group, which in turn resolves to the *tonic* of the key. A succession of fifth relations, *a la* Rameau, is produced by III → VI → II → V → I. This principle is particularly evident in Baroque music when approaching cadences. However, in phrase interiors and especially sequence passages it is not always operative. Although Roman numerals as a means of denoting such functions were foreign to thoroughbass and not even employed by Rameau, they will be utilized intermittently in this text where harmonic progressions are clearly implied. For the most part either figured bass symbols or simply vertical intervals between the outer parts will suffice. Chapter 4, will introduce some reductive techniques to better define melodic/harmonic forces in the underlying voice leading of a passage.

FIGURE 1-1 Basic classification of diatonic chords in functional harmony

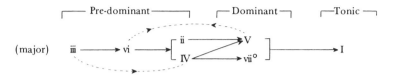

NON-DIATONIC SCALE DEGREES AND CHORDS

"Altered" chords arise from non-diatonic tones in one (or more) of the melodic lines. In most cases the inserted accidental increases the tendency of the note to "resolve" by half-step to its adjacent tone, like a "secondary" leading tone ($\sharp\hat{4} \to \hat{5}$, $\sharp\hat{1} \to \hat{2}$, or $\flat\hat{7} \to \hat{6}$). The more common of these are listed in Ex. 1-8 in both major and minor modes. This results in a category of chords known as *applied* or *secondary dominants*, since they momentarily "tonicize" a scale step other than tonic by preceding it with some form of "dominant" function. Scale degrees $\hat{7}$ in major and $\hat{2}$, $\sharp\hat{6}$, and $\sharp\hat{7}$ in minor cannot be tonicized, since they support a diminished triad.

EXAMPLE 1-8 Tonicized scale degrees and their attendant altered tones

These applied dominants may take the form of a functional V, V⁷, vii°⁶, or vii°⁷ in various inversions. A diatonic ii triad in D major is illustrated in Ex. 1-9 with these tonicizing chords. Observe the similarity between inversions of the V⁷ and vii°⁷ (V⁶₅ = vii°⁷, V⁴₂ = vii°⁴₃,). The vii° triad always appears in ⁶₃.

EXAMPLE 1-9 Various applied dominant chords (tonicizing ii in D)

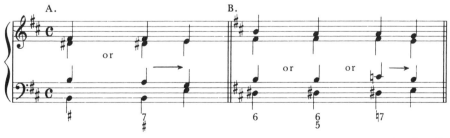

(continued)

EXAMPLE 1-9 (cont'd)

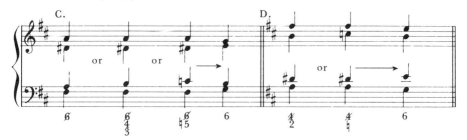

Non-dominant altered chords are much less common. The iv and bVI in major borrow tones from the parallel minor mode (b6 and b$\hat{3}$), hence the expression *mixture* chords (see Ex. 1-10A). The notorious Neapolitan sixth (bII⁶) mainly occurs in minor keys (Ex. 1-10B), as does the rare augmented sixth, a "linear" sonority employing a double half-step resolution to $\hat{5}$. Note the dual neighboring effect of f♯ and a♭ to the dominant in Ex. 1-10C; the $^6_4$ chords result from passing motion and suspension technique.

EXAMPLE 1-10 Non-dominant altered chords

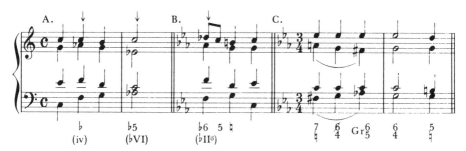

MODULATION

Modulation, or shift of tonal center, may be thought of as an extended tonicization of a particular scale degree at a higher structural level. The somewhat restless tonal nature of much Baroque music gives rise to the frequent use of modulatory procedures, particularly in longer movements where some sense of key contrast is imperative. Figure 1-2 illustrates normal key relationships (called *diatonically* -or *closely-related* keys) to the major and minor modes. Observe that the relative keys of C major and A minor hold six triads in common, each of which can serve as a potential tonic. The two diminished chords, of course, cannot be tonicized. The various accidentals necessary for the tonicization of these closely-related keys are also listed below. The total collection amounts to only five different accidentals:

C♯ D♯ F♯ G♯ B♭. This allowed the performers of that time to tune their keyboard instruments in one of the prevalent "mean-tone" tempered systems, so that by using only diatonic harmonies in the various keys related to C major or A minor, no enharmonics (which could differ from each other by as much as a ¼ of a tone) need result. One may sometimes encounter a "double" closely-related system in a piece; not only are all the keys employed related to the original tonic, but *successive* keys are also closely related.

FIGURE 1-2 **Closely related keys in major and minor modes**

C:		I	ii	iii	IV	V	vi	(vii°)	I
(keys)		C	d	e	F	G	a		
a: i	(ii°)	III	iv	v	VI	VII	i		
		B♯	D♯	B♭	F♯	G♯			
		C♯	F♯			F♯		Accidentals necessary	
		(F♯)	C♯			(C♯)		for tonicization	
			(G♯)						

(Total = C♯, D♯, F♯, G♯, B♭)

Most modulations are by *direct* key change (at the conclusions and beginnings of sections), *pivot* or common chord, and *chromatic* inflection. Examples of enharmonic tonal shifts are usually limited to more fantasia-like compositions, where non-diatonic or *foreign* modulations may abound.

CADENTIAL FORMULAS

Cadences (from *cadere*—to fall) represent rhythmic/tonal punctuations in the musical flow. Each period of music history has devised clichés associated with cadential formulas. These may include stereotyped soprano and bass melodic movements, harmonic progressions, rhythmic figuration, non-harmonic activity, and suspensions. The reference chart (Ex. 1-11) lists some of the more commonly employed cadences in the late Baroque period. Soprano scale degrees and a functional harmonic analysis for the block-chordal formulas are indicated; typical rhythmic and dissonant figuration will be appended in later chapters. The initial sonority represents one frequent approach to the cadence proper, others are also possible. Most examples are given in the major mode, but only a key signature for C minor and a consistent ♮$\hat{7}$ is necessary to convert them to the opposite mode.

EXAMPLE 1-11 Typical cadential formulas

A. Perfect authentic

B.

C. Imperfect authentic

D.

E. Half

F. Phrygian

G. Deceptive

Remember that a cadence is not merely a progression of two chords. It represents the tonal goal of its preceding phrase. The *melodic* tendency of the soprano is just as important as the harmonies which support it. Example 1-11 shows that maximum harmonic stability is preferred via the use of root-position chords. The soprano scale degrees tend to operate in close proximity to the tonic tone. The final chord of the cadence coincides with a strong metric beat.

Referring now to Ex. 1-11, the *perfect authentic* category is the most "conclusive" in effect. It is the only type of cadence allowed to *end* a movement,[12] although it can certainly occur elsewhere. Note the strong bass $\hat{5}$ to $\hat{1}$ and the stepwise approach to tonic in the upper voice, either $\hat{2}$ to $\hat{1}$ (Ex. 1-11A) or $\hat{7}$ to $\hat{8}$ (Ex. 1-11B). The remaining formulas appear only as interior punctuation. *Imperfect* cadences likewise proceed to the tonic chord but with a less conclusive soprano tone $\hat{3}$ or $\hat{5}$ (Ex. 1-11C). Example 1-11D is normally included in this group due to the absence of a fifth relation in the bass. *Half* closes are "suspensive" in nature, since they cadence on the active dominant harmony; the more restless $\hat{2}$ or $\hat{7}$ may be observed in the soprano (Ex. 1-11E). The formula of Ex. 1-11F is termed a *Phrygian cadence*, since the stepwise movement to the final octave is reminiscent of the earlier Renaissance model; it occurs only in the minor mode. Finally, *deceptive* cadences simply substitute an ascending step motion for the usual fifth found in the bass of the authentic formulas. The two instances in Ex. 1-11G are illustrated in minor to show the necessity of doubling the third in the last chord.

SEQUENTIAL PATTERNS

The use of melodic/harmonic sequence is frequent in the late Baroque period. These patterns may exhibit harmonic root movement by intervals of seconds, thirds, or fifths (fourths), either ascending or descending. Since the diatonic pitch collection consists of *seven* tones—a prime number—it produces a hierarchy of sequential motion. The top line of Fig. 1-3 represents a succession of seconds. Alternating pitches create a pattern by thirds, which in turn gives rise to fifth relations. The last line returns back to secundal movement once again, albeit now at a more advanced structural level.

A selection of the more common sequential models or paradigms are given in Ex. 1-12. They are illustrated in three- or four-voice settings. A figured bass is supplied, and occasional internal numbers clarify the intervallic relations between the outer parts. The beaming represents connec-

[12]Occasionally slow movements in sonatas or concertos may conclude with a Phrygian cadence, provided that the tonic key is minor.

FIGURE 1-3 Hierarchy of root movement in sequential patterns

C	B	A	G	F	E	D	C	B	A	G	F	E	D	C	B	A	G	F	E	D	C	B	A	G F E D C by 2nd
C		A		F		D		B		G		E		C		A		F		D		B		G		E	C by 3rd
C				F				B				E				A				D				G	C by 5th
C								B								A								G	by 2nd

(right margin: surface → structural)

tions between the more structural (stemmed) notes. Examples 1-12A through 12C illustrate *stepwise* voice-leading at the surface level. The succession of descending 6th chords in Ex. 1-12A is often elaborated by the use of 7–6 suspensions. When the upper parts are inverted, a series of parallel fifths results (Ex. 1-12B); these may be successfully "staggered" by resorting to the suspensions again. A similar problem exists in the *ascending* movement of Ex. 1-12C, which is now alleviated through the employment of a 5–6 pattern.

Examples 1-12D through 12L feature root movement by fifth, usually in descending motion. The beaming denotes an underlying stepwise framework. Example 1-12D utilizes a basic 6–5 pattern, which is maintained in E and F with different soprano lines. The latter does not complete the harmonic cycle of fifths, but stops to tonicize the dominant. Similar passages are cited in Exs. 1-12G and 12H, now incorporating only root position triads. Example 1-12I illustrates a less frequent instance of ascending fifth motion. Finally three examples of seventh-chord sequences are quoted in J through L. Note that in the first case every other chord is incomplete (with its fifth omitted), lest parallels result.

Pure sequential motion by falling thirds produces a problem with parallels (Ex. 1-12M). Two common means of elaboration are included in N and O. Other patterns are also possible, using a variety of internal root movements (see Ex. 1-12P).

EXAMPLE 1-12 Typical sequential paradigms

A. Root movement by 2nd

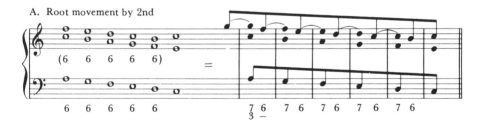

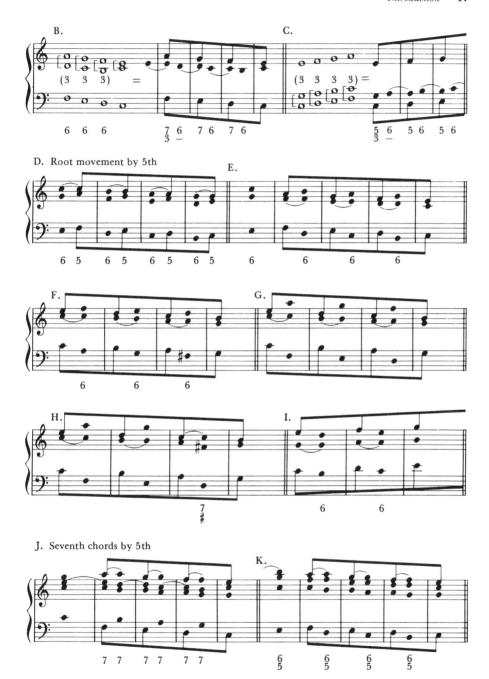

(continued)

EXAMPLE 1-12 (cont'd)

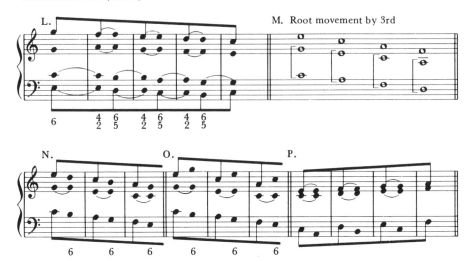

ASSIGNMENTS

1. Circle all examples of suspensions in this chorale harmonization of Bach (Ex. 1-13), noting their preparation and resolution. Add appropriate figured bass symbols for this passage.

EXAMPLE 1-13   *Danket dem Herren* (Bach harmonization)

2. Fill in the inner voices of this hypothetical chorale setting (Ex. 1-14) according to the supplied figured bass. Circle all instances of chordal sevenths and be able to explain how each is derived and resolved.

3. Add appropriate figured bass symbols to the unfigured bass lines in Ex. 1-15 to produce logical harmonic progressions. Do *not* realize the upper parts. Then "analyze" your results with functional Roman numerals.

4. Given the outer voices in the two passages of Ex. 1-16, supply an appropriate figured bass and then fill in the alto and tenor. Include a Roman numeral analysis for all "altered" chords you find.

EXAMPLE 1-14

EXAMPLE 1-15

A.

c♯:

B.

a:

EXAMPLE 1-16

A.

B.

5. Add the inner voices to this famous *Geistliche Lied* of Bach (Ex. 1-17). The figured bass has been slightly modified. Circle and identify all non-harmonic tones. Denote the various tonicized key centers and the means by which modulations are affected. You may encounter several "sticky" part-writing situations.

EXAMPLE 1-17   J. S. Bach: *Komm, süsser Tod* BWV 478

6. Several short passages from literature are quoted in Ex. 1-18. Extract and notate the basic sequential model underlying each, somewhat in the manner of Ex. 1-12.

EXAMPLE 1-18

A. Alessandro Scarlatti: *Sinfonia in G for recorder and continuo*

B. G. F. Handel: Fugue in b

C. J. S. Bach: Gavotte (French Suite in G)

D. G. F. Handel: Courante (Suite in f)

E. Dietrich Buxtehude: *Jesus Christus, unser Heiland*

(continued)

EXAMPLE 1-18 (cont'd)

F.   Dietrich Buxtehude: *Jesus Christus, unser Heiland*

2

XXXXXXXXXXXXXXXXXXXXXXXXXXXXXXXXXXXXXXXXXXXXXXX

Melody

Since polyphony is comprised of different thematic lines, we will discuss characteristics of melody in general and Baroque melody in particular.[1]

TEMPO, METER, AND PHRASING

Traditional Italian tempo markings were not common in the Baroque. Bach refrains from employing opening tempo indication in all but one of the forty-eight Fugues in the two volumes of his *Das Wohltemperierte Klavier* or *Well Tempered Clavier* (hereafter abbreviated as *WTC* I or II).[2] Those which do appear in ensemble music tend to be the faster (Allegro, Vivace, Presto) or slower (Adagio, Grave) markings. Changes of tempo which occur within the movement are clearly denoted. In the C minor Prelude of *WTC* I, one encounters a succession of Presto, Adagio, and Allegro, although the piece carries no initial designation. It was assumed that the

---

[1] Two books dealing with general melodic characteristics are Arthur Edwards, *The Art of Melody* (New York: Philosophical Library, 1956) and Leonard Meyer, *Explaining Music: Essays and Explorations* (Berkeley: University of California, 1973).

[2] The sole exception is the B minor Fugue in *WTC* I, which bears the marking Largo.

performer(s) could correctly deduce the tempo, either from external evidence or an examination of the music. The composition might bear the title of a particular dance (Allemande, Sarabande, or Gigue), each of which has a definite tempo and manner of performance. For an untitled movement a study of its texture, rhythmic figures, and notation would usually provide adequate clues to its correct pacing.

The *beat* is the underlying rhythmic unit or pulse. Although you may find a slow chordal or ricercare-like movement where durations of the beat or its multiples are employed (see Ex. 11-12D), in general the music of the late Baroque era is rather "busy" rhythmically. It is not difficult for the listener to detect the division (*background*) or subdivision of the beat. Indeed the term "motor rhythm" has been coined to describe the relentless activity at this temporal level. The so-called "walking bass", is a typical device in all tempi (see Ex. 14-1).

Faster movements tend toward the use of either *duple meter* (two beats per measure) or *quadruple meter* (four beats per measure) with the beat background either *simple* (two) or *compound* (three). Allegro *triple meter* is not as common. Thus the rhythm was usually notated in terms of the following meter signatures: $\frac{2}{4}$ $\frac{6}{8}$ $\frac{6}{16}$ (duple) or C $\frac{12}{8}$ $\frac{12}{4}$ $\frac{12}{16}$ (quadruple). *Alla breve* (¢) may contain two or four half-notes per measure. On the other hand the slower movements are usually in triple or quadruple meter, again with either background. Sometimes the tempo is slow enough to use a *divided beat*, with the background unit marking the basic pulse:

(♪) 3 4	(♪) 9 8	(♩) 9 4	(♪) C	(♪) 12 8	and sometimes	(♩) 6 4

Rhythmic and tonal forces usually indicate the meter employed by the composer. The "strong" beats of the measure are reinforced by melodic patterning, quantitative accent, harmonic change, and cadential placement. Even such diversionary tactics as *syncopation* rarely disturb the meter. Perhaps the main device employed to create momentary ambiguity is *hemiola*, either 3 against 2 or 2 against 3. Bach exploits it as a recurring motive in Ex. 2-1A, resulting in ♩. ♩ ♩. over two measures. Handel is particularly

EXAMPLE 2-1 Two examples of hemiola

J. S. Bach: Aria "Erfreute dich Seele"
(Cantata No. 21 *Ich hatte viel Bekümmernis*)
A.

G. F. Handel: Organ Concerto in d
Op. 7, No. 1, III
B.

fond of it at final cadences (Ex. 2-1B), a practice he inherited from the previous century. One may occasionally note a conflict between $\frac{3}{2}$ and $\frac{6}{4}$ in the French Courante.

VOCAL/INSTRUMENTAL CROSS INFLUENCE

During the Renaissance, existing vocal pieces frequently served as the basis for more elaborate keyboard or ensemble transcriptions. However, by the late Baroque, the perfection of technical idioms in instrumental writing had developed to the point that a kind of reverse counteraction took place. Thus passages occur in vocal works which strongly suggest instrumental origins. This is especially prevalent in *melismas*, where a single syllable of text is prolonged. Examples 2-2A and 2B are also typical of many keyboard or string pieces. In slower instrumental movements, on the other hand, it is possible to detect techniques typical of the florid operatic arias of the period. This is particularly noticeable in the highly embellished melodic lines with their written ornamental figures or symbols. In Ex. 2-3C, a simple chorale tune undergoes this treatment. Performers were expected to supply embellishments for expressive purposes at appropriate places, even when they were not indicated by the composer in the music.

EXAMPLE 2-2   G. F. Handel: Aria "The Trumpet shall sound" (*Messiah*)

G. F. Handel: Aria
"For who may abide" (*Messiah*)

O Mensch, bewein' dein' Sünde gross

(continued)

EXAMPLE 2-2 (cont'd)

(Bach's setting in his *Orgelbüchlein*)

TECHNICAL FEATURES OF BAROQUE MELODY

After the composer states the primary thematic idea(s) of a piece, he must develop them. The Germans have a useful term—*Fortspinnung*—which means the "spinning out" of a melodic line, its further extension, expansion, or evolution. One of the principle methods of *Fortspinnung* in the late Baroque era is *motivic manipulation,* in which one (or perhaps several) short melodic figures or fragments undergo extensive subsequent development. This may occur in one of five ways. The specific topics listed below are keyed to relevant passages in Bach's Two-Part Invention in C major (Ex. 2-3); note the possible division of the primary motive (M) into two sub-motives (x and y) in Ex. 2-3A.

  1. *Repetition*—immediate restatement of the motive, sometimes an octave higher or lower, without tonal or rhythmic change.

  2. *Sequence*—restatement at a higher or lower diatonic pitch level (Ex. 2-3B). Normally sequences are not extended past three such successive reiterations. The law of "good taste" would seem to prevail. Both repetitions and sequences may be slightly modified with an occasional pitch change.

  3. *Restatement in a different key*—although this appears to be directly related to the previous devices, the effect of a new key center can give the original motive an entirely different musical meaning. See Ex. 2-3C, where after a cadence in G, the motive is restated in the dominant relation.

  4. *Melodic Mirror*—a more artificial device in which the tones of the motive are literally turned upside down, so that ascending motion is replaced with corresponding descending motion, and *vice versa.* In Ex. 2-3D the melodic mirror (*inversus* in Latin) alternates with its upright version (*rectus*).

  5. *Rhythmic alteration*—although the pitch relations of the motive are retained, its rhythm is changed in some manner. This usually takes the form of a proportional *augmentation* (such as 2:1 or 3:1) or *diminution* (1:2 or 1:3)—consult Ex. 2-3E. It is also possible to exercise free *rhythmic transformations*, but aspects of the original motive must be preserved.

  These manipulations may be combined and continued in various ways, depending on the ingenuity of the composer (see Exs. 2-3F and 3G).

EXAMPLE 2-3 Motivic manipulation from Bach's Two-Voice Invention in C

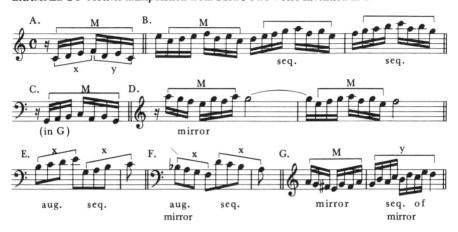

In contrast to motivic development, in which a complete movement grows out of exploitation of a theme or themes, there is also in slow tempi a less confining approach—that of an *autogenerative* melody, whose *Fortspinnung* gradually evolves different relations and perhaps entirely new ideas. Even with works of this nature, related motivic material is apt to be found lurking in the background. The familiar Air (on the G string) from Bach's Orchestral Overture No. 3 in D major BWV 1068 is a good example of this.

The older vocal practice of "melodic balance" or change of direction after a leap, so typical of the Renaissance, is not as much in evidence here. This is because of the instrumental influence mentioned earlier, where arpeggiation is frequent. Many melodies of this period exhibit a strong directional tendency, so that the various undulations of the line are actually based on an underlying stepwise movement. Although the results can sometimes be misleading, the application of reductive methods to single-line melodies can help reveal their tonal framework. This is sometimes obvious, as in Ex. 2-4. On the other hand, the reduction of Bach's fugue subject in Ex. 2-5 to an underlying scale-degree succession of $\hat{5}$ ($\hat{6}$) $\hat{5}$ $\hat{4}$ $\hat{3}$ requires some probing.

EXAMPLE 2-4   J. S. Bach: Concerto for Two Violins in d, I BWV 1043

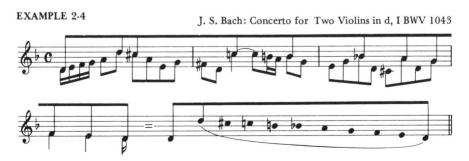

EXAMPLE 2-5

J. S. Bach: Fantasia and Fugue in g ("The Great") for organ BWV 542

Motivic development by sequence is a powerful generator of directional conjunct motion, since most sequences feature stepwise movement at some level of their patterning. Examples 2-6A and 6B are typical passages. At the other extreme of the linear spectrum are those melodies which consist almost entirely of chordal arpeggiation or broken chords, as shown in Ex. 2-6C. However, don't think that little or no sense of voice-leading occurs in such passages. Observe the chordal reduction at the conclusion of Ex. 2-6C, noting the upper line.

EXAMPLE 2-6

A typical phenomenon of the late Baroque is *compound melody*. Here a line is broken up into fragments, which suggest two (or more) individual melodic strands. This technique of *melodic unfolding* is best illustrated with sequences, where the implied two-voice patterns are restated several times.

The three passages cited in Ex. 2-7 all employ common sequential paradigms (refer back to the end of Chapter 1). The compound melody in the
top stave is split into its separate components in the middle stave, leading to
the underlying model on the bottom. The broken sixths of Ex. 2-7C are
especially common. They may also be thought of as pure descending con-
sonants without recourse to the 7–6 suspensions.

EXAMPLE 2-7 Examples of compound melody

Despite the frequency of this procedure, you may not recognize it in
non-sequential themes. Only increased exposure to the literature will
sharpen your perception. Example 2-8A, which at first might appear inappropriate for this type of analysis, reveals on closer scrutiny at least two
ways to demonstrate its underlying framework. The latter, which actually
suggests three voices, is preferred. The apparently torturous chromaticism
of the fugue subject in Ex. 2-9, following the elimination of the half-step
appoggiaturas (indicated by the composer with slurs), reduces back to a
simple diatonic two-voice setting. The Sarabande in Ex. 2-10 represents a
cross between chordal arpeggiation and the more contrapuntal aspect of
"polyphonic" melody.

EXAMPLE 2-8

EXAMPLE 2-9 Diatonic reduction of subject in Bach's Fugure in b (*WTC* I)

EXAMPLE 2-10 Polyphonic melody in Bach's Sarabande (Cello Suite No. 1 in G)

ASSIGNMENTS

1. Example 2-11 quotes the opening theme and its continuation to the first cadence in the third movement of Bach's *Brandenburg* Concerto No. 1 in F major. This passage is an excellent summary of many of the characteristics of Baroque melody discussed in this chapter. Analyze it carefully and be able to point out the following: basic motives (there may be several) and the means of their subsequent development, long-range stepwise motion by sequence or other techniques, use of chordal arpeggiation or compound melody, and finally, the employment of rhythmic deviations, such as syncopation or hemiola.

EXAMPLE 2-11

J. S. Bach: *Brandenburg* Concerto No. 1 in F, III

2. Using the opening thematic idea in Ex. 2-12, compose a short piece of about twelve measures for solo flute. Base your melodic continuation on motives or figures derived from the original passage. Incorporate one sequence employing stepwise motion either up or down.

EXAMPLE 2-12

3. Using the succession of chords in Ex. 2-13, write a melody based on arpeggiation for solo violin.

EXAMPLE 2-13

4. Analyze the two compound melodies quoted in Ex. 2-14 and extract their underlying framework. Example 2-14A implies only two parts, while the more polyphonic melody of Ex. 2-14B suggests three voices.

EXAMPLE 2-14

A.   J. S. Bach: Fugue in C♯ (*WTC* I)

B.   J. S. Bach: Chaconne (Partita No. 2 in d for solo violin)

3

※※

General characteristics of counterpoint; pedagogical foundations

The term *counterpoint* is derived from the latin *punctus contra punctum*, literally *note against note*. In the fifteenth century, Tictoris defined it as "an artistic combination of tones which arises when one is placed opposite another."[1] Although this description correctly relates the practice of polyphony to its origins in the Medieval period, the phrase "artistic combination" only hints at its more important attributes. For general purposes perhaps Walter Piston's definition of counterpoint as "the art of combining melodies" is more appropriate.[2] Four characteristics of late Baroque polyphony require investigation. In discussing the musical interplay between the various voices in contrapuntal texture, consideration must be given to: (1.) the composite melodic motion generated by the separate parts; (2.) their rhythmic interaction; (3.) their registral placement in relation to one another; and (4.) the resultant vertical sonorities (consonance vs. dissonance) and the sense of harmonic progression. Each of these will be taken up briefly and illustrated in two-voice texture.

Three types of melodic motion occur in two-part contrapuntal settings: *similar motion*, where the voices proceed in the same direction, either

---

[1]From Tinctoris *Liber de arte contrapuncti* (1477)
[2]Walter Piston, *Counterpoint* (New York: W. W. Norton & Co, Inc., 1947).

by step, leap, or both;[3] *contrary motion*, where they move in opposing directions to each other; and *oblique motion*, where one part sustains while the other moves up or down. Although similar motion carries restrictions, contrapuntal writing usually demonstrates a variety of all three. This assures the tracing of different melodic contours in each voice (see Ex. 3-1A). Instances where the parts move in extended similar motion negate the contrasting linear characteristics of the separate voices, so that the result is more that of a "doubled" single line (see Ex. 3-1B).

EXAMPLE 3-1

S = similar motion   O = oblique motion   C = contrary motion

Although the above settings fit the definition of *punctus contra punctum*, the use of melodic motion alone is only marginally helpful in maintaining the individuality of the voices. It is actually the *rhythmic* interplay between the parts that activates and separates the melodic strands. Thus as the soprano moves in shorter values, the bass may sustain a longer note, creating a kind of rhythmic balancing. Compare Ex. 3-2A, which features a succession of sixths in a note-against-note setting, with Ex. 3-2B. In the latter case the ear can better distinguish between the parts, and the similar sixths become less objectionable. The effect of the individual rhythms of each voice and their interaction is crucial in comprehending polyphonic passages. The ear switches back and forth between the various parts, listening to the one that displays shorter durations, or in some instances (such as *cantus firmus* pieces), to the one with longer notes.

EXAMPLE 3-2

[3]*Parallel motion* involves similar movement between identical interval types.

Contrast the two settings given in Ex. 3-3A and 3B. The pitch classes of the separate lines are identical in each. However, in the first example they are so close that the continual voice-crossing makes it difficult to clearly distinguish the two parts. In the latter instance this problem is rectified, since the melodies now move within their own registers. This does not imply that examples of voice-crossing will not occur in denser textures, but in general the outer voices tend to be separated spacially.

EXAMPLE 3-3

voices cross

Finally, let us consider vertical intervals produced by the parts. Each historical period has established sets of verticalities which are considered either normal or deviant, with carefully regulated procedures for consonance and dissonance. The preparation and resolution of dissonant intervals in the Baroque period is especially crucial. Example 3-4 illustrates a typical passage for two voices, showing some common occurrences of nonharmonic tones (circled in the quotation). In addition to this, the succession of implied chordal sonorities, denoted here by Roman numerals, is not random but suggests a functional harmonic progression in the key of B minor.

EXAMPLE 3-4

PEDAGOGICAL FOUNDATIONS OF BAROQUE POLYPHONY

One might assume that the best instruction of polyphony in the Baroque era would be exactly what the composers themselves learned during their early training. But *how* and from *what* sources did the masters of this period receive their instruction? These are not easy questions to answer.

To begin with, a composer during that time was first a practicing performer. He (composition was almost exclusively a male occupation) would doubtless begin his musical education as a choir boy. Should any exceptional talent become evident, he might then be instructed in some keyboard, string, or wind instrument. Only after a solid foundation of practical musicianship had been established might he be initiated into the "secret rites" of musical composition, usually under the tutorship of a famous master. History is replete with instances of young aspiring composers undertaking long and arduous journeys to study under a renowned teacher or pedagogue.[4]

Other sources of instruction were the theoretical treatises. The Renaissance writer Johannes Tinctoris began his *Liber de arte contrapuncti* (1477) with a survey of the various consonant intervals. He distinguishes between note-against-note settings (*contrapunctus simplex*) and those in which one or more voices moves against a slower part (*contrapunctus diminutus*). Although he derives a set of general "rules" to govern contrapuntal writing, his approach is more analytical than pedagogical, based on the observation of contemporary examples. In the sixteenth century the emphasis shifted to a more didactic approach with "how to write" counterpoint manuals. One such method is presented in great detail by Gioseffo Zarlino in the third volume of his *Istitutioni harmoniche* (1558), perhaps the first comprehensive treatise on the art of counterpoint. Following the survey of consonant intervals, Zarlino commences with two-voice note-against-note settings (*contrappunto semplice*) using a plainsong *cantus firmus* (see Ex. 3-5). This progresses through free counterpoint against the cantus (*contrappunto diminuto*), see Ex. 3-6, into strict imitation (*fuga*), double counterpoint, and compositions for three or more voices. Zarlino's influence is apparent in writings by Artusi, Morley, and Sweelinck.[5] These treatises were set against the backdrop of the *modal* system of the late Renaissance. Although the writers cited typical cadence formulas and dealt with consonant/dissonant relations at the surface level, there was little or no concern for larger harmonic progression *per se*.

During the seventeenth century, modality was gradually abandoned in favor of the major-minor tonal system with its hierarchy of related keys and underlying harmonic functionality. Nevertheless, most of the authors of contrapuntal treatises during this period continued to model their stud-

---

[4]See Kerala Snyder, "Dietrich Buxtehude's Studies in Learned Counterpoint," *Journal of American Musicological Society*, Vol. 33/3 (Fall 1980), pp. 544–64; and Friedrich Blume, "J. S. Bach's Youth," *Musical Quarterly*, Vol. 54/1 (Jan. 1968), pp. 1–30.

[5]Giovanni Artusi, *L'Arte del contrappunto* (Venice: 1586–89); Thomas Morley, *A Plaine and Easie Introduction to Practicall Musicke* (London: 1597); Jan Peter Sweelinck, *Compositionregeln* (c. 1600), which was compiled by his pupils and quotes liberally from Zarlino.

EXAMPLE 3-5

Gioseffo Zarlino: *Istituioni harmoniche* III

cantus in lower voice

EXAMPLE 3-6

Gioseffo Zarlino: *Istituioni harmoniche* III

ies in polyphony after Zarlino, in the style now referred to as *stilo antico*. These include Diruta (1609), Cerone (1613), Banchieri (1614), and Zacconi (1622).[6] Thus the contrapuntal instruction outlined by these theorists tend-

[6]Girolamo Diruta, *Il Transilvano* part 2 (Venice: 1609); Pietro Cerone, *El melopeo y maestro* (Naples: 1613); Adriano Banchieri, *Cartella musicale* (Venice: 1614); Lodovico Zacconi, *Prattica di musica* part 2 (Naples: 1622).

ed to look backward to the practices of the sixteenth century rather than forward to those procedures typical of the Baroque. In contrast to this trend one may mention Bernhard (c. 1650), Nivers (1667), Reincken (c. 1670), Bononcini (1673), Berardi (1681), and Purcell (1694), all of whom devoted some discussion to the so-called *seconda prattica,* in which the free dissonant treatment and certain stylistic characteristics of the Baroque period were anticipated.[7]

In addition to "contrapuntal" writings, there was another type of treatise which became significant during the late Baroque period, that of *thoroughbass.*[8] The origins of this technique may be traced to late Renaissance performance practice. Since full scores of polyphonic choral pieces were usually not available, a choir organist would take a *bassus* partbook and write in numbers in a kind of intervallic shorthand to denote what *chords* to play, in no way attempting to reproduce the exact upper contrapuntal lines on his instrument. Thus the roots of figured bass lie in purely vertical or harmonic relations.

During the experiments of the Florentine Camarata around 1600, composers advocated a return to simpler declamatory style, abandoning the polyphony of the Renaissance. A single melodic line was stressed with supporting sustained chords, the result of thoroughbass realization. The importance of the *bass line* as the harmonic foundation of the music increased with the development of the major-minor system. In Friedrich Erhardt Niedt's *Musikalische Handleitung* (1707–17), it is clear that he considered the bass the *primary* voice of the texture. The performer elaborated various soprano lines *above* it. This view was somewhat modified in Heinichen (1728) and Mattheson (1731), both of whom advocated a mutual cooperation between the outer parts.[9] We are interested in the treatises which may have formed the basis for instruction in the late Baroque period. In this regard Niedt's work is particularly significant, since we know that J. S. Bach was acquainted with its initial volume, having paraphrased it in his own little manual on figured bass.[10]

The importance of thoroughbass in polyphonic instruction cannot be

[7]Christoph Bernhard, *Tractatus compositionis augmentatus* (c. 1650); Guillaume Nivers, *Traité de la composition musicale* (Paris: 1667); Jan Adams Reincken, *Kompositionslehre* (c. 1670); Giovanni Bononcini, *Il Musico prattico* (Bologna: 1673); Angelo Berardi, *Documenti armonici* (Bologna: 1681); Henry Purcell, "Of Fuge, or Pointing" in John Playford, *An Introduction to the Skill of Musick,* 12th ed. (London: 1694).

[8]Review the section on thoroughbass in Chapter 1.

[9]Johann David Heinichen, *Der Generalbass in der Komposition* (Dresden: 1728); Johann Mattheson, *Grosse Generalbass-Schule* (Hamburg: 1731).

[10]Bach's own writings on thoroughbass instruction, probably compiled by his pupils, may be found in Philipp Spitta, *Johann Sebastian Bach* Vol. 3 (New York: Dover Publications, Inc., 1951). pp. 315–48.

overemphasized.[11] It formed the basis from which almost all theoretical training began. Kirnberger, in describing Bach's own compositional method to his pupils, states:

> Simple strict counterpoint can be in two, three, four or more parts. It is best to begin with four-part counterpoint because it is hardly possible to write in two or three parts perfectly until four-part writing has been mastered. For since the complete harmony is in four parts, something must always be missing in two-and three-part works, so that one cannot judge safely as to what is to be omitted from the harmony in the different cases which arise unless he has a thorough knowledge of four-part writing.[12]

As Jeppesen observes, "Kirnberger no longer begins with the line, as did his predecessors, but with the chords; and yet he wants polyphony. But he is entirely in the right, because the polyphony he is striving for is the harmonically conceived linear music of the late Baroque, of the Bach style."[13] This approach is verified by Bach's other pupils, Heinrich Nikolaus Gerber and Johann Freidrich Agricola. In Handel's little instruction manual written for Princess Anne,[14] he begins with thoroughbass exercises. As it proceeds to contrapuntal studies, some of the fugal problems (notated as a single line), are always accompanied with figured bass symbols.

Thus it appears that the pedagogical foundation for contrapuntal training around 1700 stems from two complementary sources, the neo-Zarlino approach with its emphasis on linear movement, and thoroughbass with its emphasis on vertical sonority. This two-fold method will form the basis for our study of techniques for writing Baroque counterpoint. We will begin with the Renaissance procedure of two voices, and then progress through three and four parts. However, a figured bass will often be appended to a two-voice passage or composition in order to clarify the chordal implications. Numbers may be added between the staves to denote the intervallic relations between the outer voices. In order to avoid confusion with larger numbers, compound intervals (more than an octave) will occasionally be reduced *within* the octave (10 = 3, 12 = 5; see Ex. 3-7). Following Kirnberger's format, note-against-note settings will be considered first

---

[11]In 1782 Kirnberger complained that "One knows from history that many countries have always had organists who, particularly in church music, have played figured bass as it must be accompanied—following thorough rules. It was as rare then to find an organist who did not understand how to play figured bass correctly as it is today to find one who does."

[12]From Johann Kirnberger *Die Kunst des reinen Satzes in der Musik* (Berlin and Königsberg: 1771-79).

[13]Knud Jeppesen, *Counterpoint* (Englewood Cliffs: Prentice-Hall, Inc., 1939), p. 45.

[14]These "Composition Lessons", dating from about 1722, may be found in *Hallische Händel-Ausgabe* Supplement Bd. 1 (Kassel: Bärenreiter, 1978).

(the old *contrappunto semplice*), moving on to chordal figuration with the addition of elaborative or "florid" counterpoint (the old *contrappunto diminuto*). Once the *cantus firmus* is dropped, free polyphony will be introduced, leading eventually to a study of imitation and the fugue.

EXAMPLE 3-7

J. S. Bach: *Schaff's mit mir, Gott* BWV 514
(*Notenbuch der Anna Magdalena Bach*)

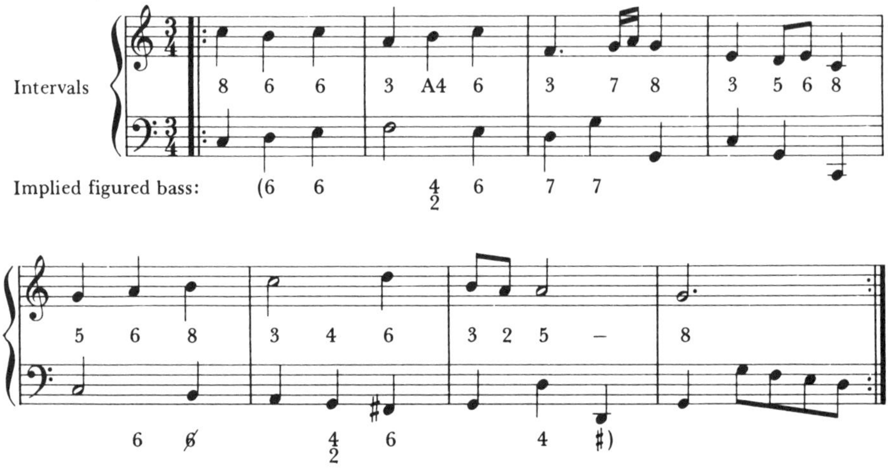

4

Two-voice note-against-note counterpoint

Introductions to two-voice polyphony have traditionally used a preexistent *cantus firmus* in note-against-note or first species contrapuntal settings. The authors of Renaissance manuals utilized a chant melody as the cantus (see Ex. 3-5). In later theoretical writings of the seventeenth and early eighteenth centuries this fixed tune is often contrived, like those in Fux's *Gradus ad Parnassum* (see Ex. 22-1). This text will draw its *cantus firmi* from two basic sources, the Lutheran chorale melodies of the late Baroque period, either as the upper or lower voice, and figured bass lines, some of which are from contemporary theoretical treatises. The German chorales represent the most common cantus tunes in the actual musical literature of the time, and they allow more freedom than the contrived models. They provide definite metrical settings in a variety of signatures, and incorporate a wider range of initial and closing formulas. By 1700 the major-minor system was well established, so implied harmonies, both as isolated chords or complete progressions, must also be considered.

TYPICAL MELODIC PROBLEMS
IN THE COUNTERPOINTING VOICE

All polyphonic compositions, especially those of the late Baroque, present the dichotomy of *linear* versus *harmonic* forces. Neither must gain the upper hand, but both should coexist euphoniously. The paradox of these elements is often a source of despair for the beginning student of counterpoint—what seems to work well melodically often results in problems of a harmonic or vertical nature, and *vice versa.* Therefore each component will first be treated separately, with increasing emphasis on the interaction between the two. With additional skill, hopefully you will see the horizontal and vertical aspects of polyphony simply as dual manifestations of the same underlying tonal framework.

Let us review characteristics of the melodic line in note-against-note settings. Since the cantus part is given and must *never* be altered, we can devote our attention to the counterpointing voice. Six specific situations to avoid are listed below, with corresponding musical examples:

1. Avoid excessive repeated notes or "static" melodic contours which have little or no overall sense of direction (Ex. 4-1A).
2. Avoid the continuous repetition of the highest or lowest note in the complete melodic profile. If possible, have them occur only once (Ex. 4-1B).
3. Avoid continuing in the same direction after larger leaps; try to affect a restoring or balancing motion in the opposite direction (Ex. 4-1C).[1]
4. Avoid awkward intervallic leaps, such as ninths, sevenths, or augmented intervals in general. Downward leaps of the diminished fifth or seventh are possible, though rare (Ex. 4-1D).
5. Avoid leaping away from active scale degrees which require immediate resolution, such as the leading tone or $\sharp\hat{6}$ in minor (Ex. 4-1E).
6. Avoid the composition of melodic lines that are either exclusively conjunct or disjunct (Ex. 4-1F). A mixture of motion by both step and leap is preferred, with some tendency toward the former.

EXAMPLE 4-1 Undesirable melodic traits in the counterpointing voice

---

[1]This may appear to contradict the statement made in Chapter 2. However, the remark here refers to note-against-note settings, not actual elaborated melodic lines.

HARMONIC INTERVALS

For the moment only *consonant* harmonic intervals will be allowed between the two voices. These include: the perfect consonances—unison, octave, and fifth (both simple and compound); and the imperfect consonances—thirds and sixths (also simple and compound). The use of dissonance, such as seconds, perfect fourths, sevenths, ninths, and any diminished/augmented intervals (including both forms of the tritone), must be explained in terms of "chordal dissonance" and will be taken up later in this chapter. Avoid them completely for the time being.

The perfect consonant intervals tend to be reserved for the initiation and conclusion (or cadence) of the phrase. If the cantus melody begins on a strong beat, the harmonic implication is almost always the tonic of the key, using either the unison, octave, fifth, or sometimes third (tenth); see Ex. 4-2A. If the phrase begins with an upbeat, the first implied triad is sometimes dominant (either in $\frac{5}{3}$ or $\frac{6}{3}$), which normally resolves to tonic on the following downbeat (see Exs. 4-2B to 2D).

EXAMPLE 4-2 Typical harmonic intervals at the opening of phrases

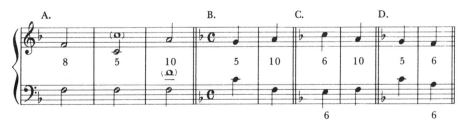

In more traditional *first species* cantus settings a double-stepwise approach to the final octave (or unison) is utilized at the cadence (Ex. 4-3A), a formula derived from the modal practice of the Renaissance. However, in chorale phrases a variety of cadential types may occur. Their two-part frameworks are grouped and listed in Exs. 4-3B through 4E, with the vertical intervals, soprano scale degrees, and implied harmonies indicated. With the exception of modal chorale settings, the complete tune ends with a perfect authentic close. All may occur as interior cadences.

EXAMPLE 4-3 Typical cadential formulas

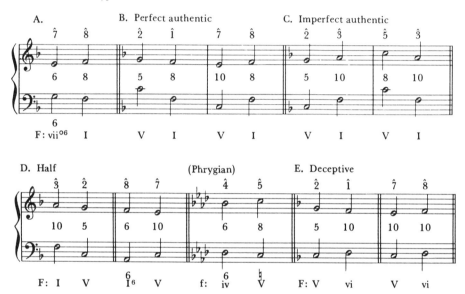

The initiation and destination of the phrase require the greatest degree of tonal stability. In the latter, the perfect consonant intervals tend to occur more frequently in the penultimate and final notes of the cadence. (Refer back to Exs. 4-2 and 4-3, observing the use of octaves and fifths at these crucial points.) Conversely, the more fluid tonal motion *within* the phrase shows a preference for imperfect consonances of thirds and sixths. Johann Kirnberger declares that "In the middle (of the phrase) the octave and fifth should be avoided;" see his setting in Ex. 4-4.[2] Perhaps this overstates the case, but any use of the octave is best relegated to a kind of passing motion ($\frac{C\ D\ E}{E\ D\ C}$) on a weaker metric position.

---

[2]From Johann Kirnberger *Gedanken über die verschiedenen Lehrarten in der Komposition* . . . . . (1782). This introduction to counterpoint has been translated by Richard Nelson and Donald Boomgaarden as "Thoughts on the Different Methods of Teaching Composition as Preparation for Understanding Fugue," *Journal of Music Theory*, Vol. 30/1 (Spring 1986), pp. 71–94.

EXAMPLE 4-4   Johann Kirnberger:
Gedanken über die verschiedenen Lehrarten in der Komposition (1782)

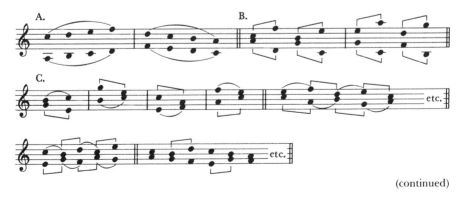

MELODIC MOTION BETWEEN CONSECUTIVE HARMONIC INTERVALS

As discussed in Chapter 3 (refer to Ex. 3-1), a good mixture of similar, oblique, and contrary motions occur in counterpoint. The latter is preferred, since it maximizes the individuality of the two melodic lines. However, you may encounter up to four-note successions of thirds or sixths in similar stepwise motion (see Ex. 4-10B). Do not overuse oblique motion.

There are no general restrictions on melodic motion employing only thirds and sixths, although the simultaneous leaping of both voices in the same direction is discouraged. Since these imperfect consonances are so prevalent in the phrase interior, a closer examination of the melodic connections between them is recommended. Aside from stepwise patterns or contrary leaps within successive thirds or sixths (see Exs. 4-5A and 5B), alternations of third-sixth (or sixth-third) involve stepwise motion in one voice, accompanied by a leap of the opposite direction in the other part. This leap may take the form of either a third (Ex. 4-5C) or a fourth/fifth (Ex. 4-5D). Study these possibilities carefully, particularly noting the potential sequence patterns.

EXAMPLE 4-5 Examples of melodic motion batween imperfect consonances

(continued)

EXAMPLE 4-5 (cont'd)

Melodic motion to perfect intervals is quite another matter. To begin with, parallel unisons, octaves, and fifths are strictly forbidden, even by contrary motion (Ex. 4-6A). Similar movement (or *direct motion*) to these intervals is also discouraged. This is not to say that the passage in Ex. 4-6B is nonexistent, but certainly the alternate solution in Ex. 4-6C is better— note the "passing" octaves. This restriction is usually relaxed at *cadential points*, where direct motion (by step and leap) to either the octave or fifth is common (see Ex. 4-6D). One rationale for this is the anticipation of elaborating the counterpointing voice, which might produce parallels (Ex. 4-6E).[3]

EXAMPLE 4-6 Melodic motion involving perfect consonances

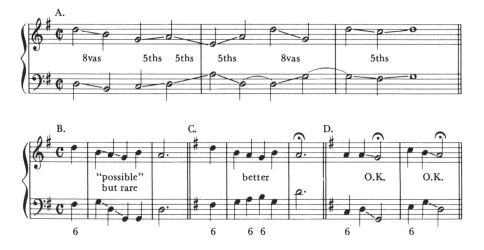

[3]Fux in his *Gradus ad Parnassum* (1725) summarized the basic "commandments" of melodic motion between consonant intervals: use only contrary or oblique motion in approaching a perfect consonance (from either a perfect or imperfect interval), and use any of the three motions in approaching an imperfect consonance (from either a perfect or imperfect interval).

HARMONIC IMPLICATIONS

There are two schools of thought on harmonic implication in two-voice polyphony. Some theorists insist that the vertical relations between two notes should be considered on purely intervallic terms, devoid of any implied chord or harmonic function. Thus the interval of a sixth is simply that and nothing more. Others have scrupulously applied the principles of functional harmony to this music. Here the intervals suggest specific tertian chords within a harmonic progression denoted by Roman numerals. Perhaps a solution lies somewhere between these two extremes. Thoroughbass manuals suggest that the interval of a sixth implies either a ⁶₃ (or first inversion, if you will) or even a ⁶₄, depending on its context (Ex. 4-7A).

The problem of functional harmonic progression is somewhat trickier. Although Roman numerals were unknown in this period, this does not mean that a sense of functional harmony did not exist. Innumerable passages occur, particularly near cadential points, where a sense of functional progression (predominant → dominant → tonic) is apparent, a fact which led Rameau to expound his theory of the underlying cycle of fifths through *fundamental bass* (Ex. 4-7B). However, keep in mind that principles of voice-leading and consonance/dissonance treatment over a bass part evolved before those of harmony. The familiar cadential formula found in Ex. 4-7C, which is traditionally analyzed as ii⁶₅ V I, actually is the result of the combination of two Renaissance clichés: the ⁶₃ sonority and the 4-3 suspension at cadences.

There are two drawbacks to applying functional analysis to Baroque polyphony. First, it is misleading to assign a Roman numeral to each chord, since the implied chords are *not* of equal structural significance within the tonal hierarchy. Secondly, there are many passages, especially sequential ones, that defy normal functional progressions (see Ex. 4-7D). Therefore this text will take a cautious approach to functional harmonic analysis in general and the use of Roman numerals in particular. For the most part only figured bass or pure interval relations will suffice. From a more practical standpoint, use of vertical intervals which clearly imply ⁵₃ or ⁶₃ triads will provide a convincing tonal/harmonic framework, as long as correct voice-leading is applied. In purely diatonic phrases, 6th chords over scale degrees

Î and 5̂ in the bass are less common and should be handled with care. The musical effect created by Ex. 4-7E is less than desirable, even though the intervallic relations are quite correct. A better setting is in Ex. 4-7F.

EXAMPLE 4-7 Harmonic implication in note-against-note settings

Several model note-against-note settings are given in Ex. 4-8. Study them carefully in light of the preceding discussion.

EXAMPLE 4-8

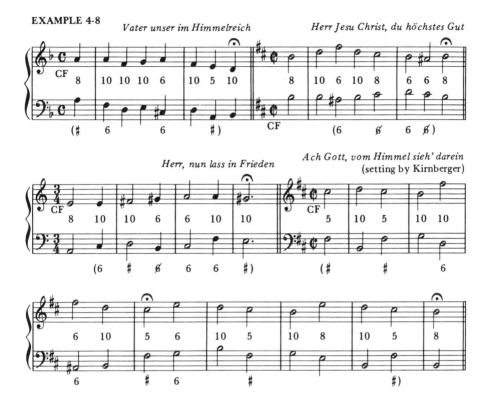

A figured bass cantus is cited in Ex. 4-9 with four hypothetical "student" counterpoints written above. The melodic contour of No. 1 is perfectly acceptable, but its comparison to the bass reveals similar motion in tenths, hardly qualifying as polyphony at all. The profile of No. 2 is static and repetitious; also note the indulgence in perfect intervals—five out of eight are either octaves or fifths. The skip from the leading tone and the recurrence of the climactic b¹ mar the overall line of No. 3, compounded by the contrary fifths at the opening and the curious skip to the fifth at the cadence. No. 4 alone is relatively free of defects, unless one wishes to quibble over the extended stepwise motion.

EXAMPLE 4-9

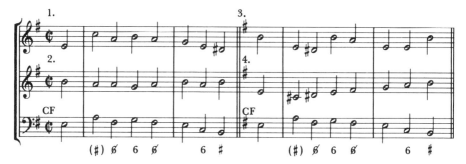

ASSIGNMENTS

1. Criticize the four lower counterpoints to the opening phrase of *Jesu, meine Freude* (Ex. 4-10) in the manner of the previous evaluations on Ex. 4-9. Which do you think is Bach's own setting?

EXAMPLE 4-10

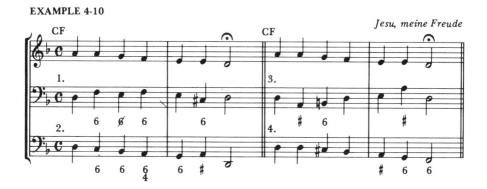

2. Compose two note-against-note settings for each of the cantus tunes quoted in Ex. 4-11. Use only diatonic tones of the key and do not modulate.

EXAMPLE 4-11

Wer nur den lieben Gott lässt walten

Nun lob', mein Seel', den Herren

Wachet auf (last phrase)

VOICE-LEADING REDUCTION

You might think that note-against-note settings are irreducible bases for contrapuntal elaboration, but it is possible to abbreviate them further. This process suggests that the individual melodic tones and the chords they imply are not of similar tonal importance. This underscores one danger of assigning Roman numerals to each chord, since it tends to foster the idea that they are equal. In Ex. 4-12A, for instance, the V⁶, vii°⁶, and V all belong to the same functional classification of the "dominant", and indeed they do resolve quite normally to tonic. However, only the last of these represents a *structural dominant;* the first two are the result of contrapuntal motion "prolonging" the tonic triad (see Ex. 4-12B). Ways of achieving voice-leading reductions and the symbols used are discussed below.

EXAMPLE 4-12

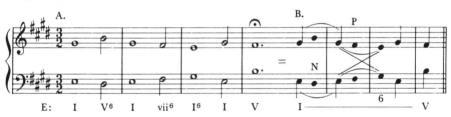

E: I   V⁶   I   vii⁶   I⁶   I   V   I ————————— 6 ————————— V

The structural tones are denoted by a stemmed black note, regardless of their original rhythmic duration (♩). Accessory tones (either consonant skips within the same triad or less subordinate harmonies) are indicated with an unstemmed black note head (●). Suspensions and non-harmonic tones (usually passing or complete/incomplete neighbors) will employ an unstemmed black note head with a slur, usually signifying its derivation and resolution; the abbreviations S, P, N, or IN (see above and Ex. 4-12B) will be incorporated at first, but as they become more obvious, these will be dropped. Example 4-13 illustrates ways in which a single harmonic sonority may be *prolonged*. In Exs. 4-13A and 13B, neighboring and passing motion is employed, while Ex. 4-13C shows a combination of the two. A pair of incomplete neighbors form the basis for Ex. 4-13D. Another important device is *voice exchange,* which is illustrated in increasing complexity in Ex. 4-13E through 13G; note the typical cross-over of lines to denote the registral exchange of parts. Ex. 4-13H cites a familiar approach to a full close. The basic notes have been stemmed and beamed, suggesting a progression of I ii^6 V I.

EXAMPLE 4-13 Some basic reduction techniques

Example 4-14 consists of several note-against-note settings, with accompanying voice-leading reductions. Study each in detail, observing triadic prolongations and the underlying structural harmonies. This method of reduction is valuable in free elaborated counterpoint as a means of revealing the basic tonal framework.

EXAMPLE 4-14 Voice-leading reductions of note-against-note settings

ASSIGNMENT

Make similar voice-leading reductions of the note-against-note settings found in Ex. 4-15, using those in Ex. 4-14 as possible models. Do not be discouraged with your results at first—further analyses and assignments will sharpen your skills in reductive technique.

EXAMPLE 4-15

CHORDAL DISSONANCE

Up to this point only consonant intervals have been allowed. In traditional first species examples, dissonance is never permitted. However, in the actual music literature involving note-against-note *chorale* settings, occasional dissonant intervals may be encountered. Their presence can be explained in terms of implied seventh chords. In each case their actual origins arise from large-scale non-harmonic motion (passing and neighboring) and suspensions. The most commonly occurring dissonance is the tritone (augmented fourth/diminished fifth), usually derived from implied $^6_5$ or $^4_2$s of major-minor seventh chords. Some typical idioms are shown in Exs. 4-16A through 14G in a kind of reduced format. Observe the occasional use of chromaticism, originating from secondary dominant sevenths. It is even possible to find instances of intervals of sevenths or seconds (= ninths) as the result of suspension technique (Ex. 4-16H and I).[4]

EXAMPLE 4-16 Instances of chordal dissonance in note-against-note settings

TONICIZATION AND MODULATION WITHIN THE PHRASE

Thus far the cantus examples have remained in the tonic key throughout. Many chorale phrases will modulate, thereby cadencing in a related ton-

---

[4]The question of chordal dissonance in note-against-note chorale settings is also discussed on pp. 247–49 of Felix Salzer and Carl Schachter's *Counterpoint in Composition* (New York: McGraw-Hill Book Company, 1969).

ality. Even instances of momentary tonicization may be noted in the interior of the phrase. In the composition of such settings, first plot out the appropriate key for the melodic cadence so that the contrapuntal and tonal motion can be directed toward it. In some cases the chorale cantus itself will suggest or even require a modulation. In other situations, however, the tune may appear to remain in the same key, but its eventual tonal destination may be averted for the sake of contrast. It is therefore important to examine melodic cadences carefully to uncover possible dual harmonic settings. For instance the tones D–E in the key of C major might support an imperfect cadence in C ($\hat{2}$–$\hat{3}$), a half cadence in D minor or ii ($\hat{1}$–$\hat{2}$), or a Phrygian cadence in A minor or vi ($\hat{4}$–$\hat{5}$). Study the phrases in Ex. 4-17 for examples of modulation or tonicization. You might wish to do a harmonic analysis to determine how the modulations were effected.

EXAMPLE 4-17 Tonicization in note-against-note settings

ASSIGNMENTS

1. Given the following three-note soprano cadential formulas in Ex. 4-18, which use only diatonic tones in B♭ major, construct cadences in two different keys for each—either in B♭ or related keys. Make sure that your cadences correspond to the conventional ones employed in the period (refer back to the cadence chart Ex. 4-3 in this chapter). In this case include both a figured bass and the implied harmonies in terms of Roman numerals.

EXAMPLE 4-18

2. Add an appropriate bass counterpoint (with figures) to this hypothetical chorale cantus. Include an example each of a perfect authentic, half, deceptive, and Phrygian cadence; this will necessitate some modulation. Add idiomatic uses of the harmonic tritone on those notes marked with an arrow. You might want to make a functional analysis to check your sense of harmonic progression.

EXAMPLE 4-19

3. Finally, Ex. 4-20 cites several *cantus firmi* which give you the opportunity for tonicization and altered chords in your contrapuntal settings.

EXAMPLE 4-20

A.   (cantus from Playford-Purcell: *An Introduction to the Skill of Musick* 1694)

5

✶✶

Simple diminution:
2:1 elaboration
of the
counterpointing voice

In Chapter 3, we saw that most of the counterpoint manuals of the late Renaissance and seventeenth century mentioned only two categories of cantus settings for two voices: *simple* counterpoint, the note-against-note technique discussed in the previous chapter; and *diminished* counterpoint, in which the added voice is rhythmically elaborated by consonant skips or stepwise dissonance (refer back to Exs. 3-5 and 3-6). Some treatises laid out a more systematic method, employing strict proportional relations of 2:1 or 4:1 with the cantus.[1] This approach, often found in variation sets of the period (see Ex. 19-4), was referred to as *diminution*. This term is not to be confused with melodic augmentation/diminution, where the note values of a theme are enlarged or reduced. In this context it denotes the rhythmic and tonal *elaboration* of a basic pitch succession, in our case the note-against-note counterpoint to a cantus. This chapter will begin the study of diminution, limited to only two notes for every one of the cantus. In contrast to more academic "second species," where only consonance and passing motion are allowed, a much wider range of dissonance will be explored, including non-harmonic tones, suspensions, and chordal dissonance. Cho-

---

[1]In particular, Diruta (1609), Banchieri (1614), and Berardi (1681 and 1689); see under Treatises in the Bibliography.

rale melodies and figured bass lines will continue as the primary sources for the cantus.

DIMINUTION WITH CONSONANT INTERVALS

This elaboration in the counterpointing voice can take the form of either consonant skips or stepwise motion involving 5–6 or 6–5. Most common of the former group is that of *chordal figuration,* where the leaps to consonance remain within the same implied triad. Since the problems of lower or upper voice elaboration are somewhat different, each will be discussed separately.

The process of chordal figuration in the bass is relatively simple: when the basic note implies a $\frac{5}{3}$, it may be followed by a $\frac{6}{3}$ of the same triad, and *vice versa.* The quotation from Kirnberger illustrates this technique (see Ex. 5-1). The beamed notes indicate the probable note-against-note setting. Observe that an elaborated tone may begin the measure.

EXAMPLE 5-1   Chordal figuration from Johann Kirnberger's
                         Gedanken über die vershiedenen Lehrarten in der Komposition

Several potential problems may arise. Leaps to the chordal fifth, even when it forms a consonant sixth with the cantus, can produce an implied $\frac{6}{4}$ (Ex. 5-2A). This type of consonant skip is permitted only when two *different* sonorities are involved (Ex. 5-2B). Be careful that the added note does not create perfect parallels with the cantus (Ex. 5-2C). (This is the main reason why similar motion to perfect intervals was covered in detail in Chapter 4.)

EXAMPLE 5-2 Problems of chordal figuration in the lower voice

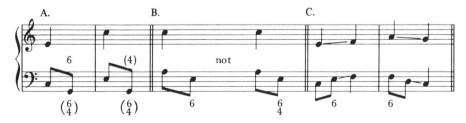

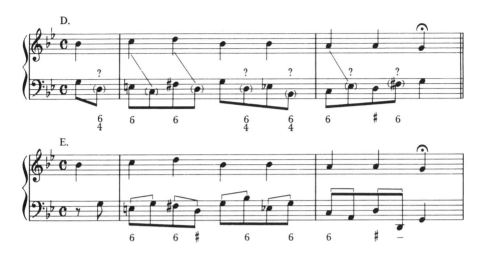

A rather poorly elaborated lower voice is given in Ex. 5-2D. Avoid parallel octaves on the first two offbeats of the initial measure. The tritone in the next measure is also questionable. The penultimate leading tone (f♯) weakens the effect of the final cadence, where root position is preferred. Now examine carefully the corrected version in Ex. 5-2E.

A few chordal figurations typical of the upper voice are illustrated in Ex. 5-3A. In Ex. 5-3B the basic notes appear on the beat, with chordal leaps relegated to the offbeats. You do not have to strictly adhere to this—in fact, the soprano line can be melodically enhanced by occasional switching of tones (Ex. 5-3C). Chordal figuration like this usually implies two distinct voices in the upper part. The resultant compound line is often referred to as a *melodic unfolding*. Consult Ex. 5-4, where the stemming denotes the separate strands. Be sure that the underlying voice-leading of all three parts is handled correctly. In Ex. 5-5A, the reduction reveals an augmented second (f^1–$g\sharp^1$) in the middle voice. This is rectified in Ex. 5-5B. An elaborated cadential section from a Scarlatti Sonata is quoted in Ex. 5-6. There appears to be a slight problem between measures 3–4. What is it?

EXAMPLE 5-3 Chordal figuration in the upper voice

(continued)

EXAMPLE 5-3 (cont'd)

EXAMPLE 5-4   Example of melodic unfolding in Johann Kirnberger's *Gedanken . . .*
(transposed to G here)

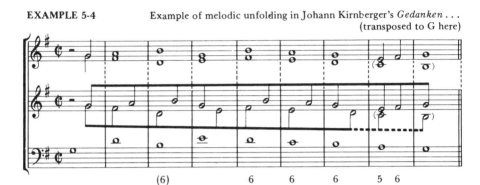

EXAMPLE 5-5

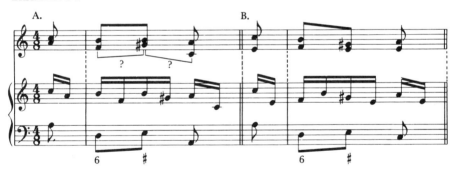

EXAMPLE 5-6   Domenico Scarlatti: Sonata in C K. 513

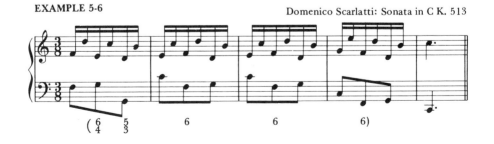

Successive stepwise consonances of 5–6 or 6–5 are common in 2:1 diminution. Some typical idioms are illustrated in Ex. 5-7. Note the frequent cadential cliché of Ex. 5-7C, implying a harmonic progression of ii^6 V I.

EXAMPLE 5-7 Examples of 5-6 or 6-5

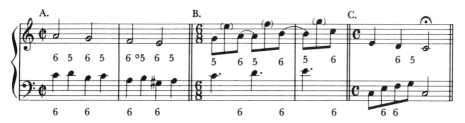

DIMINUTION WITH DISSONANT INTERVALS

The use of dissonance in the counterpointing voice may be conveniently divided into three categories: non-harmonic tones, suspensions, and chordal dissonance. The treatment of dissonance in this period always involves stepwise motion, either in its approach, resolution, or both.

In terms of 2:1 diminution *unaccented non-harmonic tones* means dissonant notes which fall on the offbeat. From an aural standpoint such non-harmonic tones have an embellishing or "nonessential" effect—that is, their weak metric placement de-emphasizes the dissonance, so that their principal effect is to generate rhythmic motion. Passing (P) and neighboring (N) tones are by far more frequent. The former are particularly useful since they create directional motion while bridging the interval of the melodic third. Some possibilities are cited in the two chorale phrases of Bach (Ex. 5-8A). Two passing tones in this example are actually consonant with the cantus, but dissonant with the implied harmony. Since the complete neighbor elaborates the same note, it is more static in nature. Do not overuse this technique. Typical idioms are given in Ex. 5-8B.

EXAMPLE 5-8 Examples of stepwise unaccented non-harmonic tones

Ach was soll ich Sünder machen (harmonized by Bach)

(continued)

EXAMPLE 5-8 (cont'd)

The remainder of the unaccented non-harmonic tones may be grouped together under the broad category of *incomplete neighbors* (IN). They are: (1.) *anticipation* (A) by step and common tone (Ex. 5-9A); (2.) *escape tone* (E) by step and leap (Ex. 5-9B); and (3.) *leaping tone* (L) by leap and step (Ex. 5-9C). Although each can be exploited motivically, all three are much less common than passing or neighboring tones. Occasionally several may be found together, as in the elaboration of the cadential $^6_4$ $^5_3$ formula (Ex. 5-9D).

EXAMPLE 5-9 Examples of other unaccented non-harmonic tones

By definition *accented non-harmonic tones* fall on the beat. Excluding suspensions, these dissonances come under the generic heading of *appoggiaturas*, which resolve by step on the offbeat, usually downward. In contrast to unaccented non-harmonic tones, appoggiaturas have a more "essential" character. The expectation of consonance on the beat is momentarily delayed by the appoggiatura, thereby rendering its resolution "sweeter". Their removal from the texture seriously deprives the music of much of its expressive quality. For instance, compare the Handel excerpt of Ex. 5-10A, which features consistent employment of on-the-beat dissonance, with the hypothetical setting of the same passage in Ex. 5-10B, using only unaccented non-harmonic tones. It hardly seems the same piece.

EXAMPLE 5-10   G. F. Handel: Gavotte (Sonata in C) (rhythm slightly modified)

A. Accented non-harmonic tones (original)   **B.** unaccented non-harmonic tones

Appoggiaturas may be approached by either step or leap. The former features accented passing and neighboring tones. Descending 7–6 and 4–3 passing motion is more common than 9–8 in the upper voice (Ex. 5-11A), while only 2–3 (or 9–10) is generally found in the bass (Ex. 5-11B). The ascending variety are possible but less frequent (Ex. 5-11C). Successive passing tones are often useful; note the voice exchange in the familiar idiom of Ex. 5-11D. The excerpt from the Bach Minuet combines both accented neighboring and passing motion (Ex. 5-11E). Appoggiaturas approached by leap, perhaps the rarest dissonance of the Baroque period, must be treated more carefully. They often tend to occur in sequences. Study the passage in Ex. 5-11F and point out any instances of accented dissonance.[2]

EXAMPLE 5-11 Examples of appoggiaturas

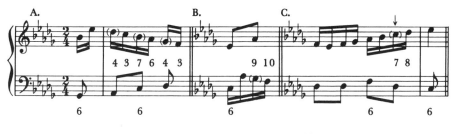

J. S. Bach (?): Minuet in G BWV Anh. 114
(*Notenbuch der Anna Magdalena Bach*)

(continued)

[2]An interesting quarter-note elaboration of a half-note bass line (2:1) may be found in the second movement of Bach's *Brandenburg* Concerto No. 6 in B♭ major.

EXAMPLE 5-11 (cont'd)

J. S. Bach: Aria "Seufzer, Tränen, Kummer, Not"
(Cantata No. 21 *Ich hatte viel Bekümmernis*)

ASSIGNMENTS

1. Add chordal figuration to the bass line of Ex. 5-12A, indicating any instances of first inversion with 6. Do the same for the soprano line of Ex. 5-12B. In the latter example be sure that the voice-leading resulting from any implied three-voice texture is treated correctly.

EXAMPLE 5-12

2. Criticize the four bass counterpoints to the chorale cantus of Ex. 5-13, pointing out specific errors or questionable practices. Which one do you prefer, and why?

EXAMPLE 5-13

Herr, ich habe missgehandelt

3. Compose a 2:1 counterpoint above Ex. 5-14A, using only consonance and unaccented dissonance. In the counterpoint below the chorale
tune of Ex. 5-14B try to include some accented non-harmonic tones. Note
the identical melodic cadences in the latter. Some tonicization or momentary modulation may be necessary to avoid monotony.

EXAMPLE 5-14

A.

B.

Wie schön leuchtet der Morgenstern

4. Example 5-15 represents a small problem in successive reduction.
In this excerpt both voices have been elaborated. Begin by identifying and
removing all non-harmonic tones; which particular one seems to be exploited here? Then identify and remove those notes which constitute chordal figuration, noting that the harmonic rhythm is one chord per measure.
What remains should form the note-against-note framework on which the
passage is based.

EXAMPLE 5-15   J. S. Bach: Prelude in d BWV 935 (*Sechs kleine Präludien*)

SUSPENSIONS IN SIMPLE DIMINUTION

The suspension is by definition an accented dissonance. Since the duration of its *preparation* (consonance), *suspended note* (dissonance), and its stepwise descending *resolution* (consonance again) are each usually a half-beat long, the study of suspensions properly belongs to the domain of 2:1 diminution. They are classified according to their intervallic dissonance and resolution between the two parts. Suspensions elaborate imperfect consonances of thirds and sixths. Typical of the upper voice are the 7–6 and 4–3, which resolve to chords of the 6th and ⅗ respectively. The only bass suspension of any consequence is the 2–3 (or 9–10). Observe the "inversional" relation of the 7–6 and 2–3 in Ex. 5-16A. Although the tie is customarily employed to link the preparation and suspended note, it is not mandatory (Ex. 5-16B). Beware of Ex. 5-16C; although the intervallic relations are 2–3, it is *not* a bass suspension; why? In Ex. 5-16D the apparent passing tone f¹ is delayed by a suspension before its final resolution to e¹, a rare case where the preparation is not consonant. Upward resolutions, sometimes called *retardations,* are rare.

EXAMPLE 5-16 **Suspensions in two voices**

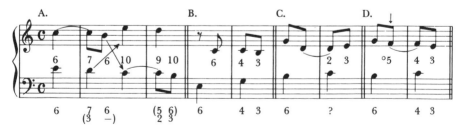

The ornamentation or embellishment of suspensions and the possibility of change of bass or upper part during resolution will be discussed in a later chapter.

CHORDAL DISSONANCE IN SIMPLE DIMINUTION

The use of chordal sevenths, producing dissonance for the duration of the beat, has been discussed in Chapter 4. They continue to appear in conjunction with diminished 2:1 counterpoint. Some typical instances feature either suspension (Ex. 5-17A) or passing (Ex. 5-17B) idioms. Although the tritone is featured in these examples, sevenths or ninths may likewise be encountered (Ex. 5-17C). In cases of this nature one can begin to see several levels of hierarchical dissonance. Consult the reductions of the three previous passages in Ex. 5-17D, noting the underlying voice-leading.

EXAMPLE 5-17

ASSIGNMENTS

1. Write counterpoints for Exs. 5-18A and 18B, utilizing as many appropriate suspensions as possible.

EXAMPLE 5-18

2. Set the unfigured bass line of Ex. 5-19 with 2:1 counterpoint. Employ at least three suspensions (7–6 or 4–3) and at least one example of a chordal dissonance. Supply the correct bass figures when completed.

EXAMPLE 5-19

3. The opening of Bach's chorale prelude *Wachet auf* poses a fascinating problem in non-harmonic analysis. Identify each note of the upper voice in terms of consonance or specific dissonances. It may be necessary to consider compound melody.

EXAMPLE 5-20

J. S. Bach: *Wachet auf* BWV 645 (*Schübler Chorales*)

6

※※※※※※※※※※※※※※※※※※※※※※※※※※※※※※※※※※※※※※

Further rhythmic diminution; two-voice chorale preludes

After examining more rhythmically active diminution procedures (3:1, 4:1, and free), this chapter will explore compositional techniques of the Baroque two-voice chorale prelude.

FURTHER CONTRAPUNTAL DIMINUTION

To bring out the slower moving cantus, faster rhythmic motion is often used in the accompanying counterpoint. It may take the form of 3:1 or 4:1 (quasi-third species) or even 6:1 or 8:1. Instances of "free" rhythmic counterpointing (fifth species) are also common.

Even a partial list of the melodic figurations resulting from 3:1 or 4:1 diminutions is impractical. Obviously, examples of chordal tones and unaccented stepwise dissonance abound, with occasional instances of appoggiaturas, mostly in the form of descending accented passing tones. Examples 6-1A through 1E cite other idioms that may occur in compound meter using 3:1. Examples 6-1A and 1B employ a pair of incomplete neighbors (usually called a *returning tone*) to embellish the oblique motion in the upper voices. Examples 6-1C and 1D are basic elaborations of a passing tone (g^2–f^2–e^2) in conjunction with chord tones that are circled. The first of these is

the classic *nota cambiata* (or *changing note*) figure. The final passing motion
in Ex. 6-1E employs an incomplete upper neighbor.

EXAMPLE 6-1 Incomplete neighbors in 3:1 settings

Now analyze the counterpointing voice in Ex. 6-2 for chordal and
non-harmonic tones.

EXAMPLE 6-2

Jesu, der du meine Seele

Example 6-3 illustrates the possible utilization of returning or changing note figures in typical 4:1 settings. Circle and explain all instances of
dissonance in Ex. 6-4 and 6-5. Are there any examples of appoggiaturas or
suspensions?

EXAMPLE 6-3 Incomplete neighbors in 4:1 settings

EXAMPLE 6-4

Von Gott will ich nicht lassen

EXAMPLE 6-5

Johann Kirnberger: *Ach Gott, vom Himmel sieh' darein*
(*Die Kunst des reinen Satzes in der Musik* 1771-79)

The greater rhythmic activity in these contrapuntal settings tends to increase problems. Guard against parallels produced by the elaboration (see Ex. 6-6A through C), and beware of "dangling" dissonance, either within or at the end of the beat (Ex. 6-6D and E). In general avoid *extended* successions of accented dissonance, as the underlying harmonic implication may be obscured. The series of descending passing tones in Ex. 6-6F is possible, but its inversion (Ex. 6-6G) should be discouraged.

EXAMPLE 6-6 Potential problems in 4:1 and 3:1 diminutions

Using more rhythmically active elaborations allows the introduction of *embellished suspensions.* Remember that the *suspended* dissonance is ornamented, *not* its resolution note. Three other common figurations are shown in Ex. 6-7 with both dotted and undotted beat-notes. In these instances the suspension resolves *within* the beat unit (see the arrows), so its preparation needs to last only part of a beat, as in Ex. 6-7A and 7B. In Ex. 6-8 the suspension now resolves on the *following* beat (again see the arrows), so the preparation should be at least one beat long.

EXAMPLE 6-7 Ornamented suspensions with resolution on off-beat

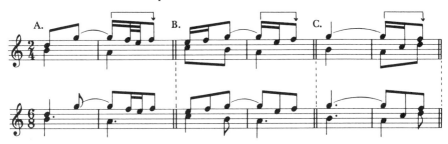

EXAMPLE 6-8 Ornamented suspensions with resolution on following beat

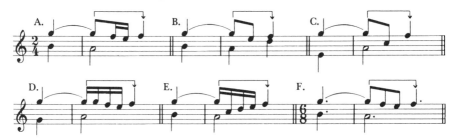

In the chorale phrase settings of Exs. 6-9 and 6-10 the rigid rhythmic restrictions are now removed, resulting in a kind of *free* (or *fifth species*) counterpoint. Both employ suspensions, some of which are embellished. Analyze each carefully.

EXAMPLE 6-9

Dietrich Buxtehude: *Vater unser im Himmelreich* (fifth phrase)

EXAMPLE 6-10

Ach wie nichtig, ach wie flüchtig

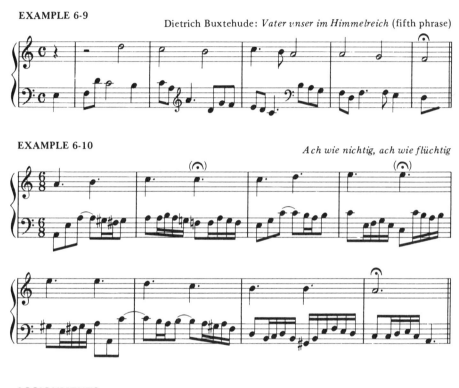

ASSIGNMENTS

1. Complete Ex. 6-11, using free counterpoint. Place either a 7–6 or a 2–3 suspension on each beat marked with an X. The suspensions will resolve on the following beat. Use as many different suspension embellishments as you can.

EXAMPLE 6-11

2. A passage from a Bach Prelude is quoted in Ex. 6-12. Although the arrows denote a succession of 7-6 suspensions, the embellishing tones (on the second sixteenth note of each beat) appear to leap randomly. Make a voice-leading reduction, indicating the passing motion on the weak beats. Can the excerpt be further simplified to show the overall movement to the final F♯ chord?

EXAMPLE 6-12

3. The 4:1 setting found in Ex. 6-13 contains six errors, as indicated by the circled notes and brackets. After explaining the nature of each mistake, compose a correct counterpoint over the same bass.

EXAMPLE 6-13

4. Compose a 3:1 setting for Ex. 6-14A and a 4:1 (or in the case of half notes, 8:1) setting for Ex. 6-14B. It may be necessary to tonicize the dominant area briefly in each.

EXAMPLE 6-14

THE TWO-VOICE CHORALE PRELUDE

Use of the German chorale tune as a *cantus firmus* formed the basis for much vocal and instrumental repertoire in the Baroque. The more general term *Choralbearbeitung* simply denotes a hymn arrangement or setting (literally a "working out"). Even in the late Renaissance, composers were employing these new Protestant melodies in motets. This activity in the vocal genre continued well into the seventeenth century, culminating in the *chorale cantatas* of the North German School—Franz Tunder and his son-in-law Dietrich Buxtehude.[1] As the Baroque development of purely instrumental idioms intensified, a host of related "forms" evolved in association with the chorale: chorale prelude, chorale fantasia, chorale fugue, and chorale variations or partitas. It is not surprising that the organ was the favorite instrument. In addition to Tunder and Buxtehude, one may trace a line of development through the numerous chorale compositions of Johann Pachelbel, Georg Böhm, Johann Walther, and J. S. Bach.

Our interest lies in the chorale prelude (*Choralvorspiel*), which implies a more contrapuntal setting as opposed to a simpler "harmonization," although one cannot dismiss Bach's 371 chorales as merely homophonic examples. Originating in the liturgical service, the performance of a chorale prelude on the organ served the practical function of reminding the congregation of the actual tune, since the hymnbooks of that time contained only text. Thus they preceded (or followed) the congregational singing in much the same fashion as an organist today often plays an introductory first verse. However, the chorale prelude quickly outgrew its original purpose and evolved into an art form in its own right. There are many examples of extended and complex works in this genre using a variety of techniques.[2]

The rare instances of two-voice chorale preludes in the late Baroque give us a chance to compose more elaborate and extended cantus settings. Chorale preludes employing only 2:1 diminution are practically non-existent, since that is usually reserved for actual chorale harmonizations, as in Bach's "371," which were mostly extracted from his own cantatas.

COMPOSITIONAL UNIFICATION IN THE CHORALE PRELUDE

In a period that prized economy of compositional means, the contrapuntal settings of hymn tunes presented somewhat of a problem. Since little internal relation exists between the melodic phrases of a typical chorale, com-

---

[1]For a discussion of the chorale cantata, see Chapter 21.

[2]Some of Bach's more important chorale prelude collections include the *Orgelbüchlein*, the "Great Eighteen", the *Klavierübung* Part III, the *Schübler Chorales*, the *Kirnberger-Sammlung*, and the recently discovered *Neumeister-Sammlung* at Yale University.

posers began to explore methods of achieving organic unity within a piece. Three such means will be discussed here.[3]

A. Anticipation of the Cantus Voice

The first method has its roots in some of the *cantus firmus* (or *tenor*) mass settings of the sixteenth century. The introduction of the fixed melody, usually in longer note values, might be preceded by a series of imitative entries (or *point of imitation*), whose theme is based on the cantus itself. The opening Kyrie to Palestrina's *Missa L'Homme arme* (a5) is a typical example. This technique continued into the following century, as you can see in the pair of excerpts from a *bicinium* chorale prelude by Samuel Scheidt (Ex. 6-15). The opening counterpoint states the cantus in diminuted rhythmic form. In the first phrase it is a fifth lower, while in the latter it is an octave removed (see the brackets in the example). The counterpointing voice finishes with its "anticipation," then continues in free elaboration with little sense of motivic development. The cadential points, with their 2-3 suspensions, look backward to the Renaissance.

EXAMPLE 6-15   Samuel Scheidt: *Da Jesus an dem Kreuze stand* (versus 3)

---

[3]Further information on various types of chorale preludes may be found in Chapters 12 and 18.

An entire composition by Johann Walther (Ex. 6-16) illustrates this device applied to a complete chorale tune. Brief interludes between the phrases, a procedure typical of most chorale preludes, allow the counterpoint (in this case 6:1) to make its anticipatory statements.[4] Compare the circled notes with the first cantus phrase. Now relate each of the remaining interludes to the chorale melody which follows it. Some may be slightly hidden within the contrapuntal elaboration.

EXAMPLE 6-16

Johann Walther: *Herr Jesu Christ, dich zu ans wend'* (Variation 7)

(continued)

[4]When the interludes are missing, it is sometimes called a *simple chorale prelude;* see Ex. 12-9C.

EXAMPLE 6-16 (cont'd)

B. Internal Motivic Development in the Counterpointing Voice

In the opening phrase of the Walther setting above, bracketing shows three distinct motivic figures, which reappear. These are labelled A, B, and C. Thus an *internal* method of unification begins to emerge—that of more consistent motivic development within the counterpointing voice itself. This technique appears again in Ex. 6-17, also by Walther. Not only is the anticipatory device still in operation (see bracketing), but now the composer takes the final figure of the opening counterpoint (shown with slurs) and uses it five more times. Even the cantus is elaborated in the third measure to conform to the motive.[5]

EXAMPLE 6-17   Johann Walther: *Durch Adams Fall ist ganz verderbt*

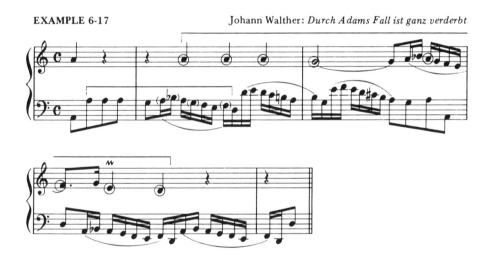

This type of motivic unity is not accidental, but must be built into the basic contrapuntal voice-leading of the parts. Returning to the first phrase of Ex. 6-16, note that motives B and C may occur in a variety of harmonic situations, *provided* there is an available chordal tone either a third lower (motive B) or a third higher (motive C) within the same beat. Motive A is an elaborated descending passing tone which may be used only when the basic voice-leading falls by third to the next beat; check other instances of A. Therefore, to make consistent use of such motivic figurations, determine the intervallic/rhythmic relation necessary for each, and then build these into the underlying framework of the counterpointing voices. Go back and analyze Ex. 6-17 in this way.

---

[5]This technique will be discussed further in Chapter 12 under "doctrine of figures" (*Figurenlehre*).

C. Ritornello Interludes

Chorale preludes may sometimes utilize interludes between the phrases of the hymn. Many of the *simple* preludes in Bach's *Orgelbüchlein* dispense with interludes altogether. When interludes are used, they may be extended and a consistent thematic idea was applied to link the cantus phrases, somewhat in the manner of a *ritornello*. A rare two-voice setting by Bach of *Allein Gott in der Höh' sei Ehr'* is an excellent example of this procedure. Only the opening ritornello theme and the first chorale phrase are quoted in Ex. 6-18. Between phrases two and three the ritornello is stated again (measures 22–27 = 1–6). It likewise appears between phrases three and four transposed a tone higher (measures 36–40 = 2–6), and finally serves as a kind of coda back in the original key (measures 56–61 = 1–6).

EXAMPLE 6-18

J. S. Bach: *Allein Gott in der Höh' sei Ehr'* BWV 711

The initial ritornello theme may accompany subsequent chorale phrases. In this case one must work out a good counterpointing voice that can stand alone on its own melodic merits (see Ex. 6-19). Here the hymn tune has been embellished; the circled notes represent the original chorale.

EXAMPLE 6-19

J. S. Bach: *Du Friedefürst, Herr Jesu Christ*
(*Neumeister-Sammlung*) BWV 1102

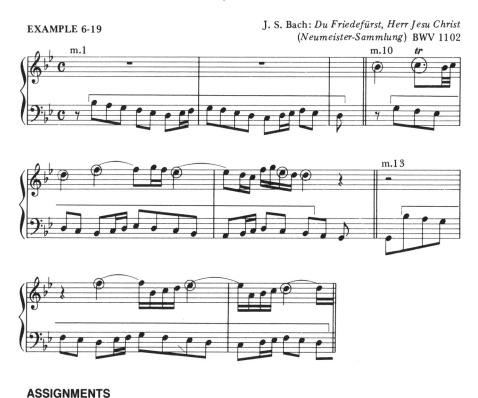

ASSIGNMENTS

1. Using the chorale tune in Ex. 6-20, anticipate each phrase with a diminuted form of its melody (at the lower octave). Then counterpoint the two phrases using a 4:1 setting.

EXAMPLE 6-20

Christ lag in Todesbanden

2. Compose a free contrapuntal setting of the tune in Ex. 6-21. Make *consistent* use of several motives. Be sure to plan your basic voice-leading toward this end.

EXAMPLE 6-21   *Herr Jesu Christ, dich zu uns wend'*

3. An opening *ritornello* theme and a short chorale melody are cited in Ex. 6-22. Use the theme to counterpoint the first phrase and then try to restate some form of the *ritornello* in successive interludes.

EXAMPLE 6-22   *Wer nur den lieben Gott lässt walten*

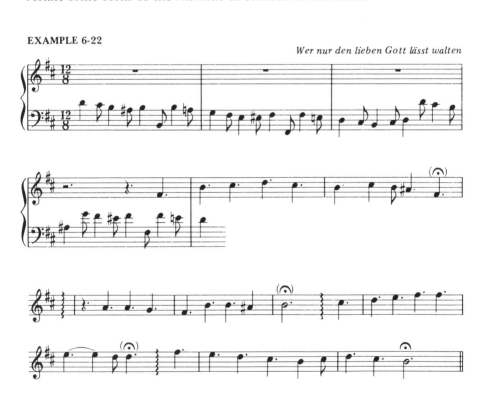

7

※※※※※※※※※※※※※※※※※※※※※※※※※※※※※※※※※※※※※

Free counterpoint;
simple two-reprise form

Now that we have applied diminution to the voice counterpointed against a cantus, the next logical step is to elaborate *both* parts, neither of which derives from a given fixed melody. You may write out either voice in complete form and then counterpoint it, or compose the two parts simultaneously. Whatever the procedure, do not be so misled by this *free counterpoint* as to forsake the underlying note-against-note setting, which determines the validity of the voice-leading. Maintain a constant rhythmic interplay or balancing between the voices, so when one is sustaining, the other is active, thereby producing a seamless rhythmic flow. Also, continue to use the technique of motivic unification discussed in Chapter 6. Limit the number of motivic figures to less than three.

Ex. 7-1A through 1C represent some typical passages of free counterpoint with elaboration in both parts. In Ex. 7-1A the simple 2:1 diminution is shared between the voices. The initial measure of Ex. 7-1B establishes two motives which continue through the excerpt; note the sequential pattern and melodic inversion. Whereas here the motivic figures are interchanged, in Ex. 7-1C the soprano and bass maintain separate musical ideas. Analyze each example carefully, extracting the basic note-against-note framework. Be able to explain the handling of dissonance or chordal figuration in the diminution process.

EXAMPLE 7-1 Examples of free counterpoint

Momentary tonicizations will often involve chromaticism.[1] Example 7-2A represents the normal situation where the augmented prime (f–f♯–g) occurs in the *same* voice. Avoid Ex. 7-2B, in which the voice switching has created an undesirable chromatic *cross relation* between two *different* parts. It is best to limit the use of cross relations to those examples where a *bona fide* voice exchange occurs (sometimes called a *chromatic voice exchange*), as in Ex. 7-2C. Example 7-2D is also possible, although rare in two-part texture.

EXAMPLE 7-2 Examples of cross relations

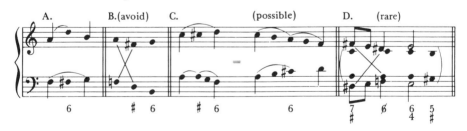

[1]For a more extensive discussion of chromaticism in general see Chapter 13.

ASSIGNMENTS

1. Given the note-against-note setting in Ex. 7-3, elaborate both voices in free counterpoint, using a meter signature of $_1{6\over8}$. Provide appropriate suspensions at the points indicated with arrows. You may wish to employ ornamental figures with the suspensions. Keep a continual flow of sixteenth-notes throughout by rhythmically alternating the voices.

EXAMPLE 7-3

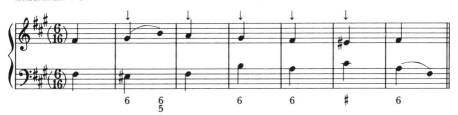

2. Compose three original note-against-note settings, and then elaborate both voices of each, utilizing various types of diminution. Choose different keys and meters. The phrases may modulate if you wish; feel free to use sequence.

SIMPLE TWO-REPRISE FORM

Short works cast in a *two-reprise* (or binary) form are common in this period.[2] They appear in a great variety of media: keyboard, solo string, chamber, and even orchestral. The term "two-reprise" refers to *two sections* of music set off with *repeat* signs. In no way does the expression "binary" signify an A B thematic structure. Brief two-reprise pieces generally consist of either sixteen measures (‖: 8 :‖: 8 :‖) or twenty-four measures (‖: 8 :‖: 8 + 8 :‖). Typical of this form are the shorter stylized dance movements of suites, usually the minuet or perhaps a slower sarabande. As the following examples will illustrate, it is difficult to make much of a case for stereotyped melodic or thematic structure. The opening material undergoes development throughout the piece, although minimal contrast can be found at the initiation of the second reprise or at the end of both sections.[3] Thus, the underlying tonal scheme is the delineating formal element in these works.

The following remarks will be limited to the first-reprise section. Its eight-measure duration is normally divided into two four-measure phrases

[2] Extended binary form will be considered in Chapter 14.

[3]Sometimes the thematic material or cadential formula may be identical at the conclusion of both sections, excepting transposition.

(‖: 4 + 4 :‖), although in some cases it is not possible to pinpoint a real cadential punctuation half-way through. Following the establishment of tonic, this section will move toward the tonal goal (or cadence) of the second phrase. Three or four typical tonal schemes exist in each mode (consult Fig. 7-1). Here the letter T denotes a tonicization of that scale degree. Thus V equals a simple half cadence, while T/V is a tonal shift to the dominant through tonicization. It is difficult to predict the cadence of the first phrase. Generally, if the goal of the first reprise is I (or i), it will normally move to V. If that goal is something other than tonic, it may cadence on I.

FIGURE 7-1 **Typical tonal schemes for the first-reprise section**

Examples 7-4 through 7-7 cite three complete minuets and a sarabanda. These will serve as typical models for analysis and simulation. The continuous walking bass in the Corelli piece (Ex. 7-6) sets it off texurally from the others.

EXAMPLE 7-4   J. S. Bach (?): Minuet in d BWV Anh. 132
                                                                (Notenbuch der Anna Magdalena Bach)

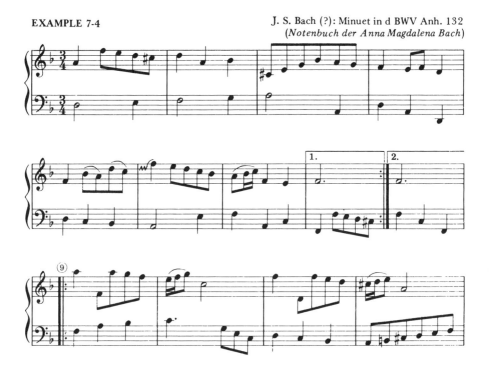

EXAMPLE 7-5

G. F. Handel: Minuet in F
(also see Minuetto Alternativo in his Concerto Grosso Op. 3, No. 4 in F)

EXAMPLE 7-6

Arcangelo Corelli: Sarabanda (Sonata No. 8 in e for Violin and Continuo)

EXAMPLE 7-7

Jean Baptiste Loeillet: Solo for Flute and Continuo in F

The following comments refer to only the first-reprise sections of the above examples. In the initial Minuet (Ex. 7-4) this period is divided into the customary 4 + 4 grouping, each concluding with an authentic cadence in tonic and the relative major respectively. Note the little *turnabout* in the first ending which leads back to D minor upon repetition. The Handel piece (Ex. 7-5) tonicizes the dominant at the conclusion of its first section. There is little sense of interior cadence, producing a seamless eight measures. The Sarabanda (Ex. 7-6) returns to a pair of four-measure phrases, punctuated first by III and then a Phrygian cadence on V. Loeillet's first reprise is likewise cast in a 4 + 4 pattern with goals of I and tonicized V respectively (see Ex. 7-7).

The student composition in Ex. 7-8 represents a possible working procedure for composing the first reprise of a small binary piece, in this case a minuet. In the upper staves the stemmed notes represent the more

EXAMPLE 7-8 First-reprise section of a student Minuet: framework and elaborration

essential tones of the framework, providing a kind of foundational note-against-note setting. The phrasing is 4 + 4 with goals on I and tonicized V. The harmonic rhythm is basically one chord per measure, although exceptions do occur, particularly near the cadences.

ASSIGNMENTS

1. Analyze the first-reprise sections of Exs. 7-4 through 7-7 in some detail, reducing each to its underlying voice-leading, observing the methods of diminution, and tracing any motivic development you may notice.

2. Point out the compositional "errors" of Ex. 7-9 in regard to the general contrapuntal norms and specific points pertaining to the above discussion.

EXAMPLE 7-9

3. Compose an original first-reprise section in the manner of Ex. 7-8. Show both your original note-against-note setting and its eventual elaboration. Choose your own key, tonal scheme, and phrasing.

The fundamental tonal plan for the second reprise is more complex. It consists of a movement away from tonic (this is essential if the first reprise remains in the home key) through either sequential patterns or the exploration of other closely-related areas, followed by a return to I during the latter part of the section. Although the restatement of tonic *may* coincide with a recurrence of the initial thematic idea at the beginning of the piece, this tends to be the exception rather than the rule.[4]

---

[4]One such example is quoted in Ex. 14-10.

Anton Reipel, in his exposition of melodic structure in binary form,[5] lists three stereotyped formulas which frequently occur at the opening of the second reprise. The *Ponte* (bridge or melodic arch) basically prolongs the dominant harmony in preparation for the eventual tonic (see Ex. 7-10A). Two sequential patterns are also possible: the *Monte* (mountain or rising contour), involving V^7 /IV IV V^7 /V V, at which point the tonic usually returns, or the *Fonte* (fountain or falling contour), featuring V^7 /ii ii V^7 I. Consult Ex. 7-10B and C.

EXAMPLE 7-10   Anton Riepel: *Anfangsgründe zur musikalischen Setzkunst* II (1755)

It is possible to move to and cadence in other closely-related keys. However, due to the brief duration of such pieces, these scale degrees are never tonicized extensively. Some typical schemes for the second-reprise section are listed in Fig. 7-2.

FIGURE 7-2 Typical tonal schemes for the second-reprise section

	⌢I		T/V			I		
Major	T/V	: :	T/ii	(V)		I		:
	V		T/vi	(ii	V)	I		

	⌢i		T/III	(V)		i		
Minor	T/III	: :	T/iv	(V)		i		:
	T/III		T/v	(V)		i		

[5]Anton Riepel, *Anfangsgründe zur musikalischen Setzkunst* Vol. 2 (1755).

The outlines of Fig. 7-2 intentionally omit phrasing indications. The placement of cadences in related keys and the return of tonic are dependent upon whether this section is divided into either a 4 + 4 or an 8 + 8 measure grouping. In some instances the phrase consistency may break down, resulting in phrasings of five, six, or seven measures.

The brief observations below refer back to the second-reprise sections of Exs. 7-4 through 7-7. Phrasing is denoted by slurs, and cadences by arrows.

(Ex. 7–4) T/III :‖: III i V V i :‖

The arrival back in tonic is delayed until quite late.

(Ex. 7–5) T/V :‖: V/IV IV V/V (V) T/vi V⁷/ii ii V⁷ I I :‖

Note the use of both *Monte* and *Fonte* sequences (in brackets).

(Ex. 7–6) V :‖: V i V/VII V I I' T / v V/iv iv V/III I I I i :‖

The last eight measures are almost an exact repetition of the first eight a fifth lower. Transposed *Fontes* are bracketed.

(Ex. 7–7) T/V :‖: vi T/ ii (ii V I IV—V) I :‖

Observe the seven-measure phrasings and the returning cycle of fifths which "overshoots" the tonic into IV.

The upper staves of Ex. 7-11 are a possible working model for the continuation of the student minuet analyzed in Ex. 7-8. The final elaborated version is given below. Here the student decided upon a second reprise of sixteen measures with the normative 8 + 8 division. The opening of this section moves immediately from the previously established dominant to the submediant key of C♯ minor, which is then maintained until the perfect cadence in measure 8. Despite the continuous rhythmic flow, there is a slight sense of punctuation in measure 4 on V of that key. Note the gradual stepwise descent from g♯² to c♯² in the soprano (shown by beaming), with the a² acting as a neighbor. The problem now is to cancel the tonicized vi and a return to the original tonic. The device incorporated here is a transposed *Fonte* sequence (measures 9–12), which descends from the previous c♯² through b¹ to a¹ in the subdominant area. The soprano d♯² (measure 14) then directs the final phrase back toward I.

EXAMPLE 7-11 Second-reprise section of a student Minuet: framework and elaboration

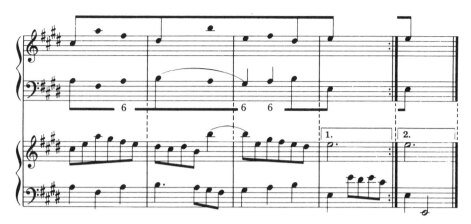

ASSIGNMENTS

1. Select several of the pieces cited in Exs. 7-4 through 7-7 and extract the basic voice-leading of the second-reprise section. The Corelli is particularly interesting in this regard.

2. Take the first-reprise assignment you did previously and now add the remaining section, plotting out a logical tonal scheme, basic framework, and eventual elaboration. Retain the same motivic ideas you developed originally.

8

✳✳

Further diminution techniques in two-voice texture

Chapter 7 introduced simple diminution in both voices, resulting in free two-part counterpoint. Chapter 8 will focus on more intricate elaborative procedures, emphasizing sequential patterns, chord-member exchange, and figurations of underlying voice-leading models.

The frequent use of compound melody, in which two separate strands may be detected, was mentioned in Chapter 2 (review Exs. 2-7 through 2-9). Examples 8-1 and 8-2 are typical. The upper part of each implies a pair of voices (refer to the reductions). This texture is common in sequential passages, such as Ex. 8-2 with its cycle of seventh chords.

In Chapter 7, diminution in the two voices occurred in a leisurely way. In fast movements, frequent subdivision of the beat often results in more rhythmically active elaborations. Here the composer's concern is how to "prolong" chords by using rapid note values without speeding up the harmonic rhythm. One solution to this problem in two-voice texture is *chord-member exchange*, but at a faster speed. Typical forms are listed in Ex. 8-3A and 3B; the quarter-note is the assumed beat unit. These may be elaborated in many ways (see Ex. 8-3C). "Chordal exchanges," in the following examples are only surface events that do not affect the underlying voice-leading of a passage.

EXAMPLE 8-1

J. S. Bach: Trio Sonata in C for Organ BWV 529, III

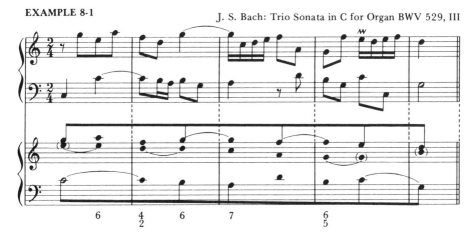

EXAMPLE 8-2

J. S. Bach: Concerto for Two Violins in d BWV 1043, I

EXAMPLE 8-3 Examples of chordal exchange and their possible elaboration

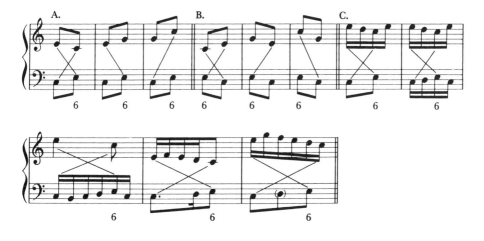

Since our aim is to develop skill in handling more active and involved rhythmic diminutions, we will study some complex elaborations, first with two *real* parts and then with three *implied* voices. Bach's Prelude in F♯ minor (*WTC* I), a virtual lexicon of these various procedures, will serve as our instruction manual. This piece is based on the sixteenth-note motive quoted in Ex. 8-4 (see brackets). The following comments refer to a series of short passages extracted from the prelude. A basic voice-leading reduction accompanies each example.

EXAMPLE 8-4   J. S. Bach: Prelude in f♯ | (WTC I), meas. 1-2

In the opening excerpt (Ex. 8-5) the initial note of each beat outlines a sequential pattern of descending fifths with alternating 6th chords (see Ex. 8-5B). Applied to Ex. 8-6, this method of reduction yields the same harmonic motion using ⅗s only. Observe the continual chordal exchanges in these two passages involving both voices. In the next quotation (Ex. 8-7), the exchange is only partial, producing a succession of 6th chords. While the two previous examples showed overall descending stepwise motion, here the basic movement is by ascending seconds (see the beamed notes).

EXAMPLE 8-5

J. S. Bach: Prelude in f♯ (*WTC* I), meas. 3-4

EXAMPLE 8-6

J. S. Bach: Prelude in f♯ (*WTC* I), meas. 16-17

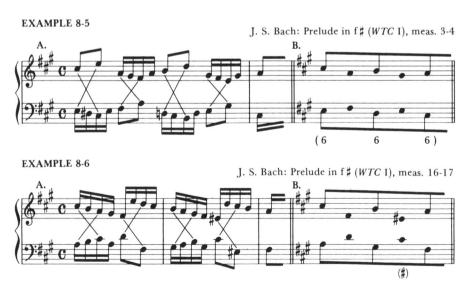

EXAMPLE 8-7

J. S. Bach: Prelude in f♯ (*WTC* I), meas. 5-6

The next two examples are not strictly sequential. Although chordal exchange is still employed in Ex. 8-8, the lower part suggests two separate melodic strands (see the circled notes), resulting in three implied voices in the reduction. In Ex. 8-9 the soprano and bass switch places from the previous passage (albeit now transposed), with the pair of implied voices in the upper part. The $^6_4$ passes through a $^4_2$ (rather than $^5_3$) on its way to a first inversion resolution.

EXAMPLE 8-8

J. S. Bach: Prelude in f♯ (*WTC* I), meas. 6-7

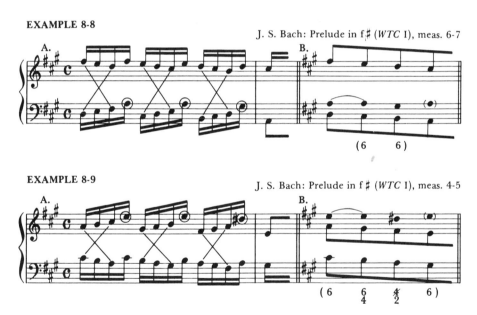

EXAMPLE 8-9

J. S. Bach: Prelude in f♯ (*WTC* I), meas. 4-5

The final pair of quotations from Bach's Prelude are more complex. If the intervals of the sixth in the bass of Ex. 8-10A are verticalized, parallel fifths are produced with the soprano (see Ex. 8-10B). More likely to be implied in the lower part is a series of 7-6 suspensions, which stagger the fifth motion (Ex. 8-10C). The reduction of the next passage also features fifths between the outer voices—compare Ex. 8-11A with 11B. Example 8-11C offers an alternate analysis: a sequence involving a pattern of $^6_5$ to $^5_3$.

EXAMPLE 8-10

J. S. Bach: Prelude in f♯ (*WTC* I), meas. 9-10

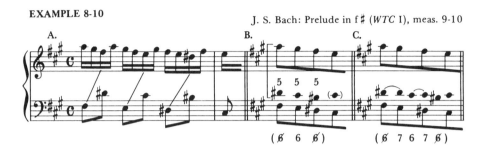

EXAMPLE 8-11

J. S. Bach: Prelude in f♯ (*WTC* I), meas. 20-21

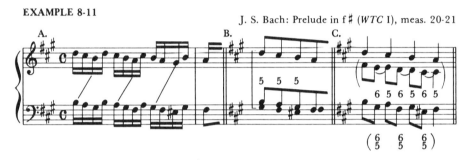

Despite the precaution of parallels noted above, such instances as Exs. 8-12A and 12B do exist in Baroque music. There is no way, however, to rationalize the fifths in Ex. 8-12C.

EXAMPLE 8-12 Possible parallel motion in elaborations

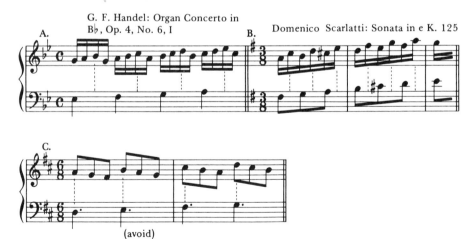

Does chordal exchange also exist at higher structural levels? In Ex. 8-13A it appears to occur within each measure (note the crossing). However, voice exchange is more appropriate here. Example 8-13B gives a clear picture of the technique. The basic voice-leading of the first measure (see the beamed notes) is interrupted by the voice exchange. But the exchange in the next measure reestablishes the original framework, and so forth. The final reduction in Ex. 8-13C reveals the tonal movement for the passage, in this case the familiar cycle of fifths with alternating 6th chords. This continuous voice exchange is common when the harmonic rhythm moves by the measure in sequential fashion.

EXAMPLE 8-13

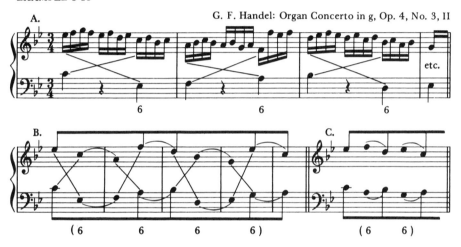

G. F. Handel: Organ Concerto in g, Op. 4, No. 3, II

ASSIGNMENTS

1. Examine Bach's Prelude in F♯ minor (*WTC* I) in its entirety, observing motivic development and overall tonal scheme.

2. Employ the melodic motive of Ex. 8-14 as the basis for an elaboration of a two-voice sequence. You may want to refer back to the paradigms listed in Chapter 1. Repeat the same assignment with a different sequence and a motive of your own. Incorporate the principle of chordal exchange in both.

EXAMPLE 8-14

3. Make a voice-leading reduction of Ex. 8-15, taking into account the possible effect of voice exchange.

EXAMPLE 8-15

FIGURATION PRELUDES

You may encounter instances of diminution where one or both parts will elaborate chords in *consistent figuration*. A basic prototype of this technique may be found in Friedrich Niedt's treatise *Musikalische Handleitung* (c. 1709). After first outlining the basic progression in block harmonies, he demonstrates several simple methods of rhythmically elaborating or "figuring" the triads in the upper staff, resulting in a basic two-voice texture. Study Exs. 8-16A through 16E.

EXAMPLE 8-16   Friedrich Niedt: *Musikalische Handleitung* Vol. II

This procedure is found more frequently in short keyboard preludes of the period, hence the expression *figuration preludes*. During the seventeenth century composers might write a series of harmonic progressions in whole notes, and the performer was expected to supply his own rhythmic elaboration. Later one may find a specific figuration at the beginning of the piece which was to apply to the remainder of the composition. Some employ a more polyphonic than figurative diminution of the model. In such cases the voice-leading of the fundamental chord progressions must be worked out more carefully, particularly in the outer voices.

Portions of three figuration preludes have been selected from the *Klavierbüchlein,* a collection of pedagogically oriented pieces which Bach wrote for his eldest son, Wilhelm Freidmann. Since the voice-leading underlying four of these preludes (the C major, C minor, E minor, and D major) is virtually identical, they may have been an attempt to demonstrate *different* figurations on the *same* framework. Several other common characteristics may be noted: the persistent employment of the original figuration; and the rather slow harmonic rhythm by either four or two beats.

In the autograph score of the *Klavierbüchlein* the arpeggiations of the C major Prelude are written out in the initial few measures and then assumed for the remainder of the piece. Example 8-17A quotes the opening eleven measures. The five-voice part writing is handled very carefully in regard to parallels. In the reduction (Ex. 8-17B) the first four measures prolong the tonic, after which a staggered descent in tenths cadences in the dominant.[1] Note the suspensions in the bass.

EXAMPLE 8-17

J. S. Bach: Prelude in C (*Klavierbüchlein*, later in *WTC* I)

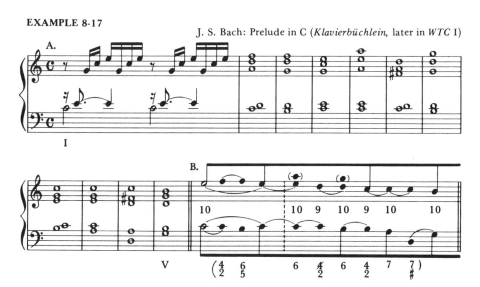

The C minor Prelude proceeds similarly (Ex. 8-18), except that its harmonic destination is now III, the relative major key. The initial tonic prolongation occurs over a pedal c. Although the implied texture suggests six voices, two of these represent *octave doublings* (not parallels) shown with black note-heads and brackets, reducing the total to only four parts. The

[1]The upper a² and g² (see the parentheses in the reduction) are actually "covering tones" which momentarily obscure the stepwise soprano. They do *not* appear in the earliest version of this prelude. The most famous analysis of this piece appears in Henrich Schenker's *Five Graphic Analyses* (pp. 36–37), published by his pupils after his death.

basic voice-leading again reveals 2–3 dissonances in the descending tenth motion.[2] This same framework also forms the basis for the E minor Prelude. Here the elaboration consists of an ostinato - like sixteenth-note figuration in the bass, above which are placed eighth-note block chords. In the more familiar version of *WTC* I Bach expands this simple soprano line into a lyrical melody, a textbook model of this procedure.

EXAMPLE 8-18

The figuration employed in the D major Prelude is more polyphonic with slight changes in the elaborative technique. The bass is a compound melody implying two separate voices. All redundant parts (through octave doublings) have been removed in the opening section quoted in Ex. 8-19, resulting in a five-voice texture. A glance at the reduction of Ex. 8-19B will confirm the similarity of voice-leading in all of these preludes. Since Bach was definitely acquainted with some of the theoretical writings of Niedt,[3] it is possible that the rather naive figurations quoted in Ex. 8-16 piqued his interest in this procedure while writing *Klavierbüchlein*.[4]

---

[2]Schenker's analysis of the *WTC* I version of the C minor Prelude may be found on pages 299–320 of Sylan Kalib's translation of his *Thirteen Essays* (see Bibliography).

[3]We are certain that he was familiar with Volume I of *Musikalische Handleitung*, since he borrowed liberally from it in his own thoroughbass manual.

[4]The employment of consistent figuration technique is relatively rare in the remainder of Bach's output.

EXAMPLE 8-19

ASSIGNMENTS
───

1. Using the above preludes as models (consult them in the *WTC* I), compose a similar short figuration prelude. First work out a harmonic progression with good voice-leading which establishes tonic, moves to a well-defined cadence on V (major) or III (minor), and returns to the original key center. You might want to add a dominant prolongation before the final cadence. Then choose a figuration to activate the chords.

2. Two additional excerpts from a pair of related preludes in the *Klavierbüchlein* are quoted in condensed form (see Exs. 8-20 and 8-21). The first of these is by Bach, and the second by Wilhelm Freidmann, perhaps as a kind of student "exercise". Make a two-voice reduction of each and compare their basic voice-leading. Do you think the father's version is superior, and if so, why?

EXAMPLE 8-20

(continued)

EXAMPLE 8-20 (cont'd)

EXAMPLE 8-21   Wilhelm Friedmann Bach: Prelude in C BWV 924a (*Klavierbüchlein*)

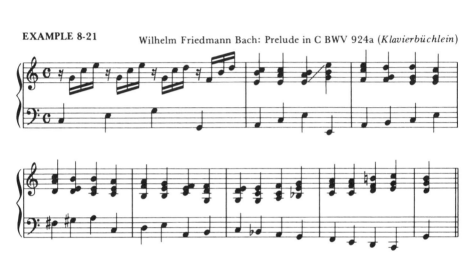

9

✕✕✕

Real imitation and double counterpoint

In preparation for the study of the two-voice canon and invention, this chapter will explore real imitation and simple invertible counterpoint at the octave. Since continual reference will be made to Bach's Two-Part Inventions, you should have handy access to these works (preferably in an edition with numbered measures).

REAL IMITATION AT THE OCTAVE AND FIFTH

Friedrich Wilhelm Marpurg, in his *Abhandlung von der Fuge* (1753–54), makes a distinction between *repetition* (the immediate restatement of an idea in the same voice and at the same pitch level or octave removed), *sequence* (immediate restatement in the same voice at a different pitch level), and *imitation* (immediate restatement in a *different* voice at the same or some other pitch level). Imitation can appear either as an incidental device or as a basic structural component in almost all genre of the period. It is particularly significant in the relationships between the voices of a fugue or invention, hence the term *imitative pieces*. In almost all such cases the work opens with a *point of imitation*. In two-part pieces the continuation of the strict imitative process rarely extends beyond the statement of the original theme or *subject* in the second voice, where the parts will usually revert to free counterpoint.

Real imitation denotes the reentry of the subject in an exact interval-for-interval relationship. During the late Renaissance the term *fuga* (literally *to flee*) was employed. In order to insure the identical melodic intervals in the imitating voice the notes of the so-called *naturale* hexachord (C D E F G A) and those of the *molle* (F G A B♭ C D) and *durum* (G A B C D E) a perfect fourth or fifth away were utilized. Study Ex. 9-1, where the same *solmization* syllables (Ut, Re, Mi, Fa, Sol, La) are retained in both the subject and its imitation (or *answer*).

EXAMPLE 9-1

Roland de Lassus: "Serve bone" (*Cantiones duarum vocum*)

In the late Baroque, this became equivalent to imitation in either the dominant (V or v) or subdominant (IV or iv), since these are the only closely related keys in the major-minor system which retain the same intervallic relations. Any other pitch level will involve a key relation which is foreign to the original tonic. Although "diatonic" imitation can occur on a scale degree other than $\hat{4}$ or $\hat{5}$, the resultant intervals will be generically equivalent rather than exact (like a minor third for major third). Of course, no problem exists if the imitation takes place at the unison or octave. Other than the octave, the dominant key is preferred for real imitation, since it is simple to return to the tonic after stating the subject on V. This is more problematic with IV. The return to I is now "weaker" and may sound like a half-cadence (I–V) on the subdominant. These statements are also valid for the minor mode. Remember, however, that the relationship is with v as a *key,* not V as a chord.

Although shorter compositions such as suite movements, inventions, or preludes may open with imitations at the unison or octave, these intervals are virtually non-existent in the fugue, which requires a dominant answer. In inventions they may take the form of either *motivic* or *thematic* imitation. With the former, the initial melodic idea is little more than a motivic figure. It is usually less than one measure long and tends to imply a single harmony, the tonic. Since the opening motive and its imitation at the octave are so brief, both are normally restated on the dominant before resolving to tonic. The C major and E minor Two-Part Inventions fall into this category. The beginning of each and their basic voice-leading are quoted in Ex. 9-2 and 9-3.[1]

EXAMPLE 9-2 Motivic imitation in Bach's Two-Part Invention in C

EXAMPLE 9-3 Motivic imitation in Bach's Two-Part Invention in e

In thematic imitation the initial melodic idea more closely resembles a short self-contained subject. It is often one to two measures long and tends to imply some simple progression like I–V or I–ii–V. The opening of the D minor Invention employs only tonic and dominant (Ex. 9-4). Note the compound nature of the theme.

[1]Notice that in Ex. 9-2 the initial three sixteenth-notes c^1–d^1–e^1 reappear at a higher structural level in the soprano framework of measures 1–3.

EXAMPLE 9-4 Thematic imitation in Bach's Two-Part Invention in d

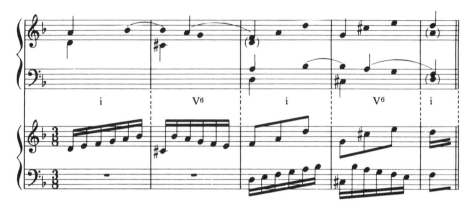

In real imitation at the fifth, the second voice entering in the domi-nant key is usually called the *answer*.[2] Either motivic or thematic formats can be found. The G major Invention opens with a tonic arpeggiation. The ensuing V then adds a seventh, which resolves immediately back to I (Ex. 9-5). The more complex B minor Invention begins with an accompanied counterpoint.[3] The answer is now in the minor dominant of F♯ minor (see Ex. 9-6). Note the miniature Phrygian cadence between measures 2 and 3 in order to prepare the dominant key. Again reductions are given.

EXAMPLE 9-5 Imitation at the fifth in Bach's Two-Part Invention in G

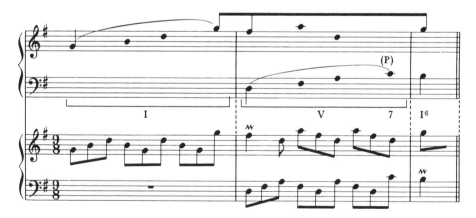

[2] The question of imitation at the dominant will be taken up more extensively in Chapter 15.

[3] This "accompaniment", as the reduction shows, is actually a simplification of the counterpoint to the answer in measures 3–4.

EXAMPLE 9-6 Imitation in the minor dominant key (Bach's Two-Part Invention in b)

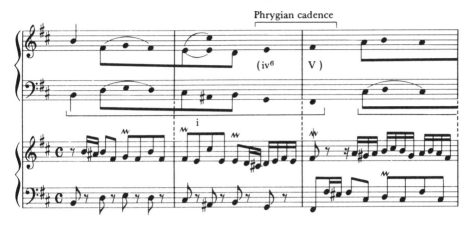

The voice-leading frameworks of the previous passages emphasized the simplicity of the harmonic background and the underlying note-against-note settings. Keep your points of imitation free of complications. Complexity tends to generate contrapuntal obscurity, while simplicity and economy of means produce the most musically effective polyphony. Try to maintain a rhythmic balance between the voices.

ASSIGNMENTS

1. In Ex. 9-7 a motivic idea is given in measure 1, which is to be imitated at the lower octave in measure 2. This process is repeated on the dominant in measures 3–4, eventually moving back to tonic. Fill in the motive and add appropriate counterpoint, noting the harmonic implications.

EXAMPLE 9-7

2. Three thematic subjects are quoted in Exs. 9-8A through 8C. Imitate each at the octave and add counterpoint. Be sure to work out the harmonic implications of each theme and then utilize it as the basis for the two-voice polyphony.

EXAMPLE 9-8

3. Add appropriate note-against-note settings to Exs. 9-9A and 9B. Elaborate the opening pitches into a suitable theme, which will then be imitated and counterpointed. Choose your own meter.

EXAMPLE 9-9

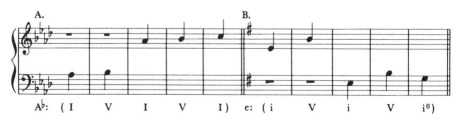

DOUBLE COUNTERPOINT AT THE OCTAVE

Sequence and imitation are only two ways to achieve recurrence and/or development of previous musical ideas. Another technique is *invertible counterpoint*. Here the music of a previous section is restated but with a textural switching or exchange of voice parts. In two-voice polyphony this is called *double counterpoint,* since each voice now serves a "double" function: as both the upper and lower part. This chapter will examine double counterpoint at the simple or multiple octave.[4]

Example 9-10 quotes Marpurg. The upper voice has been displaced an octave around the other part, although the second staff could have also been displaced an octave. The intervals have been indicated in both cases. Note that all the diatonic dyads within the octave are included. This inversional process is represented in numerical form in Fig. 9-1; remember that the unison equals 1, not 0. Once the range of the octave is exceeded, the intervals no longer invert. Thus a tenth becomes a third rather than a sixth. It is better to avoid voice-crossing in this technique.

EXAMPLE 9-10 Double counterpoint at the octave

(Friedrich Marpurg: *Abhandlung von der Fuge* 1753-54)

FIGURE 9-1 Chart of intervallic inversions in double counterpoint at the octave

3	2	1	2	3	4	5	6	7	8	9	10
10	9	8	7	6	5	4	3	2	1	2	3

In general, consonance inverts into consonance, and dissonance into dissonance: third equals sixth, seventh equals second. The major exception is that the perfect fifth becomes a dissonant perfect fourth. Thus the third and sixth are the basic structural consonances. If the fifth is to occur in

---

[4]For a discussion of double counterpoint at the tenth and twelfth, see Chapter 15.

double counterpoint, it must be treated as though it were a dissonant fourth. In the Marpurg quotation the fifths have become passing-tone fourths. The tritone remains dissonant through inversion: diminished fifth equals augmented fourth. It also occurs as a passing tone in the Marpung. Example 9-11 illustrates several ways to correct these "problem" intervals.

EXAMPLE 9-11 Treatment of the perfect fifth and tritone in double counterpoint

Example 9-12A shows a measure of potentially invertible counterpoint with the typical thirds and sixths. Suppose you wanted to invert the passage but at the dominant level of C major. It is possible, of course, to transpose the initial example first (Ex. 9-12B) and then invert the transposition (Ex. 9-12C), or invert and then transpose. However, there is a simpler procedure. Observe in Fig. 9-1 that the *sum* of each column within the octave is the "magic number" 9 (1 + 8, 2 + 7). By raising *and* lowering the two voices respectively by numbers which *total* 9, the transposition/inversion process is achieved in only one operation. Returning to Ex. 9-12A, the bass has been raised a fifth, and the soprano lowered a fourth (5 + 4 = 9), producing Ex. 9-12C. Appropriate accidentals may then be added.

EXAMPLE 9-12 Simultaneous transposition and inversion

Since the parts in two-voice polyphony are usually separated spatially, (often by more than an octave), double counterpoint at *multiple octaves* must be evoked before they are inverted. In the double octave or fifteenth *both*

voices are displaced an octave in either direction. Compare Ex. 9-13A with 13B. In Ex. 9-13C the bass has been raised two octaves. The magic numbers for transposition/inversion would then be 16 and 23 respectively. In Ex. 9-13D the upper part has dropped an eleventh and the lower part raised a twelfth (11 + 12 = 23).

EXAMPLE 9-13 Double counterpoint at multiple octaves

In imitative pieces the answer and its accompanying counterpart will most likely recur later in a switched relation. It is therefore essential that they be written in double counterpoint. This is common in the Bach Two-Part Inventions. One of several instances occurs at the beginning of the F minor Invention (compare measures 1–3 with 5–8). Also see the opening of the E major Invention, where measures 1–4 equal 5–8. The use of this technique is also frequent in episodic passages which may involve modulatory or sequential elements. It may occur either untransposed (C major Invention, measures 3–4 = 11–12) or transposed (E♭ major Invention, measures 3–4 = 14–15). The use of double counterpoint *within* a sequence is somewhat unusual (see Ex. 9-14).

EXAMPLE 9-14   J. S. Bach: Prelude in e BWV 941 (*Fünf kleine Präludien*)

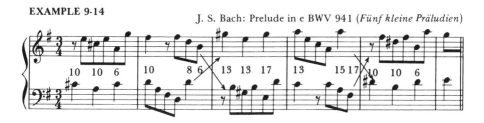

ASSIGNMENTS

1. The C♯ major Prelude (*WTC* I) is constructed on the principle of double counterpoint. Sketch out a structural diagram, indicating the inversional process. The underlying voice-leading produces strict imitation between the parts, beginning about measure 31. Can you find it?

2. Go back to those sections of two-voice counterpoint in your previous assignments on imitation in this chapter. Examine each one and see if

it will invert correctly at the octave or double octave. If not, alter it to produce acceptable double counterpoint.

      3. Compose several "invention-like" themes. Imitate them at the octave (or fifth) and counterpoint their answers. Write your two-voice polyphony so that it will invert at the octave or some multiple. Then write out the inversion. Do the same for several original episodic or sequential passages. Try to work in a couple of "correct" fifths, using that interval in the manner of a dissonance.

10

※※

The two-part canon and invention

This chapter completes our study of polyphony in two-voice texture. After studying the canon as either an incidental device or a complete piece, we will look at the compositional characteristics of Bach's Two-Part Inventions. Again you will need an edition of these works for reference.

TWO-PART CANON

The term canon (from the Greek *kanon*—rule or law) denotes the continuation of the strict imitative process beyond the restatement of the opening theme in the second voice.[1] This may be a relatively short passage either at the beginning or within a composition, or it may be the entire composition. The leading voice is called the *dux,* and the follower the *comes.* In two-voice canons the intervals of imitation are usually perfect, and, as in real imitation, they may be divided between the unison or octave as opposed to those featuring the fifth or fourth. Other diatonic intervals are possible, but they will produce only generically equivalent rather than exact intervals in the comes. They are generally encountered in cycles of canonic studies, such as

---

[1]Some historical background on the canon is included in Chapter 16.

the group in Bach's *Goldberg* Variations, which range from the unison to the ninth.[2]

Brief canonic passages at the octave appear intermittently in Bach's Two-Part Inventions. The F major Invention opens in the style of a canon and continues thus until measure 8. In the B♭ major Invention the device occurs in a transitional sequence (measures 12–14). Voice-leading reductions of both passages reveal descending thirds, which in the last case also forms a cycle of fifths. The temporal distance between entries is purely optional, varying from eight beats (see the opening of the C minor Invention) to only one beat, as in the B♭ Invention above.

Sequences is somewhat problematic in canons at the octave. To set up the pattern of fifths bracketed in Ex. 10-1A, the soprano must first be preceded by the bass dux. The bass of measures 2–3 must now reappear in the upper voice. Since measures 1–2 and 5–6 are also sequential, there is a strong possibility of overkill. For this reason, patterns involving a short temporal distance between voices seem to work better, although their number is severely limited. See Ex. 10-1B for some typical illustrations.

EXAMPLE 10-1 Sequence in canons at the unison or octave

There are several other problems in composing canons at the unison or octave. Beware of a tendency for the voices to remain within the tonic harmony with little or no sense of tonal motion or direction. It might seem that Bach got into this predicament in the opening of the F major Two-Part Invention, but after the initial thematic statements the soprano begins a descent in thirds which will eventually lead via the b♮[1] to the dominant key.

---

[2]Only one of these, the Canon at the Ninth, is actually a two-voice canon. The rest are accompanied with a supporting free voice. See the remarks on accompanied canons in Chapter 16.

Even if you can produce a more varied harmonic environment within the canonic restrictions, the question of how to modulate remains. One solution is to set up a succession of scale degrees which are susceptible to "double" interpretation in two different keys. Example 10-2 is a reduction of the opening measures of Bach's C minor Two-Part Invention. Observe how the pitches c^2–d^2–$e^{\flat 2}$ (or $\hat{1}\,\hat{2}\,\hat{3}$ in C minor) of measures 2–3 are now heard as $\hat{6}\,\hat{7}\,\hat{8}$ in E♭ major in measures 4–5 with the insertion of the $a^{\flat 2}$ in the upper voice.

EXAMPLE 10-2 Voice-leading reduction of the opening to Bach's Two-Part Invention in c

For a composition to maintain strict canonic technique, another difficulty arises at cadences. Example 10-3A represents a possible conclusion to a canon. The stereotyped bass line ($\hat{4}\,\hat{5}\,\hat{1}$) in the final two measures has to be anticipated in the dux (see measures 2–3). The *coronata* sign (⌒), not to be confused with a *fermata*, denotes the last note of the dux which is imitated in the comes. This same basic method must also be applied to interior cadences (consult Ex. 10-3B).

EXAMPLE 10-3 Candences in strict canonic texture

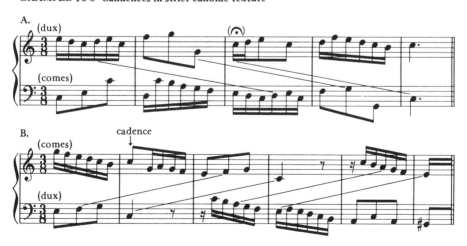

More perplexities arise with canons at the interval of a fourth or fifth. As a consequence of the comes appearing at the upper or lower fifth, the strict canonic imitation produces a conflict between the dominant (or subdominant) key and that of the original dux tonic. One way of avoiding this possible "bitonal" effect is to limit the number of scale degrees in the dux, choosing only those which share common tones with the dominant or subdominant scales. Thus in the key of C major, scale steps Î–6̂ in the dux (C D E F G A), when transposed to the dominant level (a fifth higher or fourth lower), yields G A B C D E or pitches which are still diatonic within the realm of C. This is not to say that one should avoid the B♮ (in tonic) equals F♯ (in dominant) altogether, since a B♭ in the dux will produce the normal F♮. In Ex. 10-4, observe the insertion of some chromaticism. Also examine the "anticipated" final cadence.

EXAMPLE 10-4 Canon at the fifth using restricted hexachord range

If you want to place the comes in the subdominant relation, avoid scale step 4̂ in the original key. The Corelli excerpt of Ex. 10-5 is a rare instance of canonic technique used at the opening of the second section in a two-reprise form. Can you find any places where the imitation is not strictly interval-for-interval?[3]

EXAMPLE 10-5   Arcangelo Corelli: Preludio (Sonata No. 7 in d for Violin and Continuo)

6   6   5   6

[3]Another similar two-voice canon is in Bach's Three-Part Invention in F major (measures 7–10). Why is the single pitch *f* changed in measure 9?

Sequences with canons at the fifth are easier to generate at closer temporal distances. Several are illustrated in Ex. 10-6. Go back to Ex. 10-5 and make a voice-leading reduction. Does Corelli employ any of these sequential models?

EXAMPLE 10-6 Sequence in canons at the fifth or fourth

ASSIGNMENTS

1. The basic framework for the opening of a canon at the octave is given in Ex. 10-7A. Observe the method of modulation to vi or C minor. Finish the elaboration begun in Ex. 10-7B and then continue the imitation for several more measures, plotting out the succeeding voice-leading on your own. Try for another change of key.

EXAMPLE 10-7

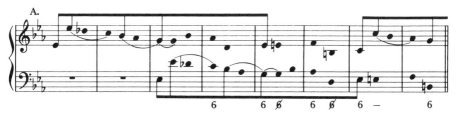

(continued)

EXAMPLE 10-7 (cont'd)

2. Use the theme cited in Ex. 10-8 to compose a complete canon at the octave, eight to ten measures long. Employ the anticipatory technique discussed previously at final cadences.

EXAMPLE 10-8

3. Compose the first eight measures of an original canon at the fifth. Sketch out the basic framework before adding any elaboration.

THE TWO-PART INVENTION

Although the term *invention* is familiar today largely through Bach's set of two- and three-voice pieces, it is rarely found as a typical genre in the literature of the late Baroque period. Used by the sixteenth century theorist Tomas Santa Maria to describe imitative procedures, it resurfaces occasionally in the works of G. B. Vitali and Antonio Bonporti, who composed ten *inventioni* for violin and continuo.

J. S. Bach conceived his "inventions" as teaching pieces in performance and compositional technique for his eldest son Wilhelm Friedmann. In his *Klavierbüchlein* (c. 1720) the two-part pieces were first entitled *Preambles,* the three-voice pieces *Fantasien.* The later version that Bach prepared for publication in 1723 was entitled *Inventions* and *Sinfonias* respectively. The original sequence was reordered thereby obscuring his former pedagogical intent. However, it is interesting that Bach did revise some minor compositional problems in the C and F major Two-Part Inventions and expanded several sections in the A minor.[4] Figure 10-1, taken from an

---

[4]See David Neumeyer, "The Two Versions of J. S. Bach's A-minor Invention BWV 784," *Indiana Theory Review,* Vol. 4/2 (1981), pp. 69–99.

FIGURE 10-1 Plan of the Preambles (Two-Part Inventions) in Bach's *Klavierbüchlein* (after Ellwood Derr)

X				Y		Z			Y'				X'	
C	d	e⌐F		G	a	b	Bb	A	g	f	E⌐Eb		D	c
4	3	4	3	9	4	4	4	12	4	3	3	4	3	4
4	8	4	4	8	4	4	4	8	4	4	8	4	8	4

unicum

scalar subjects treated à la ricercar

arpeggio subjects developed through various transformational procedures

subject w/ cptal associate exposed as invertible pair maturation of "true" episodes

emergence of periodicity

syncopation; chromaticism incresing lengths of invertible pairs concomitantly effecting greater periodicity

summary and peroration for series, culminating in the canon of the last piece

E minor Pr: as concluding member further develops details set forth in the 2nd preceding members

A minor Pr: as concluding member further develops details set forth in the 2 preceding members

A major Pr: as concluding member further develops details set forth in the 2 preceding members

E major Pr: as concluding member further develops details set forth in the 2 preceding members

article by Ellwood Derr,[5] shows the original scheme and key order as found in Friedmann's *Klavierbüchlein*.

There is no formal "model" for the invention as a genre. Even a superficial survey of Bach's Two-Part Inventions will disclose a tremendous range of structural variety, which is in keeping with his original pedagogical purposes.[6] The following are a few *general* characteristics.

1. The typical key scheme is that of tonic → related keys → tonic. Only a careful analysis of all the inventions will reveal the astonishing scope of different tonal plans and the ingenious logic behind each.

2. The opening tends to employ imitation. Chapter 9 touched upon the use of motivic and thematic subjects imitated at the intervals of the octave or fifth. In addition to several "accompanied" themes (see the B♭ major or the B minor), instances of bona fide double subjects set in invertible counterpoint do exist (see the E♭ major, A major, F minor, and G minor Inventions).

3. There are periodic restatements of the initial subject(s), usually following episodic passages and confirming cadences. This tendency has led analysts to see some of these inventions as miniature two-voice fugues. Where imitation at the dominant is found, this is not entirely inappropriate. Modulation, double counterpoint, and sequences are hallmarks of the more *episodic* sections, which tend to conclude with a well-defined cadential formula.

One might also mention the use of "codettas", often following a deceptive cadence (see the closing sections of the D major and the D minor Inventions). The E major piece uses a suite-like two-reprise form. Regardless of differences, the Two-Part Inventions share one common trait—an extreme economy of materials and means. The opening C major is a model example, since almost all of its subsequent musical continuation is based on motives found in the initial measure.[7]

Graphic analyses of three of the Inventions—the C major, B minor, and C minor—are presented in Figures 10-2 to 10-4. The format utilized here was chosen to highlight the similarity of sections and placement of cadences. A similar approach might serve as a model for your own structural analyses of other inventions. In the final C minor piece the diagram emphasizes the prevailing canonic aspect of the work. Study each of these carefully with the aid of the scores.

---

[5]Ellwood Derr, "The Two-Part Inventions: Bach's Composer's Vademecum," *Music Theory Spectrum*, Vol. 3 (1981), pp. 26–48.

[6]See Theodore Johnson, *An Analytical Survey of the Fifteen Two-Part Inventions by J. S. Bach* (New York: University Press of America, 1982).

[7]There are a number of voice-leading reductions of this familiar piece. See Richard Parks, *Eighteenth-Century Counterpoint and Tonal Structure* (Englewood Cliffs, N.J.: Prentice-Hall, Inc., 1984), pp. 321–24; Roy Travis, "J. S. Bach, Invention No. 1 in C Major: Reduction and Graph," *In Theory Only*, Vol. 2/7 (Oct. 1976), pp. 3–7; Steve Larson, "J. S. Bach's Two-Part Invention in C Major," *In Theory Only*, Vol. 7/1 (May 1983), pp. 31–45.

FIGURE 10-2 Structural diagram of Bach's Two-Part Invention in C

Subject = A   motives x and y (contained in A)
Basic keys (in terms of Roman numerals) : ⓘ ⓥ etc.

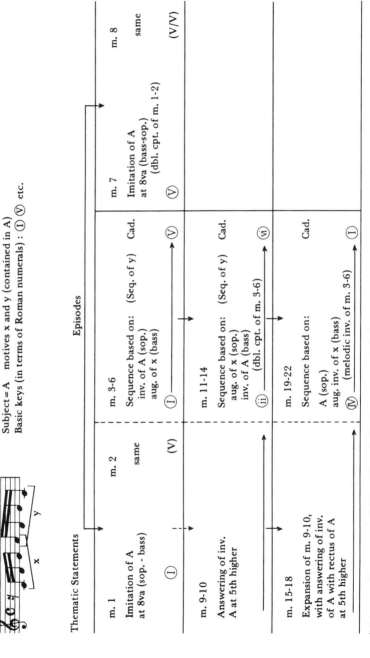

Thematic Statements

Episodes

m. 1
Imitation of A
at 8va (sop. - bass)
ⓘ

m. 2
same
(ⓥ)

m. 3-6
Sequence based on: (Seq. of y)   Cad.
inv. of A (sop.)
aug. of x (bass)
ⓘ   ⓥ

m. 7
Imitation of A
at 8va (bass-sop.)
(dbl. cpt. of m. 1-2)
ⓥ

m. 8
same
(V/V)

m. 9-10
Answering of inv.
A at 5th higher

m. 11-14
Sequence based on: (Seq. of y)   Cad.
aug. of x (sop.)
inv. of A (bass)
(dbl. cpt. of m. 3-6)
ⓘⓘ   v̂i

m. 15-18
Expansion of m. 9-10,
with answering of inv.
of A with rectus of A
at 5th higher

m. 19-22
Sequence based on: Cad.
A (sop.)
aug. inv. of x (bass)
(melodic inv. of m. 3-6)
ⒾⓋ   ⓘ

(Note overall movement of 5ths higher: I—V—ii—vi; then IV (V) I)

125

FIGURE 10-3 **Structural diagram of Bach's Two-Part Invention in b**

Subject = A   Counterpoint to answer = B (refer back to Ex. 9-6)

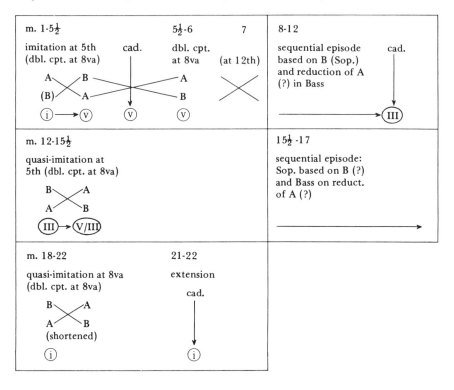

FIGURE 10-4 **Canonic structure of Bach's Two-Part Invention in c**

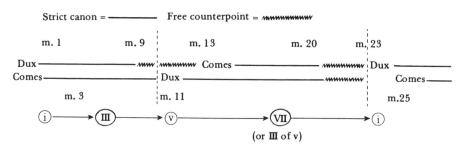

Finally, a voice-leading graph of the opening section (meas. 1−13) of the A minor Invention is given in Ex. 10-9.[8] Make a measure-by-measure

[8]A complete reduction may be found in Roy Travis, "J. S. Bach, Invention No. 13 in A Minor: Reduction and Graph," *In Theory Only*, Vol. 2/8 (Nov. 1976), pp. 29–33.

comparison with the score. The reduction to a suitable framework is more difficult in this work due to the frequent broken-chord technique.

EXAMPLE 10-9 Voice-leading reduction of the opening section of Bach's Two-Part Invention in a

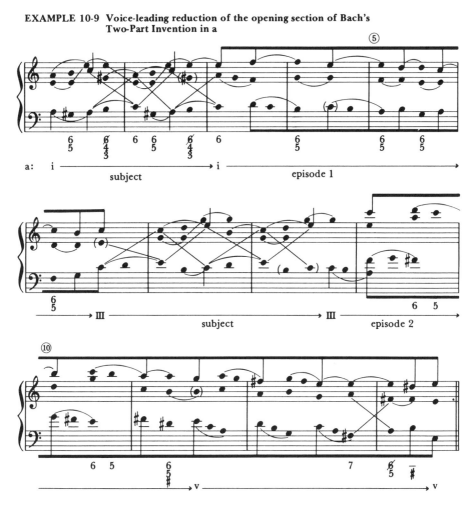

ASSIGNMENTS

1. Choose one of Bach's Two-Part Inventions to analyze structurally. The format used in Fig. 10-2 and 10-3 may serve as possible models. The following works are recommended: D major, D minor, E♭ major, E major, F major, F minor, G minor, and B♭ major.

2. Do a similar structural analysis of the following student invention in Ex. 10-10. Make note of the original materials and how they are subsequently developed (sequence, double counterpoint).

EXAMPLE 10-10

3. Example 10-11A represents one possible voice-leading "model" for the opening of a two-part invention. The reduction shows the initial imitation at the octave (measures 1–4), its immediate restatement in double counterpoint (measures 5–6), a sequential episode based on previous motives (measures 7–13), a cadence in the dominant key (measures 13–14), followed by a "switched" imitation of the original theme (measures 14–18). Its elaboration has been started in Ex. 10-11B. Finish it, using the previous example as the underlying framework.

EXAMPLE 10-11

4. Compose a similar section as the one above, using your own musical ideas. Do not neglect the underlying voice-leading. Strive for overall compositional economy. Or if you wish, write an entire invention. The use of a double subject (as in Ex. 10-10), imitation at the dominant, or even some canonic passages are possible.

11

Introduction to three-voice texture; note-against-note and simple diminution

We have already seen examples of implied three-voice texture in two-part writing, when one of the voices appears as a compound melody. Although the use of three distinct voices allows complete triads, it will also present problems, such as the simultaneous elaboration of the counterpointing parts. This chapter will begin with note-against-note settings and lead into simple 2:1 diminution technique. A cantus will be employed throughout.

NOTE-AGAINST-NOTE WITH CONSONANCE ONLY

Example 11-1A illustrates some typical spacial arrangements of complete major and minor triads. Diminished and augmented triads occur only in $^{6}_{3}$ (Ex. 11-1B), while the $^{6}_{4}$ is not strictly a consonance. Obviously, the bass can be an octave lower, or the upper voices an octave higher. It is not always possible to produce continual complete triads in three-part voice-leading. Thus triadic implication by one interval must be evoked. But in this case one of the tones of the interval will be *doubled.* In an implied $^{5}_{3}$ the bass is normally doubled, although on occasion the third is possible (see Ex. 11-1C). Empty fifths are rarely encountered. The $^{6}_{3}$ is best implied by the root and third of a triad rather than its third and fifth (Ex. 11-1D).

EXAMPLE 11-1 Complete and implied triads in three-voice texture

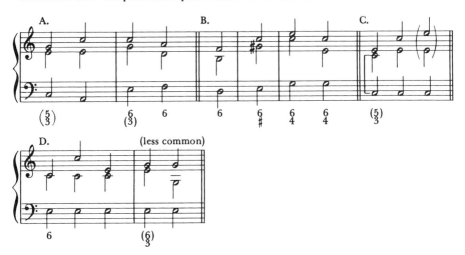

Avoid doubling *active* scale degrees in the key system. In major this is usually restricted to the leading tone (7̂), while in minor it can involve ♯6̂, ♯7̂, and ♯3̂. Contrast the two settings in Exs. 11-2A and 2B. Be cautious when approaching perfect intervals. Parallel octaves and fifths are still forbidden; even the passing ⁴₂ in Ex. 11-2C does not suffice. Beware of simultaneous leaps to fifths (Ex. 11-2D) or octaves. Example 11-2E is permissible, since the second chord has a passing function. In the perfect authentic cadence with 2̂–1̂ in the soprano, there is no choice but to *triple* the final pitch class (Ex. 11-2F). Also, note the movement into a deceptive cadence (Ex. 11-2G).

EXAMPLE 11-2 Various problems using consonance only

Several instances of note-against-note settings are given in Ex. 11-3, including two different versions of *Vom Himmel hoch*. With this chorale the tune has been placed in the middle voice, a viable possibility. Observe the use of a passing and cadential $^6_4$ in Exs. 11-3A and 3D respectively. Strive toward good melodic lines in each part but pay more attention to the outer voices. The string of static c¹'s in Ex. 11-3A is problematic, since elaboration will be difficult in subsequent diminution. Mark all chords as complete or incomplete. Three facets demand our attention: the linear characteristics of each voice; the sense of harmonic progression; and the question of complete or incomplete sonorities.

EXAMPLE 11-3 Note-against-note settings using basically only consonance

ASSIGNMENTS

1. Four different versions of the opening two phrases of *Christus, der ist mein Leben* appear in Ex. 11-4. Examine and criticize each. Some contain tonicizations, both good and bad.

EXAMPLE 11-4

Four settings of *Christus, der ist mein Leben* (first two phrases)

2. Compose note-against-note settings for the two cantus tunes in Ex. 11-5, using consonance only. *Christ lag* is a modal chorale; the first phrase should be harmonized in G minor and the last in C minor.

EXAMPLE 11-5

A.

Christ lag in Todesbanden

B.

Ein' feste Burg (last phrase)

NOTE-AGAINST-NOTE WITH CHORDAL DISSONANCE

One chordal tone must be omitted from seventh chords in three voices. It is almost always the fifth of the chord. Example 11-6 illustrates common occurrences of seventh-chord inversions in this texture, with typical approaches and resolutions of the dissonant seventh by passing, neighboring, suspension, and even leaping motion. The ⁴₃ is quite rare; since the fifth is in the bass, the third of the chord must be omitted (Ex. 11-6G).

EXAMPLE 11-6 Approach and resolution of typical chordal dissonances

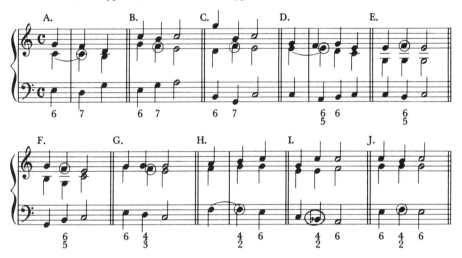

Example 11-7 represents various note-against-note settings utilizing chordal dissonance. The last passage makes considerable use of chromaticism and various altered chords; it is an "expanded" version of Ex. 11-3D.

EXAMPLE 11-7 Note-against-note settings using chordal dissonance

(continued)

EXAMPLE 11-7 (cont'd)

O Haupt voll Blut und Wunden

ASSIGNMENTS

1. Add an inner (alto) voice to make a three-part setting of Ex. 11-8. Try to employ as many complete triads as possible. In the last section the bass is unfigured.

EXAMPLE 11-8

J. S. Bach: *Wie wohl ist mir* BWV 517 (*Notenbuch der Anna Magdalena Bach*)

2. Counterpoint Ex. 11-9A using chordal dissonance where appropriate. Over the bass cantus of Ex. 11-9B insert either 7, $\frac{6}{5}$, or $\frac{4}{2}$ chords at the notes marked with arrows.

EXAMPLE 11-9

Jesu, meine Freude

SIMPLE 2:1 ELABORATION IN THREE VOICES

Many of the principles of 2:1 counterpoint with two parts hold true for three-part. Therefore only those additional techniques indigenous to three-voice writing will be discussed. Chordal figuration on the off-beat does not require extensive comment. Continue to watch for implied $\frac{6}{4}$ leaps in the bass, and make sure that the added chordal tone does not double an already sounding active scale degree (such as $\sharp\hat{6}$ or $\sharp\hat{7}$). Little more needs to be said about accented or unaccented non-harmonic tones, except the possibility of *double* passing or neighboring tones by either similar or contrary motion (Ex. 11-10A). The clash resulting from a passing tone and chordal leap is perfectly acceptable, provided the passing motion is descending (Ex. 11-10B). Even parallels formed by a simultaneous passing tone and anticipation at cadences can be tolerated (Ex. 11-10C). Avoid awkward anticipations and be wary of dissonance involving leaps (Ex. 11-10D).

EXAMPLE 11-10 Non-harmonic activity in three-voice polyphony

(continued)

EXAMPLE 11-10 (cont'd)

Typical suspensions in three-voice texture are illustrated in Ex. 11-11. Carefully note the new interval above the bass which is appended to the two-part models in Chapter 5: 5 in the 4–3, 3 in the 9–8, 3 in the 7–6, and 5 in the 2–3. Other curious non-harmonic interactions may occur. The parallel fourths in Ex. 11-11H arise from a suspension and passing tone. The infamous "Corelli clash" pits the resolution of a cadential 4–3 suspension with an anticipation (Ex. 11-11I).

EXAMPLE 11-11   Typical suspension formulas in three voices

Several settings using basic 2:1 diminutions are cited in Ex. 11-12. These may sometimes resemble chorale "harmonizations" with one voice

omitted, as in the first two modified Bach versions. Note the *suspension chain* in Ex. 11-12B. While Ex. 11-12C features unaccented dissonance, the following chorale prelude relies heavily on suspension. The final passage (Ex. 11-12E) represents a typical textural cliché, with its continuous "walking bass" and placid upper parts. Study each carefully and be able to explain the derivation of the diminution procedures.

EXAMPLE 11-12 Cantus settings using 2:1 diminution

A. *Herr Jesu Christ, du höchstes Gut*
(adapted from Bach harmonization)

B. *Herr' ist, O Mensch, ein grosser* (adapted from Bach harmonization)

C. *Herr Jesu Christ, du hast bereit*

D. J. S. Bach: *Allein Gott in der Höh' sei Ehr'* BWV 714

(continued)

EXAMPLE 11-12 (cont'd)

ASSIGNMENT

1. Example 11-13 cites a four-phrase chorale tune to be used as an upper cantus. Add two lower voices employing 2:1 elaboration. Keep the eighth-note motion continuous, even through the cadences. Supply the suspensions or seventh-chord inversions indicated above the soprano notes. Since this is a modal melody, the tonality will probably alternate between D minor and F major.

EXAMPLE 11-13

12

✖✖

Further rhythmic diminution; three-voice chorale preludes

This chapter will examine rhythmically complex methods of elaborations against a cantus, and investigate some techniques of three-voice chorale preludes.

FURTHER RHYTHMIC DIMINUTION

Examples 12-1 through 5 illustrate some of the more common textural settings in 3:1, 4:1, and even 6:1 rhythmic diminutions in the counterpointing voices. Examples 12-1 and 12-2 represent typical 4:1 elaborations with the chorale in the upper voice. Observe the rhythmic exchange between the lower activated parts. The Pachelbel passage exploits several motives, which occasionally appear in the slightly embellished cantus.

In Ex. 12-3 each of the two lower voices develop their own figures (also see Ex. 12-5B, where the hymn tune is in the middle part). In the bass setting (Ex. 12-4) the motivic unity is more subtle. Bracket each occurrence of the primary motive.

Extract the basic note-against-note foundation of the previous excerpts. In some instances, such as Ex. 12-1, there may be two harmonic changes per cantus note. Check the handling of dissonance and overall

EXAMPLE 12-1

J. S. Bach: *Nun freut euch, lieben Christen g'mein* BWV 755

EXAMPLE 12-2

Johann Pachelbel: Choral mit 8 Partiten

EXAMPLE 12-3

J. S. Bach: *O Herre Gott, dein göttlich Wort* (*Nevmeister Sammlung*) BWV 1110

EXAMPLE 12-4

J. S. Bach: *Allein Gott in der Höh' sei Ehr'* BWV 714

voice-leading. Remember that it is virtually impossible to construct an effective elaboration over a basically faulty framework.

As you might suspect, the chances of parallel motion increase as the voices become more elaborate. Example 12-5A appears innocent on the surface, but careful scrutiny discloses five instances of parallels (either octaves or fifths). List the location and nature of each, plus any other questionable voice-leading. Compare your findings with Ex. 12-5B, observing how each error was alleviated.

EXAMPLE 12-5

Es spricht der Unweisen Mund

In more extended 6:1 ♩♩♩ ♩♩♩ or 8:1 ♩♩♩♩ ♩♩♩♩ elaborations, the underlying harmonic rhythm will often move at a rate of 2:1 (♩. or ♩♩) in relation to the cantus. If the cantus has extensive ascending or descending motion, it may be possible to set up certain voice-leading paradigms involving sequential patterns. Refer back to Exs. 1-18E and 18F, which employ instances of $\frac{4\text{-}6}{2\text{-}3}$ and $\frac{6\text{-}5}{5\text{-}3}$ respectively.

ASSIGNMENTS

1. In the following Bach chorale prelude excerpt (Ex. 12-6), portions of the upper and lower voices have been omitted. Fill in the soprano (measures 2–4) and bass (measures 5–8) to complete a satisfactory three-voice setting. The upper part should feature basically sixteenth-note motion and the lower part eighth notes.

EXAMPLE 12-6   J. S. Bach: *Christ lag in Todesbanden* BWV 695

2. Several phrases are quoted in Ex. 12-7. Make a three-voice elaborated setting for each, using the following guidelines:
    Ex. 12-7A—cantus in soprano, 3:1 (but use two chord changes for ♩.)
    Ex. 12-7B[1]—cantus in bass, 4:1 (try for motivic exchange using ♪ ♫)

EXAMPLE 12-7

THREE-VOICE CHORALE PRELUDES

Organ chorale preludes are usually in four voices, although there are some in three parts. Anticipating the cantus melody in the introductory interludes is still a favorite technique. The two voices engage in imitation of

_____
[1]For some comments on this hymn tune, see footnote 12 in Chapter 20.

the diminuted hymn tune, hence the term *Vorimitation.* The initial entry is usually a fairly strict melodic statement of the chorale phrase although the rhythm may vary. The tune need not be quoted in its entirety. The imitation in the second part makes use of real or tonal answers; minor adjustments may be necessary to make the counterpoint "work". The most common intervallic distances are the fifth and octave. Since the interludes of *Vorimitation* in a three-voice chorale prelude are usually brief, modulation is rarely employed except to establish the key of the following hymn phrase. Analyze the Kuhnau piece (Ex. 12-8) phrase by phrase, studying the anticipatory imitation preceding each, real versus tonal answers, and extent of the hymn cited. The setting of chorale proper is usually in free counterpoint, as is the case here.

EXAMPLE 12-8   Johann Kuhnau: *Vom Himmel hoch* (vers 2)

(continued)

EXAMPLE 12-8 (cont'd)

In works where the interludes are either abbreviated or omitted, (sometimes called *simple chorale preludes*), compositional unity is often achieved through the continual reiteration of one (or more) melodic motives in the counterpointing voices. This procedure, already mentioned in Chapter 6, seems to have been associated with the so-called "doctrine of figures" (*Figurenlehre*), the illustration of literary or textural ideas with musical figures or motives. The use of such *figurae* is especially frequent in the polyphonic chorale settings of Walther and Bach.[2]

A simple scalar tetrachord has been chosen as the basic *figura* to illustrate this technique. The two forms of ascending motion incorporate a fourth, while the descending version uses a falling third via a neighboring tone (see Ex. 12-9A). A basic three-voice setting of the first two phrases of the chorale *Christus der ist mein Leben* (in the soprano) is sketched in Ex. 12-9B. It exploits the potential use of the above motives; brackets denote ascending fourths and wavy lines descending thirds. It is now simple to elaborate the framework rhythmically, employing our original motives. However, this has already been done in Ex. 12-9C, which is the opening of this chorale by Johann Walther.

EXAMPLE 12-9 Working model for built-in motivic unity

A.

---

[2]For a discussion of this principle with some musical examples see Vol. 3, pp. 81–91 of Peter Williams, *The Organ Music of J. S. Bach* (Cambridge: Cambridge University Press, 1984).

Three-voice skech for first two phrases of *Christus der ist mein Leben*

C. Johann Walther: *Christus der ist mein Leben* (vers 1)

The final example in this genre may well be Bach's most famous chorale prelude—*Wachet auf, ruft uns die Stimme*. This three-voice composition was originally the third movement of Cantata No. 140. It was scored for strings with the tenors of the choir carrying the chorale tune in the middle voice. Bach later arranged it for organ in the collection known as the *Schübler Chorales*. It is a remarkable specimen of *ritornello* technique. In this case the lengthy interludes consist of *four* distinct thematic ideas. These have been bracketed and labelled "A", "B", "C", and "D" in the opening twelve measures of Ex. 12-10. Although the walking bass is subordinate to the soprano, the effect of the two voices is so completely satisfying that one hardly suspects they are to function as the contrapuntal associates to the forthcoming cantus. Upon the entry of the first set of chorale phrases,

EXAMPLE 12-10   J. S. Bach: *Wachet auf, ruft uns die Stimme (Schübler Chorales)*

(continued)

EXAMPLE 12-10 (cont'd)

(continued)

EXAMPLE 12-10 (cont'd)

the *ritornello* themes continue in virtually *unaltered* form as companions to the hymn (see measures 13–21). The non-harmonic relations between the three voices are particularly interesting in this section. Analyze their interactions carefully (don't forget the bass).

Graph the overall structure of this piece in terms of alternating sections of *ritornello* and chorale. How many phrases are included in each "chorale" section? Bracket each appearance of the four original thematic ideas and label them, noting any displacement of order. Place these under the corresponding section of your overall graph. Now trace the basic tonal scheme of the work, noting any transpositions of the four thematic ideas. What "function" does "D" appear to serve? This chorale refers to the parable of the wise and foolish virgins which Jesus relates in Matthew 25:1–

13. Count the number of occurrences of the opening "A" theme, including repeats. How does this relate to the virgins?[3]

ASSIGNMENTS

1. In Exs. 12-11A and 11B a primary and secondary motive are given, followed by a basically note-against-note framework of a cantus in Ex. 12-11C. Elaborate the two lower voices, employing the primary motive when possible. In those situations where it does not seem to "fit", utilize the secondary figure. Some occasional chromatic motion is possible. Don't overdo the rhythmic diminutions; try for a good exchange or balance between the parts.

EXAMPLE 12-11

2. Now choose a chorale cantus and motive(s) of your own and repeat the above assignment.

3. Examples 12-12A through 12C quote the opening phrases of three chorales. Compose a short *Vorimitation* for each, using a diminuted form of the tune. Continue in free counterpoint for one of the phrases. Keep the opening imitation brief. In all cases it is actually possible for the second voice to enter before the conclusion of the first statement. You may wish to vary rhythmically your diminuted theme from the original chorale melody. Use the following guidelines:

Ex. 12-12A—Begin in soprano and imitate a fourth lower.

---

[3]There is evidence that Bach consciously employed symbolism. Some of these are discussed in Karl Geiringer, "Symbolism in the Music of Bach," *Lectures on the History and Art of Music* (New York: Da Capo Press, 1968), pp. 121–38. Also see footnotes 13 and 14 in Chapter 20.

Ex. 12-12B—Begin in bass (a) and imitate a fourth higher (a slight tonal alteration is useful here).

Ex. 12-12C—Begin in middle voice and imitate an octave higher or at the unison.

EXAMPLE 12-12

4. Bach's organ Variations on *Allein Gott in der Hoh' sei Ehr'* BWV 771 is an excellent source of three-voice texture in this genre. Check through each piece in the set, observing the cantus placement, accompanying *figurae,* and overall technique employed.

13

�incesccincesccincesccincesccincesccincesccincesccinces

Chromaticism

Although certain altered chords (secondary V^7 or vii^{o7}) have been used in contrapuntal settings, we have not discussed the chromatic lines that may result. This chapter will focus on the role of extended chromaticism in Baroque music.

This survey will be divided into two categories: *non-structural* versus *structural* chromaticism. The first of these is basically a melodic phenomenon. Although the more general use of the term *chromaticism* refers to extensive "half-step" motion, its meaning here will be limited to those instances of the chromatic alteration of a pitch class (C–C♯–D or B–B♭–A). Thus the subject of the B minor Fugue (*WTC* I) may not be considered chromatic in this sense (consult Ex. 2-9), since its appoggiaturas all employ minor seconds, *not* augmented primes. Its underlying reduction also reveals a diatonic framework.[1] On the other hand, the subject quoted in Ex. 13-1A does fit our qualifications. This theme illustrates another important feature of non-structural chromaticism: the altered tones may be "reduced back" to a diatonic basis, with little tendency to move beyond the closely-

---

[1]Johann Kirnberger's "reduction" of this same theme may be found in David Beach and Jurgen Thym, *"The True Principles for the Practice of Harmony* by Johann Philipp Kirnberger: A Translation," *Journal of Music Theory*, 23/2 (Fall 1979), pp. 210–211.

related key system. There is evidence that Baroque musicians viewed such passages in this manner. Note the diatonic foundation which Marpurg gives for Bach's subject in Ex. 13-1B.[2]

EXAMPLE 13-1

A.   The "Royal Theme" from Bach's *Das Musikalische Opfer* and Marpurg's reduction

B.

There are three basic principles concerning linear chromaticism in Baroque polyphony:

1. The chromatics will be thought of as alterations of diatonic scale degrees within a major or minor key (♯$\hat{1}$, b$\hat{7}$, ♯$\hat{4}$).

2. As a result of the enharmonic problems (G♯ = A♭) in the tuning systems of the early seventeenth century, a set of accidentals evolved which allowed modulation to the five closely related keys of a given tonality and their diatonic tones.[3] In the major mode these tended to be ♯$\hat{1}$, ♯$\hat{2}$, ♯$\hat{4}$, ♯$\hat{5}$, and b$\hat{7}$; b$\hat{3}$ and b$\hat{6}$ were less common. In the minor mode (remembering that ♯$\hat{6}$ and ♯$\hat{7}$ are diatonic), the typical altered scale steps were b$\hat{2}$, ♯$\hat{3}$, and ♯$\hat{4}$.

3. The nature of the diatonic pitch collection (A B C D E F G A) prohibits the extension of *strict* chromatic sequences beyond certain points without overstepping the closely related key system. In Ex. 13-2 the natural tones of C major and A minor are laid out in scalar fashion with accompanying scale steps. Two diatonic half-steps (E–F and B–C) partition the succession of pitches into disjunct tetrachords of half-step, step, step.[4] If one begins with B and initiates a strict chromatic sequence (B C C♯ D D♯ E), the next two tones will be E♯ F♯, which will move *outside* the closely related

---

[2]From Marpurg *Abhandlung von der Fuge* (1753–54).

[3]In the early seventeenth century the tuning systems based on *mean-tone temperament* produced a discrepancy of about a quarter of a tone between enharmonics. Thus if one were playing a harpsichord "recital" during this time, and the key of the first suite was C major, the instrument was tuned to that basic key, allowing modulations to its closely related system without becoming involved in enharmonics. However, if the next piece was in E major, the instrument would have to be retuned to that basic center, otherwise the original B♭ (in C) would have to function as A♯ (in E). The goal of most later temperament systems in the Baroque (such as Werkmeister III or the 1/6th comma) was the elimination of the unusable enharmonics. With the advent of *equal-temperament* about the middle of the eighteenth century this problem was eventually conquered, at some expense to the purity of the major third.

[4]The inversely related tetrachord (step, step, half-step = C D E F or G A B C) is seldom found as the basis for chromatic elaboration.

realm. For this reason most linear chromatic motion occurs *within* the tetrachords, which act as "limiters or dividers" to the further extension of exact sequential motion. In the major mode these tetrachords involve scale degrees $\hat{7}$–$\hat{3}$ and $\hat{3}$–$\hat{6}$; in minor $\hat{2}$–$\hat{5}$ and $\hat{5}$–$\hat{8}$. The chromatic movement may either ascend or descend. The basic exceptions to these is the succession C–B–B♭–A (consult Ex. 13-2), which is found as either $\hat{8}$–$\hat{7}$–♭$\hat{7}$–$\hat{6}$ in major or rarely $\hat{3}$–$\hat{2}$–♭$\hat{2}$–$\hat{1}$ in minor. These will become more apparent in the following discussion.

EXAMPLE 13-2 Tetrachordal basis of linear chromaticism in the major and minor modes, expreessed as pitch classes and scale degrees

We will now look at non-structural chromaticism, citing typical voice-leading models in the major and minor modes and then moving to the problem of extended chromatic passages and overlapping (producing double chromatics). A word about metric positioning—in general the altered chromatic note tends to fall on a *weak* beat or part of the measure, as the examples in this chapter illustrate.

NON-STRUCTURAL CHROMATICISM IN THE MAJOR MODE

Example 13-3 shows how to handle *ascending* half steps in major. By filling up the span of scale steps $\hat{7}$–$\hat{3}$ and $\hat{3}$–$\hat{6}$ with raised chromatics, movement is directed toward either iii or vi. The major second $\hat{6}$–$\hat{7}$ is problematic, since ♯$\hat{6}$ involves a tonicization of the leading tone. The underlying voice-leading is the familiar 5–6, producing successive dominants of I, ii, iii and IV, V, vi. Although the 5–6 pattern could continue through the minor-seventh span, the repeated E's break the sequence.

EXAMPLE 13-3 Ascending chromatic voice-leading in the major mode (5-6)

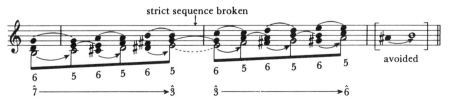

When the chromatic motion is in the *upper* part, continual voice-switching is necessary to avoid incorrect chord inversions (see Ex. 13-4A). In a two-voice texture, alternating thirds and sixths imply the above progressions (Ex. 13-4B). Applied V$_5^6$ and vii°⁷ chords may also be substituted, although the latter are rare in major (see Ex. 13-4C). For a passage using double chromatics refer to Ex. 1-18B.

EXAMPLE 13-4 Continuation of ascending chromaticism in the major mode

G. F. Handel: Sarabande (Suite in e)

J. S. Bach: Air (Overture for Orchestra in D BWV 1068)

The segmentation of the tetrachords (producing major thirds, minor thirds, and even major seconds), is common. The latter is frequently noted in chromaticized sequences of descending fifths, involving possible canonic treatment or double counterpoint (see Ex. 13-5).

EXAMPLE 13-5 Alternating chromaticization of major seconds (cycle of fifths)

J. S. Bach: Prelude and Fugue in a BWV 551

Descending motion in major uses related paradigms. Example 13-6A is simply the retrograde of Ex. 13-3, resulting in a reversal of the tonicizations (now iii, ii, I). The 5–6 motion is maintained. In the second model (Ex. 13-6B) the chromatic line consists of successive sevenths and thirds of the harmonic background. In the Baroque, this progression tends to be limited to the descending minor-third span.

EXAMPLE 13-6 Voice-leading models for descending chromatic motion in the major mode

NON-STRUCTURAL CHROMATICISM IN THE MINOR MODE

Ascending chromatic motion in minor is limited to tetrachords (or their segments) of $\hat{2}$–$\hat{5}$ and $\hat{5}$–$\hat{8}$. The voice-leading paradigm is identical with the major key (see Ex. 13-3), but now the tonicizations are III, iv, V and VI, VII, i. The Vivaldi excerpt of Ex. 13-7 employs both tetrachords with a common d. Note the use of the $\substack{6\\5}$.

EXAMPLE 13-7 Ascending chromatic motion in the minor mode

Antonio Vivaldi: Concerto Grosso in g Op. 3, No. 2, II

The most frequent occurrence of *descending* chromatics in minor focuses on the tetrachord $\hat{8}$–$\hat{5}$. It is often simply called "*the* chromatic tetrachord." Commonly associated with the half-step "sigh motive", it often appears in movements with more pathos, like: Dido's final aria (Ex. 19-7C), and the *Crucifixus* of Bach's B minor Mass (Ex. 13-8C). It also occurs as a variant of the descending *diatonic* tetrachord, used as the basis of many pieces in the period. The most common setting is given in Ex. 13-8A, but the consecutive 6th chords often give rise to 7–6 suspensions, as in Ex. 13-8B. The literature abounds with other ingenious "solutions" of great tonal variety. Two of these are quoted in Ex. 13-8C and 8D. Overlapping techniques are not unusual in this context (see Ex. 19-4 Var. 16).

EXAMPLE 13-8 Descending chromatic motion (8̂-5̂) in the minor mode

J. S. Bach: *Crucifixus* (Mass in b)

J. S. Bach: Organ Fugue in e ("Wedge") BWV 548

contrary chrom. motion

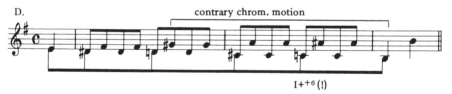

Variation No. 25 of Bach's *Goldberg* Variations is an exquisite instance of this device. The voice-leading of the original theme (measures 1–4) is sketched in Ex. 13-9A. A reduction of the opening is given in Ex. 13-9B and 9C. A pattern of staggered diminished seventh chords results.

EXAMPLE 13-9 Voice-leading comparison of opening of Aria and Variation 25 from

Bach's *Goldberg* Variations

Several more extended chromatic passages in minor are cited in Ex. 13-10A and 10B. Both have been reduced to show the underlying framework more clearly. Overlapping tetrachords will produce *double* chromaticism. They usually occur when thematic statements are overlapped in imitation, (see Ex. 16-8).

EXAMPLE 13-10 Reduced examples showing extensive chromaticism and overlapping

J. S. Bach: Contrapunctus XI (*Die Kunst der Fuge*)

(Fugue theme)

Dm   B♭

G. F. Handel: Keyboard fugue in a

STRUCTURAL CHROMATICISM

The "surface" chromaticism of the previous examples can be reduced to a diatonic framework. In several genre of the Baroque period, however, composers either tonicized non-diatonic chordal functions or explored foreign key relations, where the modulation featured highly chromatic episodes. Among these were the toccata, fantasia, and recitative. Here you may encounter ambiguous passages where it is difficult to determine the tonic orientation.

Depicting the plague of darkness in *Israel in Egypt*, Handel utilizes the unusual format of a choral recitative (consult the harmonic reduction in Ex. 13-11A). Typical of recitatives, which are not tonally closed, this movement links the C major of the previous chorus with the following A minor. It therefore opens with a unison C and concludes with an E major triad, the dominant of the next movement. The composer's setting of this foreboding passage from Exodus is ingenious. The initial C immediately functions as a dominant in F minor. After a momentary excursion to E♭ major the first section closes on V once again. Even here the tonality is ambiguous, since it could also be heard as A♭ major. Measures 10–15 are also framed by C, although now F minor is confirmed. The following section (measures 16–26) is an expansion of the first, with a change of mode on the E♭ tonicization. The C triad of measure 26 is now a *bona fide* tonic, moving through ii to iii, and cadencing on a Picardy third (E major). Observe the chromatic voice-leading bracketed in Ex. 13-11A. A summary of this chorus in Ex. 13-11B shows how the F minor and two E♭ tonicizations act as "double leading-tones" to frame the eventual dominant of A minor.

EXAMPLE 13-11

G. F. Handel: "He sent a great darkness" (*Israel in Egypt*) - reduction

The last passage is taken from the first movement of Bach's Fantasia and Fugue in G minor ("The Great"), measures 31–39 (see the reduction in Ex. 13-12A). The dominant of G minor begins a strict sequence of descending perfect fifths, utilizing alternating chromaticism in the upper

voices (refer back to Ex. 13-5). However, there is no tritone between E♭ and A to force the pattern back to the tonic, so by the time a D♭ minor triad is reached, the sense of tonality has already been destroyed. In measure 35 the sequence is finally broken with the ambivalent diminished-seventh chords propelling us to the climactic E minor $^6_4$ of the following measure. Had the pattern of fifths continued, this would have been the resultant enharmonic key (D♭m–G♭m–C♭m–F♭m = Em). The bass now spans a tritone. The last F supports a vii$^{o4}_2$ in A minor, a fifth removed and only one away from the original starting point of D. This chord is respelled, functioning now as vii^{o7}/iv in the tonic key of G minor, to which the movement returns. A further reduction (Ex. 13-12B) outlines the basic tonal scheme of the passage. The section beginning at measure 36 was presented earlier (measures 21–25) in E♭ minor—another foreign relation. The use of the half-step in the tonal design of this movement bears close scrutiny.

EXAMPLE 13-12 Reduction of measures 31-39 of Bach's Fantasia in g ("Great") BWV 542

ASSIGNMENTS

1. Continue the sequence begun in Ex. 13-13 and analyze chord functions.

EXAMPLE 13-13

D:

2. Add a second voice to Ex. 13-14 to create double counterpoint.

EXAMPLE 13-14

F:

3. Elaborate (4:1) the pattern of diminished sevenths in Ex. 13-15 for two parts.

EXAMPLE 13-15

C: 7   ♯4/♭   ♭7   4/♭   6

4. Add two counterpointing voices above the given bass in Ex. 13-16.

EXAMPLE 13-16

5. Example 13-17 represents a reduction of the second movement of *L'Autunno* from Vivaldi's cycle of concerto grossi *Le quattro stagioni* (The

Four Seasons). The piece opens on i and eventually moves to V of D minor, but the succession of sustained chords takes a most unusual harmonic route. Bracket chromatic lines, noting irregular resolutions of $^4_2$ chords. Trace the basic tonicizations throughout the movement, indicating the modulatory procedures used. Do any large-scale patterns emerge?

EXAMPLE 13-17 Slightly reduced version of Antonio Vivaldi: second movement

Ubriachi domienti of *L'Autunno* from his *Le quattro stagioni*

14

✳✳✳

Free counterpoint in three voices; extended two-reprise form

This chapter will abandon the use of a given cantus in three-voice polyphony and concentrate on free counterpoint. This leads to a reconsideration of two-reprise form, and its general relationship to the suite.

FREE COUNTERPOINT IN THREE-VOICE TEXTURE

The absence of a fixed cantus frees the composer so that the independence of the resultant free counterpoint creates a variety of harmonic, rhythmic, and textural possibilities. Examine some of the three-part pieces in Bach's keyboard Suites (French, English, and Partitas), the Three-Part Inventions, and certain preludes from the *WTC*. Example 14-1 cites a common setting. The typical walking bass in eighth-notes is contrasted with the pair of slower-moving upper voices, a frequent procedures in trio sonatas. Observe the change-of-bass suspensions, the voice crossing from measure three, and the final sequence of seventh chords.

Some different sequential elaborations are given in Exs. 14-2 through 14-4. Extract the underlying voice-leading and the sequential model upon which each is based.

EXAMPLE 14-1

Arcangelo Corelli: Allemanda (Trio Sonata da Camera Op. 4, No. 5 in a)

EXAMPLE 14-2

Jean-Philippe Rameau: Gavotte (*Les Indes Galantes*)

EXAMPLE 14-3

Antonio Vivaldi: Giga (Trio Sonata in d)

EXAMPLE 14-4   François Couperin: Vivement (*Troisiéme Ordre*: "L'Impériale")

    The initial seven measures of Bach's Three-Part Invention in F major (Ex. 14-5) employ extensive imitation. This invention could be categorized as a miniature three-voice fugue. After tracing the entries of the opening theme, study carefully the reduced framework supplied above the music. Do any sequential paradigms occur, and if so, where?

EXAMPLE 14-5   J. S. Bach: Three-Part Invention in F

ASSIGNMENTS

1. Choose three of the sequential patterns listed at the end of Chapter 1 and elaborate them in a free polyphonic settings for three voices.

THE BAROQUE SUITE

Up to this point we have discussed only two "dance" movements indigenous to the Baroque suite—the minuet and sarabande. Collections of such stylized dance movements were very popular at this time, going under various designations: *Suite, Partita* (in Germany), *Ordre* (in France), *Lesson* (in England), and *Sonata da Camera* (in Italy).[1] During the German High Baroque four dances occurred almost always in the sequence of allemande, courante, sarabande, and gigue. Consult the miniature four-movement suite cited in Exs. 14-6A through 6D for a typical example; only the first reprise of each dance is quoted.[2] The sarabande, the usual "slow movement" of the group, is often followed by one (or perhaps more) optional dance(s). The minuet, bourrée, or gavotte are more frequent. One may find a *varied* form of a movement (usually entitled *Double* or *Agréments*) immediately following the original, often with additional embellishments or ornaments. Sometimes an expanded introductory movement is appended. It might take the form of a free *prelude*, two-part *overture*, or even a *toccata*.[3] With the exception of this precursory movement, however, all of the dances in the suite are in two-reprise form.

EXAMPLE 14-6

A. Allemande   Johann Froberger: Suite No. 26 in b (first reprises only)

[1]An excellent account of the historical background and characteristics of this genre may be found in the *New Grove Dictionary* under "Suite".

[2]Although Johann Jacob Froberger has been called the "father of the German Suite", only a few of his thirty-plus suites employ the "standard" sequence of Allemande-Courante-Sarabande-Gigue. Suite No. 26 in B minor (Ex. 14-6) does.

[3]All of Bach's six Suites for Unaccompanied Cello open with a Prelude, while in his six keyboard Partitas the initial movement is continually varied.

B. Courante

C. Sarabande

(continued)

EXAMPLE 14-6 (cont'd)

D. Gigue

Suite movements find their bases in various nationalistic dances. Each is distinguished by metric and rhythmic characteristics related to the original dance steps or patterns. For a discussion of the more frequently encountered of these consult Appendix 1. Although many of these dances are set in consistent three-voice texture, composers did not always feel obligated to conform in movements employing free counterpoint. It is not unusual to find a continuous fluctuation in the number of parts, with no need to account for their absence by rests. This procedure is termed free-voiced (from the German *Freistimmig*) texture.

Although the movements of a suite are unified through a common tonic key (parallel major or minor is permitted), the tonal scheme, thematic material, and phraseology will normally differ from one dance to the other. In the historical origins of this genre, however, there were deliberate relationships between the movements. In the older pairing of a slow and fast dance (such as pavan/galliard, passamezzo/saltarello, Tanz/Nachtanz) the latter was usually a livelier variation of the former. In the late Baroque a remnant of this procedure was called a "variation suite". Here the movements share common initial motivic material or even similar tonal designs.

The D minor French Suite of Bach is a sophisticated demonstration of this technique. Consult Exs. 14-7A through 7E, noting the underlying use of scale degrees î 5̂ 6̂ 5̂ or their retrograde.

EXAMPLE 14-7   Inciptis from Bach's French Suite in d

ASSIGNMENTS

1. Analyze the *Minuet* quoted in Ex. 14-8 as follows: (1.) rhythmic activity and motivic interplay between voices; (2.) spacial or registral distribution of parts; (3.) detailed treatment of non-harmonic material (there are several curious spots); (4.) underlying voice-leading.

EXAMPLE 14-8   J. S. Bach: Trio to a Minuet by G. H. Stölzel (*Klavierbüchlein*) BWV 929

(continued)

EXAMPLE 14-8 (cont'd)

2. Can you find any traces or tendencies of "variation suite" technique in the four movements of the Froberger Suite (Ex. 14-6)?

EXTENDED TWO-REPRISE FORM

The binary pieces discussed in Chapter 6 seldom exceeded twenty-four measures (8 + 16). Allemandes, courantes, gigues, and even *sarabandes* are often longer. The proportions between the two repeated sections may vary from 1:1 to as much as 1:3. Although the tendency toward phrase periodicity decreases as length increases, the basic tonal scheme is retained. An extended two-reprise dance is less likely to close the first section in tonic, and will often explore more closely related keys during the second part. Several other features may be noted. Sometimes the closing of the initial reprise will be repeated exactly (or nearly so) at the end of the final reprise, although now transposed back to the tonic center. Douglass Green refers to this as a *balanced binary form*.[4] See Exs. 14-9A and 9B for a typical example; there are very slight alterations in the last passage.

EXAMPLE 14-9

A. Meas. 10–11   G. F. Handel: Allemande (Suite in A)

[4]See Douglass Green, *Form in Tonal Music,* 2nd edition (New York: Holt, Rinehart, and Winston, 1979), pp. 78–79.

B. Meas. 21—22

As observed in Chapter 6, the return of the tonic key in the second part seldom coincides with a return of the original *opening theme* of the piece. This so-called *rounded binary form* is actually more typical of the minuets in the later Classical period. Nevertheless, they do occur infrequently in the Baroque as illustrated in Ex. 14-10. Both of the above procedures are common in the "Sonatas" of Dominico Scarlatti,[5] but these two-reprise pieces are in many ways already anticipating the Rococo period.

EXAMPLE 14-10   J. S. Bach: Trio I to the Minuet (*Brandenburg* Concerto No. 1 in F)

(continued)

[5]The traditional title for these one-movement compositions is somewhat misleading. They should more properly be given their original name, *Esercizii* (Exercises).

EXAMPLE 14-10 (cont'd)

ASSIGNMENTS

1. Listed below are several more extended movements in two-reprise form. Trace their tonal schemes, use of initial material (does it return exactly?) or recurrent motives, phraseology and important cadential points, and possible use of "balanced" conclusions at the end of the two sections.

  a. Gigue (Bach's French Suite in G)
  b. Prelude in B minor (*WTC* I)

2. Using the opening of the *Sarabande* given in Ex. 14-11, complete the piece in similar style. Choose the relative major key as your destination at the conclusion of the initial section. Incorporate characteristics of either the balanced or rounded binary form (or both). Strive for non-periodic phrasing.

EXAMPLE 14-11

Sarabande (after Johann Mattheson)

15

Tonal imitation:
further studies
in invertible counterpoint

Before studying the three-voice fugue, we will examine several of its compositional devices. Tonal imitation will be explored first, followed by a continuation of invertible counterpoint, featuring double counterpoint at the tenth and twelfth and triple counterpoint.

TONAL IMITATION

As discussed in Chapter 9, most imitation at the perfect fifth or fourth during the Renaissance involved real (or strict interval-for-interval) answers. Occasionally, subjects opening with a fifth were answered with a fourth, and *vice versa*. This "incidental" tonal modification usually resulted from harmonic or melodic considerations. For instance in Ex. 15-1A the composer tries to retain the G minor triad, while in Ex. 15-1B the adjustment allows Palestrina to stretto his theme. This procedure would not have been possible with a traditional real answer.

Another aspect of tonal imitation results in a crucial principle of the major-minor system. In the *authentic* octave species of the older modal system the distance from the *finalis* ("tonic") to the *repercussio* ("dominant") was a pentachord or perfect fifth (see Ex. 15-1C). The upper tetrachord (or

EXAMPLE 15-1 Tonal imitation in Renai ssance music

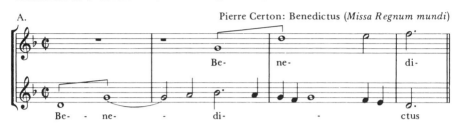

A.   Pierre Certon: Benedictus (*Missa Regnum mundi*)

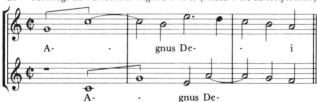

B.   Pierluigi da Palestrina: Agnus Dei II (*Missa Dies sanctificatus*)

C. Octave species of Dorian mode

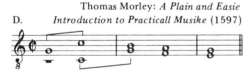

D.   Thomas Morley: *A Plain and Easie Introduction to Practicall Musike* (1597)

fourth) then completed the octave span. In the *plagal* form of the same mode (here Dorian) the basic range was a fourth lower. Thus the lower fifth of the authentic was balanced by the corresponding fourth of the plagal. Since two *adjacent* voice parts in polyphonic texture adhered to the authentic and plagal forms, an opening leap of a fifth or fourth in one would often be answered by its counterpart—a fourth or fifth. Thus Thomas Morley stated at the end of the sixteenth century (see Ex. 15-1D) that "This (answer) riseth five notes and the plainsong (subject) but four."[1] This procedure was acceptable for "fugue" but not for canon, where exact imitation had to be maintained.

As the major-minor system evolved in the seventeenth century, the

[1]From Thomas Morley *A Plaine and Easie Introduction to Practicall Musicke* (1597).

tendency of the imitating answer to appear in the dominant *key,*—not just on the fifth of the mode—precipitated adjustments in the older theory. The dominant ($\hat{5}$) now divides the scalar octave into a lower pentachord ($\hat{1}$ up to $\hat{5}$) and upper tetrachord ($\hat{5}$ up to $\hat{8}$). Notice in Marpurg's chart (of about 1750) how scale steps $\hat{4}$ and $\hat{5}$ are interchangeable with $\hat{1}$ or $\hat{8}$. (consult Fig. 15-1). Since the pentachord-tetrachord arrangement on the two scales is switched, tonal adjustments were necessary with certain types of subjects and answers in the dominant area. This technique is referred to as *tonal* (versus *real*) imitation, or *tonal answers.*[2]

FIGURE 15-1 Chart for imitation at the dominant from Friedrich Marpurg's
Abhandlung von der Fuge **(1753-54)**

Scale on the first degree	$\hat{1}$	$\hat{2}$	$\hat{3}$	$\hat{4}$	$\hat{5}$	$\hat{6}$	$\hat{7}$	$\hat{8}$	
Scale on the fifth degree	$\hat{5}$	$\hat{6}$	$\hat{7}$	$\hat{8}$	$\hat{2}$	$\hat{3}$	$\hat{4}$	$\hat{5}$	

The conditions necessitating tonal answers were discussed as far back as Nivers (1667), through Masson (1699), Rameau (1722), to Marpurg in the middle of the eighteenth century.[3] A summary of their conclusions are presented below as four general "rules". In the subject $\hat{1}$ or $\hat{5}$ are answered by $\hat{5}$ and $\hat{1}$ respectively; these are denoted with brackets in the musical examples. All scale degrees listed below relate to the tonic key.

1. If the subject begins on the dominant note ($\hat{5}$) but does *not* modulate, then the answer begins on the tonic ($\hat{1}$) and modulates to the dominant key:

Subject (in tonic key)		Answer (modulates to dominant key)
$\hat{5} \longrightarrow \hat{1}$ (or $\hat{3}$)	then	$\hat{1} \longrightarrow \hat{5}$ (or $\hat{7}$)

Usually, only one interval adjustment is necessary at the very beginning of the answer. The initial note of the answer (or $\hat{1}$) will support a tonic triad, which acts as a common-chord pivot, affecting the modulation to the dominant key. In Ex. 15-2A the modulation takes place immediately after the common chord (i = iv), while in Ex. 15-2B it is delayed until near the end of the answer. The descending sixth in Ex. 15-2C changes into a diminished fifth in order to preserve the motion $\hat{1}$ to $\hat{5}$.

---

[2]See Imogene Horsley, *Fugue: History and Practice* (New York: The Free Press, 1966). For a more comprehensive survey of the topic see Charles Naldin, *Fugal Answer* (London: Oxford University Press, 1969).

[3]Consult the Bibliography under Treatises.

EXAMPLE 15-2 Tonal answers baginning on $\hat{5}$

Giovanni Pergolesi: "Fac ut ardeat cor meum" (*Stabat Mater*)

J. S. Bach: Fugue in E♭ ("St. Anne") from his *Klavierübung* III

J. S. Bach: *Wie nach einer Wasserquelle* (*Neumeister-Sammlung*) BWV 1119

2. If the subject opens with scale degrees $\hat{1}$ to $\hat{5}$ or $\hat{5}$ to $\hat{1}$ and does *not* modulate, then the answer will reverse the order and modulate to the dominant key:

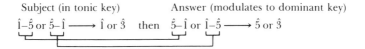

A "double" intervallic adjustment is sometimes necessary here. Example 15-3A utilizes only one change, while the octave span of Ex. 15-3B (g^1–d^2–g^2 is answered by d^1–g^1–d^2) requires two. The tonic pivot is still in effect (I = IV) to prepare the dominant modulation.

EXAMPLE 15-3 Tonal answers beginning with î-ŝ or ŝ-î

Johann Pachelbel: Fugue No. 11 (on the *Magnificat primi toni*)

Guillaume Nivers: *Magnificat*
(*Traité de la composition musicale* 1667)

3. If the subject either concludes on scale degree ŝ *or* modulates to the dominant key (during its course or near its conclusion), the answer will then conclude on scale degree î, thereby affecting a harmonic movement back to the tonic:

Subject	Answer
(tonic modulates to dominant)	(dominant modulates to tonic)
î ——————→ ŝ	ŝ ——————→ î

In Ex. 15-4A the subject concludes on ŝ although a modulation is not explicit; a probable accompanying counterpoint (missing in the original example) has been supplied. The use of the c♯² in Ex. 15-4B forces the subject to cadence in the dominant key. The initial î ŝ ŝ of the subject has *not* been tonally adjusted. Since the answer begins *immediately* in the new dominant key, no pivot is necessary. This form of tonal imitation is problematic, for any necessary tonal adjustment(s) must take place somewhere *within* the answer. It is not always possible to pinpoint the exact intervallic change, since this depends largely on the original subject. In fact several "solutions" are sometimes plausible. Strive to maintain the basic contour shape of the subject. Example 15-4C offers three feasible answers to the given theme. Study each carefully. Which do you favor and why?

EXAMPLE 15-4 Tonal answers which move from $\hat{1}$ to $\hat{5}$ or modulate

Jean Philippe Rameau: *Traité d'harmonie* (1722) - countersubject added

A.

J. S. Bach: *Herr Jesu Christ, dich zu uns wend'* BWV 749

B.

C.

Three possible answers for a modulating subject

4. Sometimes if the subject opens with scale steps $\hat{8}$–$\hat{7}$, then the initial tones of the answer will be modified to $\hat{5}$–$\hat{3}$. The original theme does no' usually modulate in this case. Often a double adjustment is needed:

Subject (in tonic key)	Answer (modulates to dominant key)
$\hat{8}$–$\hat{7}$ $\longrightarrow$ $\hat{1}$ (or $\hat{3}$) then	$\hat{5}$–$\hat{3}$ $\longrightarrow$ $\hat{5}$ (or $\hat{7}$)

A tonal answer seems to originate in the harmony of the pivot chord. In Ex. 15-5 the leap of f♯¹ to d♯¹ in measure three clearly implies the tonic (IV), while a real answer of f♯¹ to e♯¹ would hardly suffice.

EXAMPLE 15-5　　　　　　　　　　　　　J. S. Bach: Fugue in B (*WTC* I)

Notice the qualifier "sometimes" in point 4. In Ex. 15-6 the initial e^1 is clearly a non-structural neighboring tone, with the leap $\hat{1}$ to $\hat{5}$ taking precedence. Thus the answer responds with the typical $\hat{5}$ to $\hat{1}$. Also observe the b♭ (not b♮) in the middle voice, since the pivot chord is still tonic.

EXAMPLE 15-6

J. S. Bach: Fugue in F (*WTC* II)

The four general categories cited above will help you derive appropriate tonal answers. However, the topic is complex. It is possible to discover surprising and innovative solutions devised by masters of the period. Exceptions to the rule abound. Examine the subject of Bach's "Little" G minor Fugue for Organ (BWV 578), cited in Ex. 15-7A. You might expect the opening $\hat{1}$–$\hat{5}$ fifth to be answered with a tonal $\hat{5}$–$\hat{8}$ fourth. What is generally overlooked, however, is that the theme *modulates* to the dominant key of D minor, so that no harmonic pivot is necessary. Hence the real answer is completely appropriate. Had the subject been condensed, as in Ex. 15-7B, it would have required a tonal adjustment. Incidentally, a very similar situation to the G minor Fugue arises with the opening Ricercar a 3 of Bach's *Das Musikalische Opfer.* Although it has the same opening triadic basis and concluding modulatory link, the composer gives it a *tonal answer!*

EXAMPLE 15-7

A. No tonal answer employed

J. S. Bach: Organ Fugue in g ("Little") BWV 578

(continued)

EXAMPLE 15-7 (cont'd)

B. Modified subject requiring tonal answer

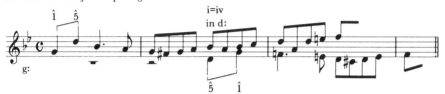

The continuing subject voice which accompanies the answer is called the *counterpart* or *counterpoint*. It should form a rhythmic complement to the answer, using structural intervals that imply a normal harmonic progression. If the counterpart is reemployed consistently with each appearance of the subject, it is called a *countersubject*. Additional thematic statements or reentries in tonic are "subjects" and those in the dominant are "answers," although "subject" also refers to entries of the original theme in other closely related keys.

If the subject does not contain any of the characteristics noted in the four categories, it will usually be given a *real* answer. The D major Fugue (*WTC* II) is a curious instance. It opens with the downward leap of a fifth, but the scale degrees involved are $\hat{1}$ down to $\hat{4}$, not $\hat{5}$ down to $\hat{1}$. Thus real imitation suffices.

Answers at the subdominant are rare. Although they may occur at the composer's whim, there is usually a good reason for them.[4] What do you think is the logic for the answer in G minor (iv) in Ex. 15-8A? Some scholars believe that this fugue may have been written for solo violin in A minor. What idiomatic string device would tend to support this, and how does it substantiate the subdominant answer? The opening of a chorus from Handel's *Samson* appears to be answered in the subdominant, but as Ex. 15-8B shows, the subject is actually in the dominant key, which is then imitated in tonic. Note the potential double counterpoint in the counterpart to the answer.

[4]Examine the subject to the G♯ minor Fugue (*WTC* I) and explain the logic of Bach's answer.

EXAMPLE 15-8 Real answers in subdominant or tonic (!)

ASSIGNMENTS

1. Go through the fugues in both volumes of *WTC* and for each piece determine whether a real or tonal answer is utilized. What characteristics of the subject necessitated the use of tonal imitation? Do a harmonic analysis of several, observing pivot tones or chords. Are there any tonal answers which do not fall within the basic four classifications discussed above?

2. A number of initial chorale phrases (for possible *Vorimitation*) and several fugue subjects are cited in Ex. 15-9. Write out an appropriate answer at the dominant for each; most but *not all* will require tonal adjustments. Then choose three of your solutions and add a counterpart.

EXAMPLE 15-9

(continued)

EXAMPLE 15-9 (cont'd)

DOUBLE COUNTERPOINT AT THE TENTH AND TWELFTH

Chapter 9 dealt with the possibility of double counterpoint at the simple or multiple octave. However, there are several other invertible relations in two-voice texture that may be encountered in Baroque polyphony.[5] An "inversion chart" for counterpoint at the tenth is given in Fig. 15-2. This form is less frequent because of two problems. All thirds and sixths invert into octaves and fifths respectively, therefore any instances of similar imperfect consonances (sixth to sixth) will produce *parallel* perfect intervals (fifth to fifth). Suspensions are almost impossible to generate since 7–6 = 4–5, 4–3 = 7–8, and 2–3 = 9–8. One example is cited in Ex. 15-10. During the inversional process the original soprano becomes the lower part, being held in the same octave, while the other voice is moved a tenth higher (or 1

---

[5]Examples of double counterpoint at the tenth and twelfth may already be found in the sixteenth-century treatises of Zarlino and Vicentiono.

+ 10 = 11, the "magic" number for this type of double counterpoint). Note that the result is a *complete* three-voice piece. Also consult the discussion on Contrapunctus X (Bach's *Die Kunst der Fuge*) in Chapter 20 (see Ex. 20-10).

FIGURE 15-2 Chart of intervallic inversions in double counterpoint at the tenth

3	2	1	2	3	4	5	6	7	8	9	10	11	12
12	11	10	9	8	7	6	5	4	3	2	1	2	3

EXAMPLE 15-10

Johann Fux: *Gradus ad Parnassum* (1725)

Counterpoint at the twelfth is more frequent. Its inversional relationships are illustrated in Fig. 15-3. Here the problem interval is the sixth, which inverts into a seventh. Therefore all sixths must be treated as though they were originally dissonant in nature. The use of thirds and tenths is very common in this technique. Why? Although the 7–6 becomes a 6–7, other suspensions are possible: 4–3 = 9–10 and 2–3 = 11–10. Example 15-11 is a typical passage employing the various suspensions. Here the method of inversion is 1 + 12 (which is 13 or the "magic" number). More usual is 8 + 5 (= 13). This is illustrated in the chorale setting of Ex. 15-12. Here the cantus falls an octave while the counterpoint is raised a fifth.[6]

FIGURE 15-3 Chart of intervallic inversions in double counterpoint at the twelfth

3	2	1	2	3	4	5	6	7	8	9	10	11	12	13	14
14	13	12	11	10	9	8	7	6	5	4	3	2	1	2	3

[6]Also consult the discussion of Contrapunctus IX (Bach's *Die Kunst der Fuge*) in Chapter 20, associated with Ex. 20-11 and Fig. 20-3.

EXAMPLE 15-11 Double counterpoint at the twelfth with suspensions (12+1)

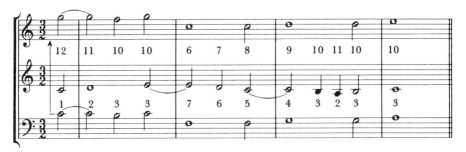

EXAMPLE 15-12

Samuel Scheidt: Bicinium (Cantio sacra: *Warum betrübst du dich*)

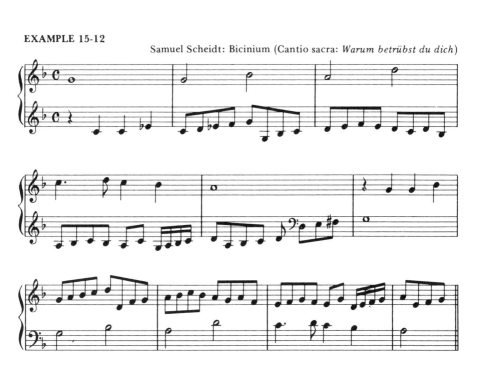

Often the two voices are constructed so that they will work in *multiple* double counterpoint. For instance Ex. 15-13 shows the possible use of both counterpoint at the twelfth *and* at the double octave. What is the "secret" of this passage?

EXAMPLE 15-13 Multiple double counterpoint at the twelfth and double octave

at double octave

at twelfth

TRIPLE COUNTERPOINT

As the term implies, three voices are utilized in this invertible procedure. There are six possibilities for triple counterpoint (3! or $1 \times 2 \times 3 = 6$). At first it would seem that the restrictions of this technique would result in insurmountable obstacles. The use of a complete triad must be avoided, since two of its permutations will produce second inversion chords (see Ex. 15-14). There are two ways to skirt this problem. All of the triads can be *incomplete*, although the resultant succession of thirds and sixths creates a rather "threadbare" texture with continual doubling of one of the inter-vallic pitches (see Ex. 15-15A). However, since the use of seventh chords in three voices normally omits the fifth, which is responsible for the trou-blesome second inversions, these sequences offer one frequent solution (see Ex. 15-15B). The passage in Ex. 15-15C consists of both incomplete $^6_5$ and $^6_3$ chords, allowing it to be inverted in all six arrangements without fear of second inversions. Such examples may be termed *strict* triple counter-point.

EXAMPLE 15-14 Six permutations of a triad

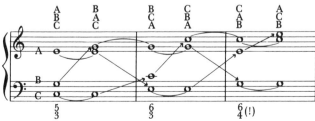

EXAMPLE 15-15 Strict triple counterpoint

In actual practice, triple counterpoint with complete triads is common. In Ex. 15-16 Bach employs all six permutations, despite the fact that $^6_4$s result in two different places (denoted with arrows). This procedure is best called *apparent* triple counterpoint; for another illustration see Ex. 17-8.

EXAMPLE 15-16 Apparent triple counterpoint (arrows denote complete triads)

This device sometimes plays an important role in subject reentries of fugues.[7] Entire pieces may be based on the principle of triple counterpoint. Example 15-17 analyzes the opening measures of one such composition,

---

[7]See the discussion of subject reentries in Bach's Fugue in C minor (*WTC* I), in Chapter 17.

EXAMPLE 15-17   J. S. Bach: Prelude in A (*WTC* I)

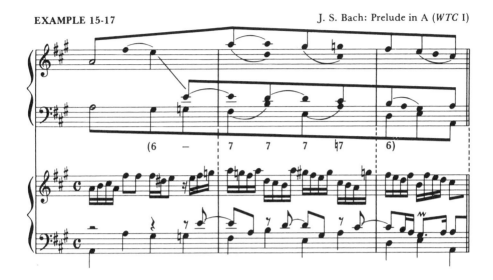

Bach's Prelude in A major (*WTC* I). Examine its voice-leading reduction and comment on the basic technique. In Bach's ingenious Three-Part Invention in F minor, both the opening three subjects and the episodic passages are set in triple counterpoint (see the reduction in Ex. 15-18).

EXAMPLE 15-18 Episodic triple counterpoint in Bach's Three-Part Invention in f (measures 9-10)

Finally, the last example illustrates a possible "working method" for composing strict triple counterpoint. Example 15-19A shows a note-against-note version featuring incomplete triads and seventh chords, while Ex. 15-19B gives one plausible elaboration. Only one permutation is cited in Ex. 15-19C. Ideally there should be three distinct levels of rhythmic activity as well as contrasting melodic contours so that each voice can stand on its own as an independent thematic idea.

EXAMPLE 15-19 Working model for triple counterpoint

ASSIGNMENTS

1. Comment on the use of multiple double counterpoint in the passages cited from the fugues listed below:

a. C♯ minor (*WTC* II)—measures 48–49 and 55–56 (in particular, note the treatment of sixths here).

b. G minor (*WTC* II)—measures 5–7, 13–16, 28–30, 32–35, and 45–48 (one passage exploits a type of double counterpoint not discussed above).

2. Compose a counterpoint in continuous eighth notes below the provided cantus (Ex. 15-20) that will work in double counterpoint a tenth higher. Copy out the inverted form. Does your solution form a complete three-part passage?

EXAMPLE 15-20

3. A possible fugue subject is cited in Ex. 15-21. Provide it with tonal imitation (why?) in the tenor voice and then counterpoint your answer so that it can be inverted at *both* the twelfth and double octave. Show both inversions.

EXAMPLE 15-21

4. Trace the triple counterpoint in the following compositions, listing the permutations employed and the order in which they occur. Do there seem to be any patterns?

a. C♯ minor Fugue (*WTC* I)—beginning in measure 51
b. A major Prelude (*WTC* I)
c. B♭ major Fugue (*WTC* I)—beginning in measure 9

5. Compose a short passage (about two measures of quadruple meter) of original *strict* triple counterpoint. Copy out one of the permutations.

16

※※※※※※※※※※※※※※※※※※※※※※※※※※※※※※※※※※※※※※

Additional
contrapuntal devices:
further study of canon

This chapter will concentrate on artificial contrapuntal devices used in the late Baroque. The first three—melodic inversion or mirror, stretto, and augmentation-diminution—occur in works stressing imitation (such as fugue), while the remainder are associated with canon.

MELODIC MIRROR (*PER MOTUM CONTRARIUM*)

The use of *melodic* (or contour) *mirroring* as a common device in motivic development was discussed in Chapter 2. In imitative compositions, it may be applied to more thematic statements or subjects, where it is termed *moto contrarius* (contrary motion). The original "upright" form is called the *rectus* and its mirror as the *inversus*. When the two versions of the same theme are compared, one scale degree will be common to both, the so-called *axis tone*. The most common axis is the third scale degree of the mode (see Exs. 16-1A and B), since the implied harmonic functions between the subject and its mirror are closely allied. This can be seen in Ex. 16-1C; note the exchange of V and iv. Due to the resultant thirds, fifths, and diminished sevenths in the minor mode (refer back to Ex. 16-1B), it is possible to present the *rectus* and *inversus* simultaneously. Indeed, entire fugues may be inverted, as occurs in Contrapuncti XVI to XVIII of Bach's *Die Kunst der Fuge*.

EXAMPLE 16-1 Scale degree $\hat{3}$ as the inversional axis in major and minor modes

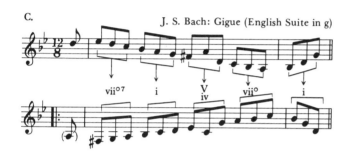

Selections from two interesting compositions of Dietrich Buxtehude are quoted below. The first is a keyboard fugue consisting of three inter-related sections. The opening points of imitation for the first two are given in Ex. 16-2A and B, contrasting upright with mirrored forms of the subject. Observe the tonal answers and how they figure in the inversional process. On what scale degree is the axis tone? Trace the subject entries in the opening part of the final section(Ex. 16-2C).

EXAMPLE 16-2

A. Rectus section   Dietrich Buxtehude: Organ Fugue in G

(continued)

EXAMPLE 16-2 (cont'd)

B. Inversus section

C. Rectus and inversus section

The second movement of Buxtehude's setting of the chorale *Mit Fried und Freud ich fahr dahin,* written on the death of his father, consists of Contrapunctus II and its exact mirror version, entitled *Evolutio.* The initial phrases of each are quoted in Exs. 16-3A and 3B. The texture is literally turned upside down, with the Dorian hymn tune in the soprano mirrored in the bass voice. What is curious about the "axis" in this case, and how may it explain the use of a one-sharp signature in the *Evolutio*?

EXAMPLE 16-3

Dietrich Buxtehude: Contrapunctus II and Evolutio
(*Mit Fried und Freud ich fahr dahin*)

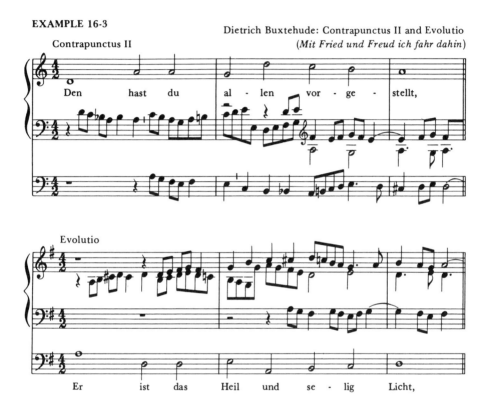

STRETTO

The term *stretto* is the past participle of the Italian *stringere*, to draw close or tighten. In essence it constitutes a temporal compression of the original point of imitation, so that the answer enters *before* the subject is finished. This device usually occurs later in a fugue, where the foreshortening of the imitation increases tension—events are now happening at a faster rate. One may even see it at the opening of an imitative piece (see Ex. 16-4), although such instances of *stretto exposition* are more typical of the Renaissance.

EXAMPLE 16-4

Johann Fischer: Fugue in f (*Ariadne Musica*)

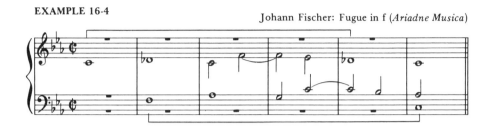

When two voices are involved in stretto, they generally occur at perfect relations (octaves, fifths, or fourths), although other intervals are possible. The stretto need not maintain the same relation found in the original imitation. Instances of tonal answers are frequent in stretti. Indeed, a composer may take tonal liberties by changing a note or two to make the stretto "work". Rhythmic adjustments, however, are quite rare. In the examples which follow, only those voices directly involved in the stretto will be quoted. Composers may construct a lengthy subject in order to produce an extended stretto later in the piece. In Ex. 16-5 the original theme is sequential, so that when combined in stretto, the two voices create a harmonic cycle of fifths, using thirds and sixths. This example is somewhat of an exception, since most stretti employ shorter subjects and hence "easier" solutions. A pair of more typical instances are cited in Exs. 16-6 and 16-7, extracted from organ fugues of the period. The original theme is enclosed with brackets in each case.

J. S. Bach: Fugue in E♭ (*WTC* II)

EXAMPLE 16-5

EXAMPLE 16-6

Johann Pachelbel: Organ Fugue in C

EXAMPLE 16-7   Dietrich Buxtehude: Prelude and Fugue in g

original subject

Stretti involving *more* than two voices are more difficult to generate, since the temporal distance between entries may be so brief that thematic overlapping can occur with the first and last parts. The chromatic subject of Ex. 16-8 offers one such example. Instances of *multiple* stretto procedures on the same subject test the craft of the composer even further. Examine this technique in Ex. 16-9, noting the various intervallic and temporal distances between entries. When this device is continually stressed throughout the composition, the term *stretto fugue* is often applied. One may even encounter a rare instance of *double stretto*, where the technique is used with two *different* thematic ideas. This usually occurs in textures of four or more voices, as is the case of the C♯ minor Fugue (*WTC* I); see measures 94–100.

EXAMPLE 16-8   Johann Christoph Bach: Prelude and Fugue in E♭

EXAMPLE 16-9
                                              J. S. Bach: Three-Part Invention in B♭

Stretti must be calculated before composing begins. Good ones seldom, if ever, happen accidentally. Several points should be kept in mind:

1. The interval between entries is usually an octave, fifth, or fourth (no tritones). The metric positioning of strong versus weak beats is normally maintained.

2. Small tonal liberties may be taken with the original subjects, but avoid changing the rhythm.

3. One must continue to employ good harmonic progression and rhythmic interplay or balance between the voices.

AUGMENTATION AND DIMINUTION
(*PER AUGMENTATIONEM—DIMINUTIONEM*)

Proportional rhythmic expansion or contraction are possible devices in motivic development. Those infrequent instances where a subject may be augmented (usually in a proportion of 2:1) are normally found near the conclusion of imitative pieces. The effect is one of an overall broadening of the pace (see the D♯ minor Fugue, *WTC I*, in Chapter 17). Diminution is even less common. Both are usually found with other artifices. Point out the various contrapuntal devices in Ex. 16-10 and 16-11.

EXAMPLE 16-10

J. S. Bach: Prelude and Fugue in C BWV 547

original

EXAMPLE 16-11   J. S. Bach: Contrapunctus VII (*Die Kunst der Fuge*)

original

ASSIGNMENTS

1. Given the subject in Ex. 16-12, compose a counterpoint to it in continual quarter notes. Then mirror and switch the parts, using $\hat{3}$ as the axis. Does your counterpoint still "work"?

2. After examining the opening subject/answer, find *all* instances of stretto in the following fugues, noting the intervallic and temporal distances between entries: C major Fugue (*WTC* I), D major Fugue (*WTC* II), B♭ minor Fugue (*WTC* II).

EXAMPLE 16-12

3. Using the subjects in Ex. 16-13, find at least three different ways to use stretto in two voices.

EXAMPLE 16-13

4. Try composing a three-voice stretto on an original subject. The successive entries should involve perfect intervals and be less than a measure's distance.

ADDITIONAL STUDY IN CANON

As mentioned in Chapter 10, the origins of imitation and canon are intertwined. During the fourteenth century the secular *caccia* (a two-voice vocal canon over a free instrumental bass) and the *rota* (a round accompanied by a ground or *pes*) were well-established genre.[1] By the time of Dufay's canonic Gloria (*Et in terra ad modum tubae*) about a century later, the term *fuga* was applied to both secular and sacred accompanied canons. The early masters of the Renaissance—Ockeghem, Obrecht, and later Josquin—frequently used canonic techniques with melodic mirror, prolation, and crab motion.[2] By the mid sixteenth century these artificial means were in decline, relegated to more "intellectual, puzzle-like" pieces. Zarlino (1558) refers to the canon as strict imitation at some perfect interval (*fuga legate*), in which "the parts can be written as one." With the exception of obvious changes in musical style, canonic forms remained largely unchanged until the late Baroque period.

Instances of *complete* pieces utilizing strict canonic technique with three or more voices are quite rare. On the other hand, there are incidental canonic passages within larger works. The ingenious example worked out by Handel in his counterpoint lessons to Princess Anne (see Ex. 16-14) was later incorporated into the final Amen of the *Messiah*.

EXAMPLE 16-14

G. F. Handel: Canonic passage (*Counterpoint Lessons for Princess Anne*)

---

[1]The famous six-part rota *Sumer is Icumen In* may have been composed as early as 1240.
[2]See the prolation (*prolationum*) and canonic (*ad fugam*) masses of this era.

Canons at the unison and with equally spaced entries present no special difficulties. Such pieces (we would call them *rounds* today) were usually set to text. The simplest method of writing a round is first to set the opening phrase of text to a melodic line. The second phrase is then counterpointed below it, and the final phrase added to fill out the harmonic and rhythmic "holes". Good melodic connections should prevail between the end of one phrase and the beginning of the next. However, if the entries are of *different* intervals and distance, the problems multiply. Study the opening of the three-voice canon in Ex. 16-15. The voices enter on Î, 5̂, and Î, with distances of one and two measures respectively.

EXAMPLE 16-15

Gottfried Heinrich Stölzel: Canon a 3

If the canon is strict *throughout,* all cadences, both final and internal, must be predetermined. In fact, it would seem easier to compose a three-voice canon by working backwards from the final cadence. Accidentals are somewhat scarce, as there is always the danger of the music wandering off into remote tonal realms and never being able to return. It is almost impossible to generalize about the technical aspects of such pieces, since their specific problems are determined by the opening thematic idea and the tonal entries of the remaining voices. Nevertheless, a successful canon should at no time "smell of the lamp"; the best compliment to the composer's craft may be the listener's inability to detect the canon.

Accompanied Canon

Baroque composers often embedded a two-voice canon within the texture of three or more parts—a common technique in the Renaissance.[3] One usually finds a single *free* or accompanying voice, which plugs rhy-

---

[3]The entirety of Palentrina's *Missa Repleatur os meum laude* is based on this principle.

mic holes and fills out the harmony of the two-part canon. Bach's *Goldberg* Variations feature a set of nine interspersed canons ranging from the unison through the interval of the ninth. With one exception, all are *accompanied* two-voice examples. This group is remarkable since the canons, being variations themselves, share the same harmonic basis as the original aria or theme. Variation 15 is especially interesting, since it represents a mirror canon at the fifth (see Ex. 16-16). Note the quasi-chromatic tetrachord in the "free" bass part.

J. S. Bach: Variation 15 (*Goldberg* Variations)

EXAMPLE 16-16

Perpetual Canon (perpetuus)

This type of canon is constructed so that the voices overlap to create an endless cycle. Thus repeat signs are employed. The basic problem in their composition is that the conclusion of the *comes* must be able to work in counterpoint with the opening of the *dux* upon repetition. The illustration in Ex. 16-17 comes from an amusing collection of pieces by Telemann, a kind of Baroque musical joke.

EXAMPLE 16-17

Georg Telemann: Canon perpetuus (*Der getreue Musikmeister*)

Modulating or Spiral Canon (per tonas)[4]

This form modulates by the use of a consistent intervallic relation (usually fifths), so that the voices eventually arrive back in the original tonic key upon completion of the cycle. In the first nine measures of Kirnberger's

---

[4]The term *per tonas* refers to the resultant superimposition of two fifth modulations: C major–(G major)–D major.

canon (Ex. 16-18), what is the interval of transposition in the successive entries and how does it explain the different key signatures? What pitches would make up the next four entries?

EXAMPLE 16-18

Johann Kirnberger: Modulating Canon

Augmentation Canon (per augmentationem)

Here the *comes* part is in rhythmic augmentation (usually 2:1) to the *dux*. It may enter after the presentation of the initial theme in the *dux* (for example, see Contrapunctus XIV in Bach's *Die Kunst der Fuge*), or both voices may begin together and then unfold in different rhythmic proportions. Although this is not difficult with only two parts, its problems intensify with the addition of more voices. Compare the relatively simple illustration in Ex. 16-19 with the highly sophisticated technique found in the *Canon per augmentationem* of Bach's *Vom Himmel hoch* variations. In the latter case the imitative voices develop over the hymn cantus in the bass.

EXAMPLE 16-19 Augmentation canon (2:1)

Retrograde Canon *(cancrizans, al rovescio, per recte et retro)*

So-called "crab" canons are a contrapuntal curiosity. The voices move forward to a certain point, where they then switch places and run backwards to the end. Trace this procedure in Ex. 16-20, which is based on a chromatic tetrachord. This type of canon is fraught with obstacles; upon retrogression, consonance may become dissonance (Ex. 16-21A), and suspensions become anticipations (Ex. 16-21B). Even dotted notes are often problematic, since such figures as ♩. ♪ invert into the awkward ♪ ♩..

EXAMPLE 16-20 Retrograde canon

EXAMPLE 16-21 Typical situations arising when composing crab canons

In addition to these techniques, the use of melodic mirror in the *comes* (*contrario motu*) may be noted. It is even possible to combine several different devices: *canone al contrario riverso* (mirror/retrograde). In four-voice texture one can encounter a *double canon,* in which a pair of different two-part canons are unfolded; this is also called a 4 in 2 canon.[5]

Puzzle Canons

In strict canonic technique it was often customary to write out only a single line (the *dux*) and indicate how the remaining parts imitated it. Multiple clefs were sometimes written before the music to denote the various intervals of imitation. Thus the second space in the staff would be c in the bass clef but g in the tenor clef. A *presa* sign (𝄇) normally indicated the point(s) at which the various voices entered. The artifice of the canon was often associated with "intellectual games" (*ludus ingenni*), so that specific instructions for realizing the canon from the given *dux* might be missing, except from an occasional cryptic phrase or clue. Hence the term *puzzle canon.* Examine the ingenious double set of six canons in Bach's *Das Musikalische Opfer,* all of which were originally notated in this fashion.[6]

ASSIGNMENTS

1. Given the opening thematic idea in Ex. 16-22, compose a strict three-part canon about ten measures long. The remaining entries should take place on $\hat{5}$ and $\hat{1}$; the choice of temporal distance is optional. The voices may become free at the final cadence or remain strict. In the latter case, use the anticipatory technique mentioned in Chapter 10.

EXAMPLE 16-22

[5]One example of a 4 in 2 canon is Ex. 18-15. Also see Mozart's double canon in Ex. 23-8, which features mirroring.

[6]See Hans Theodore David, *J. S. Bach's Musical Offering; History, Interpretation, and Analysis* (New York: Dover Publications, Inc., 1972).

2. Write out the realization of the two-part canon which appears in Bach's *Das Musikalische Opfer* (see Ex. 16-23).

EXAMPLE 16-23

J. S. Bach: Canon a 2 (*Das Musikalische Opfer*)

3. Example 16-24 cites the dux of a two-voice "puzzle" canon based on BACH. Realize the canon by adding the other part. What type of canon is it?

EXAMPLE 16-24

etc.

4. Compose one of the following, using two-voice texture:

a. perpetual canon
b. augmentation canon (2:1)
c. retrograde or crab canon

17

✄✄

The three-voice Fugue

This chapter concludes our study of three-voice polyphony. An examination of the general characteristics of the fugue will be followed by an analysis of two selections by Bach.

HISTORICAL BACKGROUND

The earliest theoretical mention of the term *fuga* (literally *to flee*) occurs in Jacobus de Liege's *Speculum musicae* (c. 1330), where it is listed as a vocal form in conjunction with the *rondellus* and *caccia,* both of which feature canonic imitation. Its association with strict canon continues into the Renaissance, where a mass setting composed entirely in this style was designated as a *missa ad fugam.* About the same time Tinctoris (around 1477) began to apply the term to the *procedure* of strict imitation rather than as a *formal* design. Some eighty years later Zarlino defined it as strict imitation at some perfect interval (evoking hexachordal theory), as opposed to *imitatione,* in which the intervallic relations are not exact.

The shift of the fugue from a predominately vocal medium into an instrumental one began with the transcription of choral motets into keyboard *ricercare.* Whereas the livelier polyphonic *chansons* evolved into the *canzonas* of instrumental ensembles with well-defined sections and multiple themes, the more "serious" *ricercar* worked out a single subject in a rigorous contrapuntal setting, often introducing various polyphonic devices, such as inversion (mirror), stretto, or double counterpoint. During the middle Baroque extended fugal sections appeared in keyboard pieces like fantasias or toccatas, but later the fugue emerged as a separate movement, as in the typical Prelude and Fugue. Most of the "fugues" of the latter seventeenth century consisted of an original point of imitation, based on tonic-dominant relations, followed by a succession of subject reentries, also usually at I or V. Instances of this procedure occur in Johann K. F. Fischer's *Ariadne musica,* a series of preludes and fugues in various keys that may be considered a forerunner of Bach's *WTC.*[1]

THE FUGUES OF J. S. BACH

Despite the great accomplishments of the late Baroque masters, their efforts in the area of fugue pale against the achievements of J. S. Bach.[2] Just as Palestrina is the model for sixteenth-century counterpoint, so is Bach for the fugue. In the hands of Bach the fugue does *not* represent any single formal stereotype. The organ fugues, which span his entire creative output, progress from early examples which stress continual subject/answer reentries (perhaps based on his study of Frescobaldi's works) to the late pieces, which tend toward ternary structure (see the famous "Wedge" Fugue in E minor BWV 548, which features an *exact da capo* of the first section). Its subject is quoted in Ex. 13-8D.)

Despite the diversity of the fugue there are some typical characteristics. Keep in mind that the fugue still represents a *compositional procedure* rather than an actual *formal model:*

1. The *monothematic* fugue is a composition in strict polyphonic texture, where an exact account of the voices is maintained. This chapter will be limited to the three-voice monothematic fugue.

2. The opening theme or *subject* is followed by its imitation at the dominant (very rarely at the subdominant) with either a real or tonal *answer.* The remaining voices enter at tonic or dominant until the initial point of imitation is completed. This section is referred to as the *exposition* of the fugue.

---

[1]This outline highlights just a few of the historical developments of the fugue. In addition to the excellent article on "Fugue" in the *New Grove's Dictionary,* see the surveys of Mann and Horsley, listed under History of the Fugue in the Bibliography.

[2]The fugal output of J. S. Bach is staggering. Aside from the collections (two volumes of the *WTC,* the seven Toccatas and Fugues for keyboard, and *Die Kunst der Fuge*), there are at least forty significant fugues for organ. These do not include the numerous choral movements cast in fugal style from cantatas or oratorios. See Alan Dickinson, *Bach's Fugal Works* (Westport, CT: Greenwood Press, Inc., 1979).

3. The remainder of the piece consists of either single or double *reentries* of the subject, usually in closely related keys or the tonic. Each of these is normally separated by *episodic* passages that serve as modulatory links. There may be some truth in Edward Cone's hypothesis that restatements of the tonally static subject and its counterpoints constitute a *tutti/ripieno* (related to the *concerto grosso*), while the episodes correspond to the texturally lighter and essentially modulatory *concertino* sections.[3]

4. Various contrapuntal devices, such as stretto and inversion—while not mandatory—may be encountered during a fugue. Double counterpoint, as we shall see later, is extremely important.

5. The recurrences of the subject in the tonic key will often (but not always) signal the conclusion of the piece. A brief codetta is not unusual.

Most of the above points will now be examined with closer scrutiny, with examples of three-voice texture drawn from literature of the period.

THE EXPOSITION

This opening section of the fugue constitutes the initial point of imitation with successive entries at tonic/dominant levels. Referred to as the *repercussio* by theorists of that time, it was first given the title *exposition* by Anton Reicha in 1825. Each of its components will be treated in some detail below.

1. The Subject

According to Padre Martini,[4] the subject (*subjectum*) falls into one of two categories: the *soggetto,* coming out of the *ricercar,* which is a relatively short theme (usually two measures or less) employing longer note values; and the *andamento,* which is a longer, livelier melody in faster tempo, perhaps related to the older *canzona.* The latter was sometimes referred to as a *caprice* by theorists in the period. Several instances of each type may be found in Exs. 15-2B, 15-3A, 16-4, 20-3 (*soggetto*) and Exs. 2-5, 15-6, 15-7, 20-5 (*andamento*).

The range of a typical subject lies approximately within an octave. Wider spans can create problems in composing an accompanying line in double counterpoint. It almost invariably opens with either scale degree $\hat{1}$ or $\hat{5}$ (rarely $\hat{3}$) and will normally close or cadence on either $\hat{1}$, $\hat{3}$, or a tonicized $\hat{5}$ (implying a modulation to the dominant). It is useless to speculate on the extent of a subject—that is, where the subject ends and the counterpart for the answer begins. Some subjects that cadence convincingly on $\hat{1}$ or $\hat{5}$ may be followed by a tiny melodic link connecting it to the ensuing counterpoint (see Ex. 17-4).

[3]See Edward Cone, *Musical Analysis and Musical Performance* (New York: W. W. Norton & Co., Inc., 1968), pp. 70–71.

[4]*Esemplare o sia saggio fondamentole prattico di contrappunto* (1774–75).

From the vast range of linear and rhythmic variety of fugue subjects, several striking melodic idioms recur like a "scarlet thread" throughout the literature. The first of these is the use of a diminished seventh in the minor mode, usually between scale steps $\sharp\hat{7}$ and $\flat\hat{6}$, either in rising or falling motion. This leap occurs in innumerable fugue themes, of which Ex. 17-1A and 1B are typical (also consult Exs. 13-1, 20-3, and 20-9). It even carries over into the Classical period (see Exs. 23-6, 23-7, and 23-12). The other melodic stereotype is actually a reduced framework which underlies many fugal subjects in the eighteenth century. It consists of scale degree $\hat{5}\,\hat{6}\,\hat{5}\,\hat{4}\,\hat{3}$ ($\hat{2}\,\hat{1}$) in either mode, the final descent to tonic being optional. In addition to those illustrated in Ex. 17-2, also see Exs. 2-5, 15-2, 17-4, and 17-6.

EXAMPLE 17-1 Fugue subjects which employ leap of dim 7th

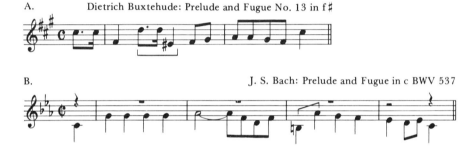

A.   Dietrich Buxtehude: Prelude and Fugue No. 13 in f♯

B.   J. S. Bach: Prelude and Fugue in c BWV 537

EXAMPLE 17-2 Fugue subjects employing underlying $\hat{5}\,\hat{6}\,\hat{5}\,\hat{4}\,\hat{3}$

J. S. Bach: Fugue in F (*WTC* I)

A.

B.   G. F. Handel: Fugue in c (*Six Grandes Fugues*)

The above idioms may represent only two melodic prototypes which form the structural basis for most of the fugue subjects of the late Baroque. Certainly Marpurg, in his treatise on the fugue, emphasizes examining the initial subject from the outset, noting its adaptability to accompanying counterparts or contrapuntal devices. One is reminded of K. P. E. Bach's tribute to his father: "When he listened to a rich and many-voiced fugue, he could soon say, after the first entries of the subjects, what contrapuntal devices it would be possible to apply, and which of them the composer by rights *ought* to apply, and on such occasions, when I was standing next to him, and he had voiced his surmises to me, he would joyfully nudge me when his expectations were fulfilled."[5]

Three rather unusual fugue subjects are quoted in Ex. 17-3. Example 17-3A is a chromatic theme based on Bach's own name: BACH = B♭ A C B♮. Observe how this half-step segment appears in disguised form in measure two. The final pair represent their respective composers in a more humorous mood. Why do you think that Ex. 17-3C was entitled the "Cat's Fugue" by Scarlatti?

EXAMPLE 17-3 Unusual fugue subjects

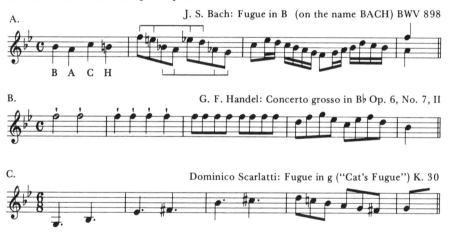

2. The Answer

The answer (*vox consequens* in Latin, *réponse* in French) is normally in the dominant key. The conditions that determine either a real or tonal answer were discussed in Chapter 15. The voice part set against the answer is termed the *counterpart* or *counterpoint*. If it is retained in subsequent reentries of the subject it is called the *countersubject*.[6] In this case it will be written in double counterpoint, so that it may appear either above or below the theme.

---

[5]Contained in a letter from K. P. E. Bach to Johann Forkel, the first biographer of J. S. Bach. See Hans David and Arthur Mendel, *The Bach Reader* (New York: W. W. Norton & Co., Inc., 1945), p. 277.

[6]This usually comes under the designation of a double fugue, which will be discussed in chapter 20.

3. The Episode following the Answer

If the answer cadences convincingly in the dominant key, the composer will often write a short episode, on either new or related material, which links the tonal motion to tonic in preparation for the next subject. All expositions, however, do not contain such episodic passages. Example 17-4 is typical.

EXAMPLE 17-4 Use of episode (v - i) between second and third entries in Bach's
Fugue in f♯(*WTC* II); also note link between subject and answer.

4. The Subject Re-entry

The original subject (in tonic) is now restated in the third or remaining voice. It may be accompanied by new counterparts, the countersubject (transposed to tonic), or it may form triple-counterpoint with the other parts. With this latter technique, subject restatements can "hold" or reiterate the counterpointing voices, but with textural distributions of the different parts.

With the last tonic entrance the three-voice texture is complete. Here the spacial/rhythmic relations between the different parts are particularly crucial. Sometimes the counterparts are "paired" together in rhythmic opposition to the subject (see measures 7–8 of Ex. 17-9). More often, however, each separate line pursues its own melodic contour and rhythmic identity. This is illustrated in Ex. 17-5; the reduction of the voice-leading is interesting.

EXAMPLE 17-5 Second subject entry in Bach's Fugue in A♭ (*WTC* II)

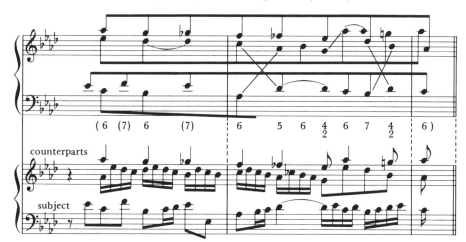

Concerning the registral entries during a three-voice exposition, the two upper parts tend to enter first (upper/middle or middle/upper), followed by the lower subject. Prout notes that the last entry appears in an outer voice about 87 percent of the time.[7]

5. Redundant Entries

Sometimes an extra or *redundant* entry exists, usually in the dominant, after the subject restatement in tonic. It may or may not be preceded by a brief episode.

Once the initial point of imitation is complete the exposition proper is concluded. There is rarely any cadential punctuation to indicate closure, however. In most cases the voices will initiate some sort of modulation. Examples 17-6 and 17-7 quote the expositions of two well-known fugues by Bach, the C minor and the D♯ minor (sometimes notated in E♭ minor) of his *WTC* I, along with a graph of the former's basic voice-leading. Both employ short episodes between the second and third entries. Whereas the C minor makes use of apparent triple counterpoint during its final subject entry, thereby retaining the countersubject, the D♯ minor employs new counterparts. The latter also features a curious redundant answer, for although it is stated in the dominant, it is harmonized in the tonic. Study each carefully.

[7]See Ebenezer Prout, *Fugue* (London: Augener, Ltd., 1891), p. 82.

EXAMPLE 17-6 Exposition of Bach's Fugue in c (*WTC* I) with reduction (meas. 1-9)

EXAMPLE 17-7 Exposition of Bach's Fugue in d♯ (*WTC* I)

THE COUNTER-EXPOSITION

Occasionally the composer may restate the material of his original exposition, retaining the tonic/dominant relations. In this case the other voices usually continue in free counterpoint, so that the *counter-exposition* is somewhat "hidden" within the texture. Consult measures 18–29 of the F major Fugue (*WTC* I), observing the stretto near the conclusion of the counter-exposition. In measures 20–31 of the G major Fugue (*WTC* I) the restatement is now a mirror version of the original exposition with the last subject entry incomplete.

RE-ENTRIES OF THE SUBJECT

Following the initial exposition are restatements of the subject in different voice parts and usually in closely related keys. In many cases the theme will enter after a rest in one of the voices; this is especially true in four- or five-part fugues. The rhythmic placement of subsequent entries must retain the same basic metric position as the original subject. Thus in Bach's F major Fugue (*WTC* I) and his C major Fugue (*WTC* II) all thematic presentations occur as $\frac{3}{8}$ ♪ | ♫♩ | and $\frac{2}{4}$ ♪ ♫♫ respectively, holding the same relation of weak to strong. In quadruple meter (such as $\frac{4}{4}$ or $\frac{12}{8}$), which features a pairing of strong-weak relations, the entries may occur on beats 1 and 3 *or* 2 and 4. The only exception to this generality occurs in close stretto passages, like those in the opening fugue of *WTC* I.

In the C minor Fugue (*WTC* I) there are four restatements of the subject—in E♭ major, G minor, and two in the concluding tonic. Since Bach has set the final subject of the exposition in triple counterpoint, he retains the counterparts in all subsequent entrances while switching their textural relations to each other. How many of the six possible permutations does he employ in Exs. 17-6 and 17-8? Note that the triple counterpoint is not "strict". Why?

A final subject entry occurs in the last three measures (Ex. 17-8E). This is actually a short "codetta" over the tonic pedal; the counterpointing voices are abandoned. See if you can find any similar examples at the conclusions of other fugues of the *WTC*.

EXAMPLE 17-8 Subject reentries in Bach's Fugue in c (*WTC* I)

A. Meas. 11-12 (in E♭)

B. Meas. 15-16 (in g)

C. Meas. 20-21 (in c)

D. Meas. 25½-27 (in c)

E. Meas. 29½-31 (codetta in c)

EPISODES

The *episodes,* which join the subject re-entries, are especially interesting. The composer's craft and imagination are tested in these passages. They are often sequential and may be based on previous material or introduce new motivic elements. Their basic function is that of transitional modulation, linking the various keys of the recurring subject. Indeed the most likely place for cadences within the fugue is at the conclusion of an episode. Marpurg states that: "If no episode precedes the cadence, one may introduce an episode rather than a thematic entrance on the cadence in order to increase the listener's anticipation of the new thematic entrance."[8] Since episodes "prepare" the subject re-entries, it is not surprising that their texture is sometimes reduced by one voice.

The episodes of the C minor Fugue, including the one found in the exposition (see Ex. 17-6) are illustrated in Ex. 17-9, with their voice-leading

[8]From Alfred Mann, *The Study of Fugue* (New York: W. W. Norton and Co., Inc., 1965), p. 141.

reductions. In this piece the construction of the episodes is extremely "tight", since all of the motivic material may be found either in the original theme or in its countersubject. Trace their derivation in Ex. 17-9 back to the first six measures of Ex. 17-6. Episodes 1 and 3 are related, as are 2 and 5, although in a different way. How? What use of double counterpoint is made between these pairs of episodes? Study the voice-leading carefully, noting the underlying sequential models on which they are based.

EXAMPLE 17-9 Episodes in Bach's Fugue in c (*WTC* I) with reductions

A. Episode 2 (Meas. 9-11)

B. Episode 3 (Meas. 13-15)

C. Episode 4 (Meas. 17-20)

(continued)

EXAMPLE 17-9 (cont'd)

D. Episode 5 (Meas. 22-26)

CONTRAPUNTAL DEVICES

The employment (or non-employment) of various contrapuntal devices and their placement within the fugue depend on the composer's whim. The use of double (or even triple) counterpoint is extremely common. In fact the C minor Fugue discussed above might well be subtitled "A Study in Invertible Counterpoint." The other more frequent procedures are stretto, usually near the latter part of the fugue, and inversion or melodic mirror. Proportional rhythmic changes in the subject (like augmentation) are uncommon, although one may note short canonic passages, sometimes embedded within an episode.

It is not unusual for the fugues of Bach to stress one particular device. Thus the C major (*WTC* I) and the D major (*WTC* II), both four-voice pieces, are examples of *stretto fugues*. The three-voice D minor and four-voice A minor (both in *WTC* I) emphasize inversion and stretto. The B♭ major (*WTC* I) in three parts employs triple counterpoint throughout, while the three-voice F♯ minor (*WTC* II) is a triple fugue.

THE OVERALL STRUCTURE OF THE FUGUE

Based on tonal centers alone, one *might* be inclined to partition a "typical" Baroque fugue into three sections:

> Opening Section (or Exposition)—tonic and dominant
> Middle Section—modulation and related keys
> Concluding Section—return to tonic

Many fugues of this period tend to adhere to this pattern. However, theorists of the nineteenth and twentieth centuries have attempted to devise a stereotype for the fugue,[9] even to the extent of evoking sonata-form terminology ("development" for the middle section). They assign contrapuntal procedures or devices to each part of the "ternary" structure. This "academic fugue" (*fuge d'ecole*), with its contrived rigidity is diametrically opposed to the free and imaginative approach favored by Baroque masters. A glance at the structural diagram of the D♯ minor Fugue (*WTC* I) in Fig. 17-2 will confirm that this in no way resembles such an artificial edifice; note the significant recurrence of tonic in the middle of the work.

As in the Bach Inventions, the "structure" of individual fugues differs greatly. Although they will usually exhibit some basic characteristics, the way in which the thematic elements are integrated with different contrapuntal devices, and tonal schemes stresses their *unique* rather than their *common* properties. Therefore in diagramming a fugue's structure, one must seek to discover its intrinsic qualities rather than force it into a predetermined mold.

Two schematic graphs of previously discussed fugues, the C minor and D♯ minor of *WTC* I, are presented in Figs. 17-1 and 17-2. The usual partitioning of the C minor Fugue results in a conventional triparte structure, where Exposition (in i and v) equals measures 1–8, Middle Section (entries in III and v) equals measures 9–19, and the Final Section (two

---

[9]See the annotations under Gedalge and Prout in the Treatise section of the Bibliography.

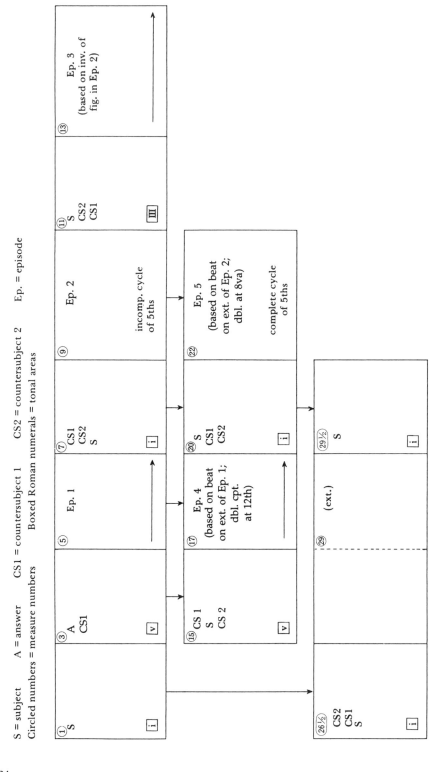

FIGURE 17-1 Structural diagram of Bach's Fugue in c (*WTC* I)

S = subject   A = answer   CS1 = countersubject 1   CS2 = countersubject 2   Ep. = episode

Circled numbers = measure numbers   Boxed Roman numerals = tonal areas

entries in i and codetta) equals measures 20–31.[10] However, if one constructs a diagram relating the entries and episodes through their similar material, use of double counterpoint, and tonal centers, a highly ingenious plan of a different sort emerges (see Fig. 17-1). The succession of entries and episodes in measures 3–10 returns in measures 15–26 in slightly expanded form. The two-measure groupings are consistent up to this point, where the extension of Episode 5 displaces the last two entries onto the third beat.

The D♯ minor Fugue is divided into three large sections of approximately the same length (30, 31, and 25 measures) with concluding cadences on III, V, and i respectively.[11] The initial part opens with the usual Exposition. Following a cadence (on v), there are three, two-voice stretti of the subject at a distance of two beats using various intervals. Whereas the first division of the fugue utilizes only the upright or *rectus* form of the subject, the middle section now concentrates on its *inversus*. A similar scheme is employed: a quasi-exposition of the *inversus* subject is succeeded by stretti in two and three voices, now at the distance of only one beat. The last major part of the fugue consists of a three-fold presentation of the subject *per augmentationem* in the lower, middle, and then finally upper voices, counterpointed with double statements of either the *rectus* or *inversus* versions of the theme. It is worth noting that throughout this piece (perhaps the most masterful three-voice fugue that Bach ever wrote), the composer maintains a sense of rhythmic tension by framing the original subject, which strongly suggests triple meter ($\frac{3}{4}$ ♩ |♩. ♫♫ |♫♩ ♩ |♩. ♪♩ |♩; see Ex. 17-10), in a consistent quadruple barring.

Some of Bach's Three-Part Inventions and various Preludes from the *WTC* are actually *bona fide* fugues in disguise—like the Three-Part Invention in F major. Its exposition, initial episode, and pair of subject entries in the dominant have been quoted earlier in Ex. 14-5 (measures 1–3, 4–5½, and 5½–6½ respectively). The remainder of the "fugue" consists of a succession of three episodes and pairings of subject statements (in ii, vi, IV, and eventually I). The second episode is an interesting two-voice canonic interlude, while the latter two are modelled on the 5–6 sequencing of the initial episode.

---

[10]This piece has almost become the "textbook model" for all fugal procedure in the late Baroque. It has been analyzed in many contrapuntal manuals; two more recent examples appear in texts by Kent Kennan (1972) and Richard Parks (1984). A more penetrating examination was done by Heinrich Schenker in his essay "The Organic Aspect of the Fugue" (see the Bibliography listings).

[11]See Wallace Berry, "J. S. Bach's Fugue in D♯ minor (*WTC* I No. 8): A naive approach to linear analysis," *In Theory Only*, Vol. 2/10 (Jan. 1977), pp. 4–7.

FIGURE 17-2 Structural diagram of Bach's Fugue in d♯ (*WTC* I)

S = subject   A = answer   IS = mirror of subject   AS = augmentation of subject   ASx = rhythmic modification of AS
Ep. = episode   2V = two voices, etc.   Circled numbers = measure numbers   Boxed Roman numerals = tonal areas   ↓ = cadences

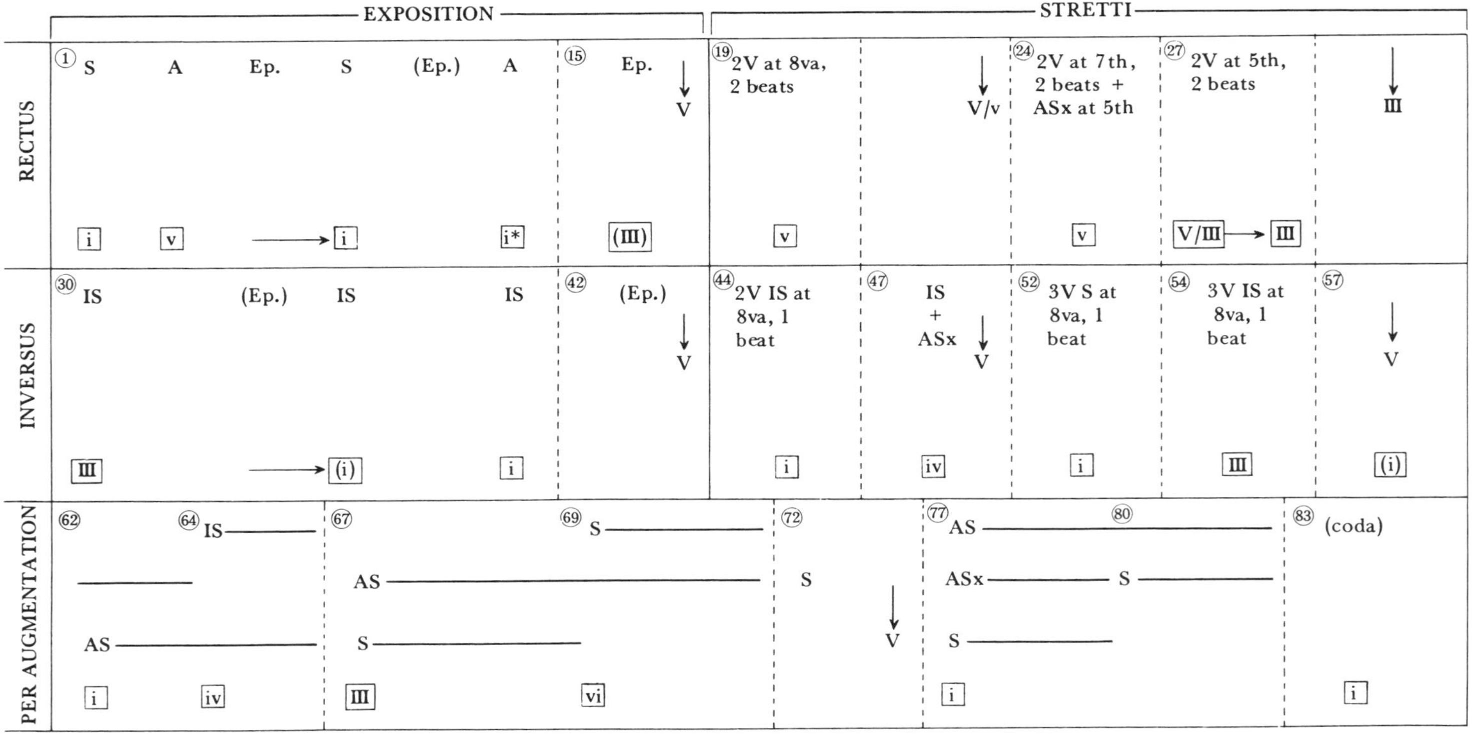

*The theme is at the Answer level, but is harmonized in tonic.

226

ASSIGNMENTS

1. Go through the three-voice fugues in both volumes of Bach's *WTC*, examining each exposition. Focus on the characteristics of the subject itself; its requirements for either a real or tonal answer; the answer and its accompanying counterpart (is double counterpoint possible?); the presence or absence of an episodic passage to the next entry; the final subject statement and its counterparts (has a countersubject been retained?); and any redundant entries. Make note of the overall registral layout of each exposition.

2.a. Using one of the subjects in Ex. 17-10, write a fugal exposition in three-voice texture. Employ double counterpoint for the answer and its counterpart. You might try some triple counterpoint with the last subject entry. The choice of a linking episode between entries two and three is optional, depending upon the subject you pick.

EXAMPLE 17-10

b. Write a short stretto using your subject from above. It can be for two voices with an accompanying free counterpoint, or it might even involve all three parts. You may wish to review the section on stretto in Chapter 16.

c. Compose an episode, utilizing motivic material from your previous exposition. Cadence in a related key and begin a subject entry.

3. If you feel more adventuresome, in lieu of assignment 2 write a complete three-voice fugue on an original subject. In order to avoid an

excessive length it may be better to use a more compact *soggetto*-like theme. Make a structural diagram *before* you begin to compose actively, plotting out possible episodes, re-entries, and an overall key scheme. Above all, examine your subject carefully in regard to contrapuntal settings and devices (like stretto or inversion).

4. Employing the graphic diagrams in Figs. 17-1 and 17-2 as models, do a structural analysis of one of the following fugues:

    a. D minor (*WTC* I)
    b. F major (*WTC* I)
    c. G major (*WTC* I)
    d. B♭ major (*WTC* I)[12]
    e. C major (*WTC* II)
    f. D minor (*WTC* II)

[12]See Carl Schachter, "Bach's Fugue in B♭ Major, *Well Tempered Clavier* Book I, No. XXI," *Music Forum*, Vol. 3 (1973), pp. 197–237.

18

✖✖✖

Introduction to four-voice texture; further study in chorale prelude

In some respects, four-voice texture was the norm of the late Baroque. Figured bass realization, choral writing (including chorale harmonizations and imitative movements in the usual SATB), the majority of instrumental fugues, and most polyphonic settings for organ are in four parts. After looking at simple diminution technique, investigation of the chorale prelude will be followed by some general characteristics of free counterpoint in four voices.

CONTRAPUNTAL DIMINUTION OF NOTE-AGAINST-NOTE SETTINGS

In Chapter 1, we reviewed principles of four-voice chorale harmonization, a familiar task to harmony students. One might think it would be simple to elaborate a typical note-against-note harmonization melodically and rhythmically into an acceptable piece of polyphony. Thus the addition of chordal and non-harmonic tones to Ex. 18-1A results in a phrase similar to Bach's harmonizations (Ex. 18-1B). However, it becomes more difficult to elaborate this setting *beyond* a basic 2:1 diminution. Because of frequent common tones and prevalent stepwise motion in the parts, the separate voices resist further rhythmic or tonal embellishment.

EXAMPLE 18-1 Note-against-note setting and its 2:1 elaboration

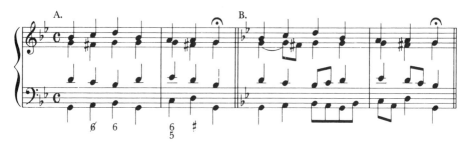

More "breathing room" would allow the expansion and activation of the parts—for both a more open structure and for larger intervallic leaps. Example 18-2A might seem strange as a preliminary first-species harmonization (note some of the chord doublings), but it is a better workable foundation for further diminution (see Ex. 18-2B).

EXAMPLE 18-2 Note-against-note setting and its 3:1 elaboration

Two other illustrations are provided in Exs. 18-3 and 18-4. The chorale tune (in the soprano) is identical in each case. There are only minor variances in the voice-leading frameworks, but Bach's contrapuntal elaborations are very different. Each setting exploits a single motivic figure.

EXAMPLE 18-3   J. S. Bach: *Christ ist erstanden (Orgelbüchlein)*, vers 1

EXAMPLE 18-4   J. S. Bach: *Christ ist erstanden (Orgelbüchlein)*, vers 2

Contrapuntal elaboration in four voices is not much different from three parts. In general, doubling is not a problem; watch for active scale degrees, excessive chordal thirds, and strive for complete seventh-chord inversions. Exercise care with parallels, not only because of the additional voice part but the frequent use of open structure, which seems more conducive to this type of error. Two useful techniques are illustrated in Exs. 18-5 and 18-6. The first excerpts simply introduce chordal figuration (compare Ex. 18-5A to 5B), which may then be elaborated further (see Exs. 18-5C through 5E). The other procedure uses two different harmonies per cantus note. This chordal interpolation converts the simple I–V–I cadence in Ex. 18-6A into the more convincing I–vi–ii⁶₅–V–I in Ex. 18-6B, which is then embellished contrapuntally (Ex. 18-6C). A similar situation occurs in Ex. 18-7. Note the use of suspensions in the last pair of examples.

EXAMPLE 18-5 Elaboration using chordal figuration

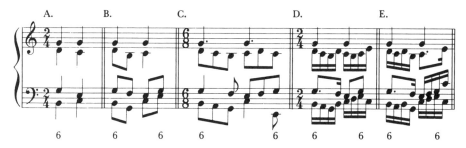

EXAMPLE 18-6 Elaboration using two harmonies per cantus note

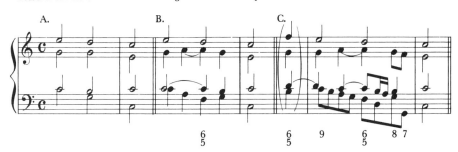

EXAMPLE 18-7 More complex elaboration

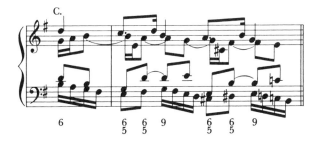

ASSIGNMENTS

1. Example 18-8 is a reduction of the initial two phrases of the chorale prelude *Christ lag in Todesbanden*, found in Bach's *Orgelbüchlein*. The unifying motive used throughout the piece is also included. Contrapuntally elaborate the framework, using this figure (or some closely related derivative). It is possible for the soprano cantus to participate in the diminution. Try to distribute the sixteenth-note motion between the various parts; don't overdo it.

EXAMPLE 18-8   J. S. Bach: *Christ lag in Todesbanden*
(*Orgelbüchlein*) - reduction

2. Choose several opening phrases from different chorale melodies (perhaps some found earlier in this text) and give them a four-voice note-against-note setting. Then elaborate each, using an underlying 3:1 or 4:1 rhythmic motion. Try to maintain some degree of motivic unity.

THE FOUR-VOICE CHORALE PRELUDE

Most organ chorale preludes in this period are in four voices. Of the many examples of *Vorimitation,* only the opening of Bach's *Vor deinen Thron tret' ich* will be quoted (see Ex. 8-9). The number of separate attack-points in the first phrase of the cantus is fourteen, while in the entire chorale tune there are forty-one. Can you explain the significance of these numbers?[1]

EXAMPLE 18-9

J. S. Bach: *Vor deinen Thron tret' ich* BWV 668

[1]See footnote 14 in Chapter 20.

Bach's setting of *Gott und Herr* BWV 693 is a masterpiece of integrated *Figuren* development and *Vorimitation* (consult Ex. 18-10).[2] The opening diatonic tetrachord of the chorale melody is exploited as a recurring motive throughout the piece, occurring twenty-four times during the first eight measures in *rectus, inversus,* and various rhythmic transformations (these do not include the cantus itself). See how many you can find.

EXAMPLE 18-10

J. S. Bach: *Gott und Herr* BWV 693

In addition to the usual simple and ritornello chorale-prelude types (see Bach's *Jesus Christus, unser Heiland* [*Orgelbüchlein*] and *Komm, heiliger Geist* [*Great Eighteen*] respectively) one may also note the use of an *embellished* (or *ornamented*) cantus voice. Example 18-11 illustrates the opening measures of Bach's *Wenn wir in höchsten Nöten sein* (the same tune as *Vor deiner . . .*). The basic notes of the chorale tune occur at the beginning of each beat in the soprano. Observe how the accompanying counterpoint is based on the *rectus* or *inversus* of a figure derived from the initial cantus notes: G G A B.[3] *O Mensch, bewein' dein Sünde gross* (*Orgelbüchlein*), one of Bach's loveliest instrumental compositions, should also be studied carefully.[4]

[2]This work has sometimes been attributed to Johann Walther.

[3]Melodic figuration derived from a chorale melody's accompanying counterparts is a frequent characteristic of Bach's chorale prelude technique. In particular see *Dies sind heil'gen zehn Gebot'* (*Orgelbüchlein*) with its curious repeated notes. See Alexander Brinkman, "The Melodic Process in Johann Sebastian Bach's *Orgelbüchlein*," *Music Theory Spectrum*, Vol. 2 (1980), pp. 46–73.

[4]The last few measures in the autograph of this piece contain an often quoted example of organ *tablature*.

EXAMPLE 18-11   J. S. Bach: *Wenn wir in höchsten Nöten sein (Orgelbüchlein)*

The final compositional technique applied to chorale preludes, that of canon, finds its origins in previous centuries. In some cantus pieces of the Renaissance, the basic melody was set in canon with itself; see the *Hosanna* of Josquin's *Missa L'Homme arme* (sexti toni). Baroque composers continued this tradition with the German chorale. At least one in six of the pieces in Bach's *Orgelbüchlein* employ this device. *Gottes Sohn ist kommen* (Ex. 18-12) employs a canon at the octave between soprano and tenor (in the pedal), although the interval of the fifth is also common. The counterpoint here is almost "species-like" in its rhythmic treatment. What is the problem in measure five and how does Bach solve it? The third variation of Bach's *Vom Himmel hoch* studies is an accompanied canon in three parts; the chorale in the soprano is answered by an inverted *comes* at the sixth (see Ex. 18-13). A less common procedure is to set up canonic relations between the *accompanying* contrapuntal voices rather than the cantus itself. One brilliant solution to this thorny problem is vers 2 of Walther's *Gott und Herr* (Ex. 18-14). A crowning *tour de force* is Bach's *In dulci jubilo* (*Orgelbüchlein*), two passages of which are quoted in Ex. 18-15. It is a *double canon* (4 in 2) at the octave, which continues strictly throughout the piece until measure 26, where the canonic imitation in the inner voices is broken. Consulting Ex. 18-15, can you explain why?

EXAMPLE 18-12

J. S. Bach: *Gottes Sohn ist kommen* (*Orgelbüchlein*)

EXAMPLE 18-13

J. S. Bach: Canone alla sesta e al rovescio
(*Canonic Variations on Vom Himmel hoch*)

EXAMPLE 18-14

Johann Walther: *Gott und Herr*, vers 2

EXAMPLE 18-15   J. S. Bach: *In dulci jubilo* (*Orgelbüchlein*)

Other genre associated with polyphonic settings of the chorale are *fughettas* or fugues, trios, variations, partitas, and fantasias.[5] Chorale prelude technique also resurfaces in many of the choral movements of cantatas.

ASSIGNMENTS

1. Choose one of the chorale phrases in Ex. 18-16 and compose a *Vorimitation* (in diminution) for three voices. When the cantus (or fourth

---

[5]A survey of Bach's contribution to this field may be found in Robert Tusler, *The Style of J. S. Bach's Chorale Preludes* (New York: Da Capo Press, 1968), and Peter Williams, *The Organ Music of J. S. Bach*, Vol. 2, (Cambridge: Cambridge University Press, 1980).

voice) enters, continue the accompanying counterpoint through the phrase. The first example might be somber with longer note durations, while the latter could be a livelier diminished version of the chorale tune.

EXAMPLE 18-16

2. Utilizing the pair of phrases in Ex. 18-17, write the opening section of a four-voice chorale prelude employing a canon with the given cantus. An "introduction" to the chorale entry is possible but not essential. Work out the voice distribution between the canon and accompanying counterparts, which should display motivic interplay or unity.

EXAMPLE 18-17

FREE FOUR-VOICE COUNTERPOINT

Keyboard preludes and suite movements are rich instrumental sources of free four-voice counterpoint (the fugue will constitute a separate topic in Chapter 20). A typical illustration is provided into Ex. 18-18; study the voice-leading in the reduction of the first reprise.

In strict polyphonic pieces such as the fugue, the individual voices are accounted for by rests. However, in many pieces of "free" counterpoint, the number of parts may vary throughout the composition, evoking the term *freistimmig* (or free-voiced) texture. In general, the denser textures occur near the conclusion of points of imitation or at the cadences of well-defined divisions, as in the two-reprise form. A good example of *freistimmig* technique may be found in the Froberger Suite quoted in Ex. 14-6. Here it is impossible to tell whether the pieces are in basically three or four voices.

EXAMPLE 18-18

J. S. Bach: Sarabande (French Suite in d) - partial reduction

(continued)

EXAMPLE 18-18 (cont'd)

TEXTURES IN EXCESS OF FOUR VOICES

Although you may encounter five-voice fugues (there are three in the *WTC*) or chorale preludes, examples of six-voice texture are rare in keyboard pieces. One must then examine the ensemble/orchestral (*concerto grosso*) or choral (divided choir) literature.[6] As expected, more parts present a further test of the composer's contrapuntal skill. The increased possibilities of parallels, to cite but one problem, abound.

ASSIGNMENTS

1. Complete the voice-leading framework begun in Ex. 18-18, using the previous analysis as a model. Try to reduce it further.

---

[6]See Bach's Motets, most of which are written for double four-part choir. In typical *tutti* passages involving all eight voices, the basses are usually doubled at the unison.

2. Given the opening of a keyboard prelude (Ex. 18-19), continue the piece for at least twelve more measures, utilizing consistent four-voice texture (it is possible for a voice to rest out several beats before reentering with a thematic statement). Exploit the original motivic material. Be sure to sketch an underlying voice-leading framework first!

EXAMPLE 18-19

Prelude (after Bach)

etc.

3. Choose one of the previous chorale phrases and give it a five-voice contrapuntal setting.

19

※※※※※※※※※※※※※※※※※※※※※※※※※※※※※※※※※※※※

Variations

Variation technique was briefly mentioned in the *Doubles* or *Agréments* sometimes found in suite movements. This chapter will focus on variation as the controlling device for an entire composition.

HISTORICAL BACKGROUND

Space does not permit a detailed history of variation before the late Baroque.[1] However, two earlier prototypes which establish the basis for most variations deserve brief comment. Collections of keyboard variations, usually based on chorales or folk and popular songs, are often encountered in the late Renaissance, particularly in England. Usually there are no more than a dozen separate movements in such sets. Each variation tends to be differentiated by a definite cadence. Occasionally the theme is used as a

---

[1]For some historical background consult "Variation" in the *New Grove's Dictionary;* Thomas Walker, "Ciaccona and Passacaglia: Remarks on their Origin and Early History," *Journal of American Musicological Society,* Vol. 21/3 (Fall 1968), pp. 300–320; and Robert Nelson, *The Technique of Variation* (Berkeley: University of California: 1962), pp. 28–54. The latter also contains an excellent discussion of continuous variations in the Baroque (pp. 55–78).

"fixed" cantus tune, with varied counterpoint around it. In these cases the separate sections may "spill over" into one another; consult Antonio Cabezón's *Diferencias Cavallero*.[2]

During the early seventeenth century, fixed bass-line patterns evolved, which were repeated below the vacillating upper parts. Usually four- or eight-measures long, some of the more frequent stereotypes were given titles. The typical *Romanesca* and the *Folia*[3] are quoted in Ex. 19-1. In compositions like this the rhythmic flow is continuous since each variation follows with little or no pause. Out of this procedure arose the concept of the *continuous variations* in the late Baroque.

EXAMPLE 19-1 Recurring bass patterns in the 17th century

A. *Romanesca*

B. *Folia*

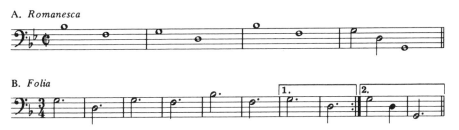

CONTINUOUS VARIATIONS

Theorists have attempted to distinguish between continuous variations, in particular the *passacaglia* and the *chaconne*, on the basis of their *supposed* "fixed elements". In the former a single *melodic* line is held constant, while in the latter it is the *harmonic* progression. It is true that certain seventeenth- and eighteenth-century writers, such as Mattheson, pointed out traits of each, based largely on possible disparities in tempo or mode. However, the musical literature during this period reveals little if any differing characteristics in the basic variation technique employed in the chaconne, passacaglia, or for that matter the English *ground*. In each case an *underlying* theme, about four to eight measures long, functions as the fixed or constant element that recurs in each variation. Note the qualifier *underlying*, since it may not always be clear from the opening statement what constitutes the basic tonal framework of the "theme" (for instance, see the beginning of Bach's Chaconne in D minor in Ex. 19-6 and the following

---

[2]Variations were often called *differences, divisions,* or *partite* during this period. Cabezón's "Cowboy Variations" appears as No. 134 in *Historical Anthology of Music* Vol. 1, ed. by A. T. Davison and W. Apel (Cambridge, MA: Harvard University Press, 1949).

[3]Perhaps the most famous set of variations on *La Folia* may be found in Corelli's Sonata No. 12 for Violin and Continuo in D minor ("Follia").

analysis). Since it is normally relegated to the bass voice, anything written above this melody is limited, thereby producing a relatively constant harmonic progression. But composers did sometimes vary the harmonies. In his Passacaglia in C minor, Bach makes very few alterations in the recurring progressions (see the later analysis of this work), while in the *Crucifixus* to his B minor Mass the harmonies above the chromatic tetrachord undergo continual change.

The theme, normally in slow triple meter, may change its mode during a middle section, but rarely modulates to other tonal centers.[4] The individual variations tend to be based on one (or perhaps several) melodic motives. If the theme is only four measures long, it is not unusual to find either the repetition of each variation (see Ex. 19-3) or "pairings" of variations sharing similar material (see Fig. 19-3 and Vars. 1–2 of Ex. 19-4). The rhythmic momentum in the cadential measure of each variation continues over into the next, hence the term *continuous*. If the fixed melody cadences on V (as in Ex. 19-3), the motivic element(s) are usually self-contained within the individual variations. However, when the theme cadences on tonic, the final measure often acts as a motivic "bridge" or "link", anticipating the ideas of the succeeding variation (this technique occurs throughout Bach's C minor Passacaglia).

One of the more frequent "themes" during this period is the so-called *descending tetrachord,* moving stepwise from tonic to dominant. It may appear in either a diatonic or chromatic version (the latter has already been briefly discussed in Chapter 13). Sometimes a short extension is added, as in Ex. 19-7C. The more traditional harmonic settings of the tetrachord are given in Ex. 19-2. However, the composer could certainly employ other possibilities (see Exs. 13-8C and D, 19-4 Var. 16, and 19-6).

EXAMPLE 19-2 Typical settings of the descending tetrachord (in minor)

A. Diatonic   B. Chromatic

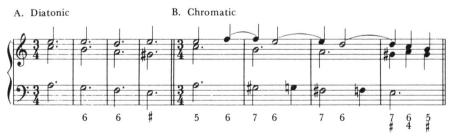

---

[4]Buxtehude's organ Passacaglia in D minor is a notable exception. The theme, quoted in Ex. 19-7B, is presented seven times each in the respective keys of D minor, F major, A minor, and finally D minor again (i–III–v–i).

The opening variations of a Ciacona in F minor by Johann Kuhnau are quoted in Ex. 19-3. Due to the brevity of the theme each variation is repeated. Successive variations develop their own new musical material. Although the rhythmic motion continues in the cadential measure, there is no overlapping of motivic elements. The number of voices varies from two to four, with no apparent textural scheme for the entire piece.

EXAMPLE 19-3   Johann Kuhnau: Ciacona in f (Vars. 2 - 5)

Many composers during this period recognized that the continual reiteration of the bass theme, when coupled with a gradual increase in textural complexity and rhythmic acceleration, could produce an over-powering sense of tension and climax. Indeed this concept is probably as close as the Baroque era ever came to the realization of a musical "crescendo". Hence no subsequent variation is distinct, but each builds on the preceding one. In this procedure the variations are interrelated, thereby achieving a unified "shape" for the entire composition. Four sets of continuous variations will be briefly examined below to demonstrate how the overall structure is realized.[5]

The Chaconne from Handel's *Trois Leçons* (1733) consists of twenty-one variations on an eight-measure theme, phrased 4 + 4. The fixed elements for the following variations are not obvious in the opening Theme (see Ex. 19-4). An analysis of later variations reveals the underlying framework, which is circled in the bass line. In the Theme the initial descending tetrachord in the bass (8̂ to 5̂) is balanced in the next phrase by the ascending motion 3̂ 4̂ 5̂ before the cadence on the tonic; note the harmonic scheme.[6] The soprano voice-leading is retained in some but not all of the variations. The succeeding variations are divided into three well-defined sections of 8 + 8 + 5, with the second group of eight in the parallel minor. The initial set of eight is grouped in pairs, following an almost "species-like" progression rhythmically: Vars. 1–2 = ♩♩ , Vars. 3–4 = ♫³ , Vars. 5–6 = scalar ♬ , and Vars. 7–8 = ♬ with an internal pedal.

In each pair the initial rhythmic elaboration in the soprano is transferred to the bass voice in the second (compare the opening of Vars. 1–2 in Ex. 19-4). Following this successive buildup, the opening of the minor section (Vars. 9–16) drops back to eighth-note motion. In Vars. 11–13 the secundal bass motion is now converted into a harmonic cycle of descending fifths (see Var. 11 in Ex. 19-4). During the final variation of this middle part the tetrachord is chromaticized. A reduction of the opening portion of this variation is given in Ex. 19-4 (see Var. 16). The concluding five variations now resume the sixteenth-note motion of the first section, continuing the internal pedal of Vars. 7 and 8 before giving way to the broken chords of the final three variations. Thus the overall shape assumes a kind of "double climax", from Vars. 1–8 and 9–21. This profile occurs frequently in Baroque continuous variations where attention is paid to the overall structure of the piece.

The theme for Bach's monumental Passacaglia in C minor is actually a four-measure extension of a subject employed earlier by André Raison in a short three-voice *Passacaille* (see Ex. 19-7D).[7] For the most part the same

---

[5]The Bach and Handel Chaconnes and the Purcell Aria may be found in the fourth edition of Charles Burkhart, *Anthology for Musical Analysis* (New York: Holt, Rinehart, and Winston, 1986).

[6]This bass line was a favorite for variations among Baroque composers. It is the basis for the first reprise of Bach's *Goldberg* Variations theme, and occurs in Purcell's *A Ground in Gamut*. All three are in G major.

[7]This brief Trio, part of an organ mass in the Dorian mode, is quoted in Douglass Green, *Form in Tonal Music*, pp. 120–21.

EXAMPLE 19-4 G. F. Handel: Chaconne in G (*Trois Leçons*)

(continued)

EXAMPLE 19-4 (cont'd)

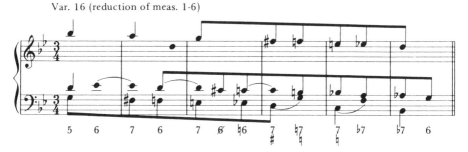

harmonic progression is retained throughout the work. Several small but significant changes occur near the opening of the variations in Ex. 19-5. The use of the Neapolitan sixth in Var. 9 is particularly interesting, as it foreshadows the climactic chord near the end of the following triple fugue. Figure 19-1 graphs the entire piece, showing placement of the theme, number of voices, and basic motives. The twenty variations following the presentation of the bass subject appear to be divided into three main sections of 10 + 5 + 5.[8] The pairing of the first two variations (refer back to the Handel above) is followed by a grouping of 3 + 3 before the climactic Vars. 9 and 10. Notice the gradual rhythmic acceleration from ♩♩ to ♫♫♫ .

In the next five variations, the theme is displaced in the upper voices. It is gradually embellished and moved downward until it forms the first note of the arpeggiations in Vars. 14–15. In the final section of five variations the subject reappears in its original form in the bass, achieving the eventual highpoint in the last two variations with their insistence on the tonic triad in the upper parts. The overall shape of this work resembles an interrupted single climax (see Fig. 19-2). The energy accumulated in Var. 10 is gradually dissipated in the next section, only to return with a vengeance in Var. 16 to the final climax.

[8]In his comments on this work in *Form in Tonal Music*, Douglass Green prefers a grouping of 13 (including the initial theme) and 8 (3 + 5), thereby evoking Fibonacci numbers—3 5 8 13 21; see pp. 123–24.

FIGURE 19-1 Structural Design of Bach's Passacaglia in c

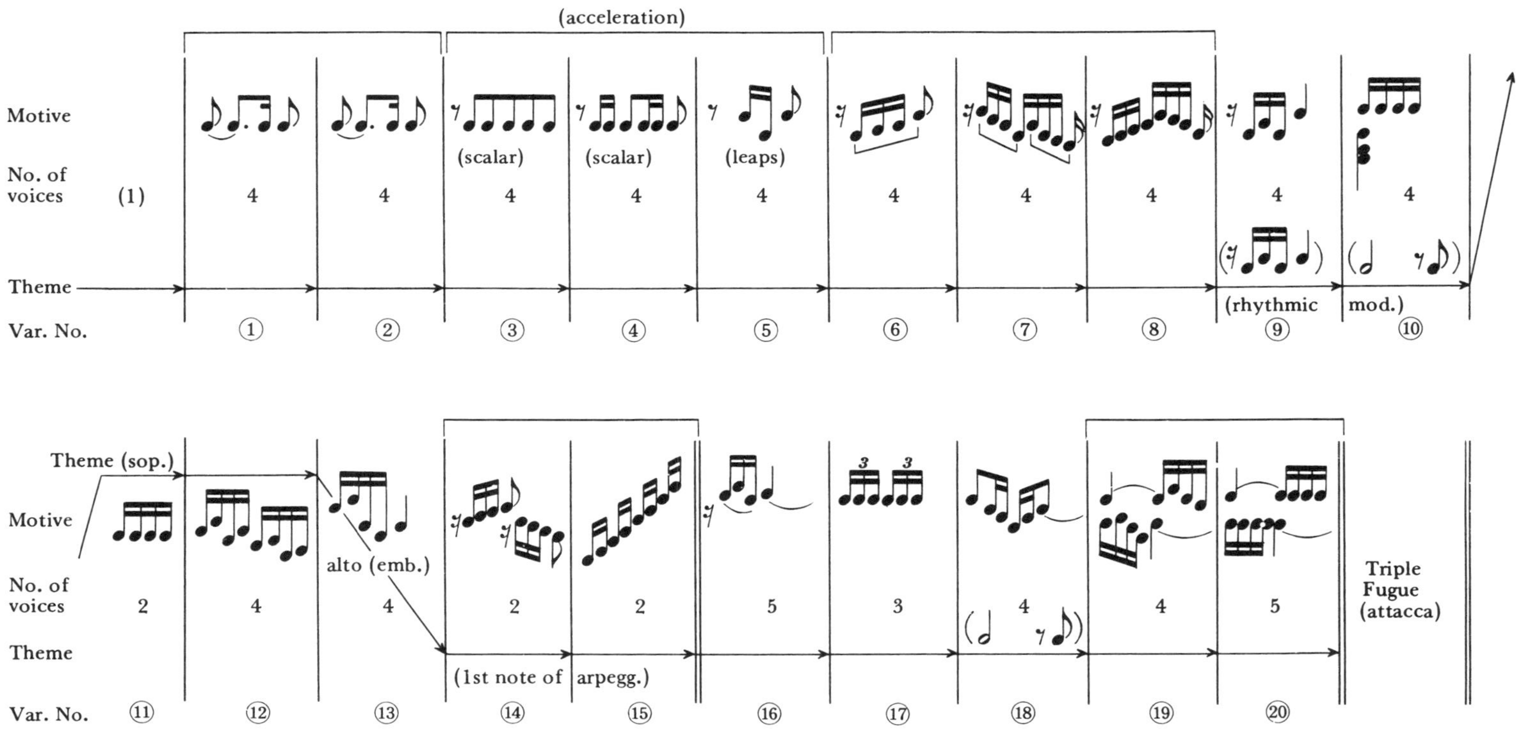

FIGURE 19-2 Interrupted single-climax profile of Bach's Passacaglia in c

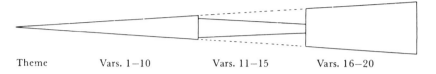

Theme   Vars. 1—10   Vars. 11—15   Vars. 16—20

EXAMPLE 19-5 Harmonic modifications in Bach's Passacaglia in c

The great Chaconne from the D minor Violin Partita may well be Bach's supreme achievement in the continuous variation genre. There are sixty-four statements of the opening four-measure phrase. As in the Handel variations, the thematic/harmonic basis is not revealed until later in the set (see the opening statement in Ex. 19-6A). It turns out to be the familiar descending tetrachord, sometimes diatonic and sometimes chromaticized. Here Bach's ingenuity of harmonic settings above the basic tetrachord is apparent. Several of the more interesting variations have been selected and presented in Ex. 19-6. Extract the voice-leading framework of the tetrachordal settings and analyze the harmonies.

EXAMPLE 19-6 Opening theme and selected variations from Bach's Chacome in d

Figure 19-3 diagrams the overall structure of the D minor Chaconne. The initial double-thematic presentation (Vars. 1–2) is restated at the close of the first large section (Vars. 31–32). An initial climax is reached during the "arpeggiation" variations (Vars. 22–29). The mode shifts to major for another thematic pairing (Vars. 33–34), which is echoed in the final two statements (Vars. 63–64), although now back in the tonic minor. A second highpoint occurs in the chordal section (Vars. 50–51). Other groupings of variations, some of which are not as obvious, are shown in the diagram.[9]

FIGURE 19-3 Structural design of Bach's Chacome (Violin Partita in d)

Variations	Grouping	Basic Characteristics
Minor		
1–2	2	Double theme
3–6	4	"French Overture" style ♪
7–8, 9–10	4	♪♪ followed by varied ♫♫
11–14	4	♫♫
15–19	5	Quasi-cycle of 5ths ♪♪ to ♫♫
20–22	3	Transition ♫♫ to ♫♫
23–30	8	Arpeggiation (1st climax) ♫♫
31	1	Transition ♫♫ scales
32–33	2	Double theme
Major		
34–35	2	Double theme
36–37	2	♫♫
38–40	3	♫♫
41–44	4	♫♫ repeated notes
45–46	2	♫♫
47–50	4	Chordal ♩. ♪
51–52	2	Chordal arpeggiation (2nd climax?)
Minor		
53–54	2	♩. ♫♫♫
55–57	3	♫♫
58–60	3	Bariolage on a² ♫♫♪
61–62	2	♫♫
63–64	2	Double theme

[9]Some of these were suggested to the author by violinist Zvi Zeitlin. Also see Rudy Marcozzi, "Deep-level Structures in J. S. Bach's D minor Chaconne," *Indiana Theory Review*, Vol. 4/2 (1981), pp. 69–99.

The *ground bass* technique employed in the final aria ("When I am laid in earth") of Purcell's *Dido and Aeneas* more properly belongs to the mid-seventeenth century. The fixed theme is again a chromaticized tetrachord which has been extended to five measures, cadencing on the dominant (see Ex. 19-7C). Above this recurring subject is the solo vocal line, cast in a clear A A B form. Interestingly, the phrasing of the voice part does not always coincide with that of the bass theme, being 6 + 3 + 1 (A) and 4 + 3 + 4 (B) measures respectively. This was a favorite device of Purcell's. Examine the aria "Ah, My Anna" from the same opera, in which the non-synchronizing technique is utilized even more extensively. A brief orchestral coda shifts the chromatic tetrachord into the upper voices as well via imitation. There is no sense of the "double-climax" observed previously.[10]

Several other movements may be cited for further study. In addition to a fine Passacaglia in F minor, Johann Pachelbel's popular Canon in D major is an example of strict canonic imitation placed over a recurring bass theme, hence the possible description "ground round". The *Crucifixus* to Bach's B minor Mass, mentioned previously, is actually a reworking of a movement from his earlier Cantata No. 12 *Weinen, Klagen, Sorgen, Zagen.* The initial chorus of his Cantata No. 78, *Jesu, der du meine Seele,* is a large chorale prelude set over a chromatic chaconne bass. Some unusual chromatic passages can be found in Bach's Capriccio in B♭ major (*On the Departure of a Beloved Brother*) BWV 992.

In composing continuous variations, you should first examine carefully the theme chosen as the fixed element. Restrict the length of the bass melody to four measures. The theme should support a strong functional harmonic progression capable of continual reiteration. You may wish to experiment with occasional harmonic modifications, although on the whole it is best to retain the basic chord succession. One of the major difficulties is the *consistent* development of one (or two) melodic/rhythmic motives during the course of each individual variation. It may be necessary to test several possibilities with the voice-leading and harmonies in the upper counterpoints to discover a setting best suited to your chosen motive(s). A typical rhythmic acceleration may move from occasional ♪♪ through ♫♫ to consistent ♫♫♫, with each figure assigned a definite melodic shape. The number of voices between variations may vary. Even though the parts are usually accounted for by rests, there is no obligation, for instance, to continue a variation in constant four-voice texture throughout. The entry and exit of voices creates a pleasant interplay which even allows fleeting moments of imitative writing. If the theme cadences on tonic, the new motive(s) for the succeeding variation are normally anticipated in the last measure, providing a seamless overlap.

[10]A Schenkerian reduction of this aria may be found in Richard Parks, *Eighteenth-Century Counterpoint and Tonal Structure* (Englewood-Cliffs, N.J.: Prentice-Hall, Inc., 1984), pp. 307–9.

ASSIGNMENTS

1. Example 19-7 cites several themes for continuous variations. Choose one and compose at least four interlocking variations for organ (two manuals and pedal). Try to achieve a gradual rhythmic acceleration and increase in textural density.

EXAMPLE 19-7

A.

B.   Dietrich Buxtehude: Passacaglia in d

C.   Henry Purcell: "When I am laid in earth" (*Dido and Aeneas*)

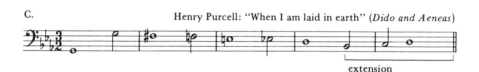

extension

J. S. Bach: Passacaglia in c

D.   Raison's theme   Bach's extension

2. Using a diatonic (or chromatic) tetrachord as your thematic basis, write at least four continuous variations for solo violin in D or A minor.

THEME AND VARIATONS

The tradition of *theme and variations* for keyboard instruments based on either preexistent or original melodies continued into the late Baroque. The use of chorales, popular/folk songs, and arias in two-reprise form are especially common. Here the theme is usually a short, self-contained piece, so that each succeeding variation is treated as a separate entity with no rhythmic overlap. Although the phraseology and underlying melodic/harmonic voice-leading is usually retained, no one voice acts as a cantus throughout the set; the bass part undergoes the least modification. There is little sense of gradual buildup noted above in the continuous technique. Composers would often write many variations, from which the performer could choose and thereby create an original *collage* of successive variations.

Johann Kuhnau's Variations on *Jesu, meine Freude* is a typical example of this genre. Several variations on the opening *Stollen* of the hymn are quoted in Ex. 19-8. The original chorale tune is in the inner voice of Ex. 19-8B, while in Ex. 19-8A it occurs in embellished form in the soprano. Example 19-8C is an excellent instance of the chromatic elaboration of an underlying diatonic framework.

EXAMPLE 19-8

Johann Kuhnau: Variations on *Jesu, meine Freude*

(continued)

EXAMPLE 19-8 (cont'd)

Variatio 9

Although J. S. Bach also wrote several sets of chorale variations or partitas, his output in the area of theme and variations is mainly limited to only two significant works: the *Variations in the Italian Style* BWV 989, and the celebrated *Goldberg* Variations BWV 988, named after the music connoisseur who supposedly commissioned them to provide entertainment during his bouts of insomnia. The original theme (or Aria) for the latter is cast in the usual two-reprise form. Since the successive buildup indigenous to the passacaglia/chaconne was no longer available in this case, Bach achieved unification by grouping three distinct types of genre which follow one another in a well-ordered plan. Variations 1, 2, 4, 7, and every third number through 25 consist of a series of "character" pieces, bearing such titles as *forlana, fughetta, aria, ouverture, barcarolle,* and several invention-like movements. Every third variation from No. 5 through 26 (and including 28 and 29) are based on a complex pattern of increasing rhythmic acceleration within a basic 3/4 meter; they are scored for two keyboards. The remaining pieces—every third variation from No. 3—are accompanied canons at successive intervals from the unison to the ninth. The meters here vary according to an intricate relation of beat to sub-division. The final *quodlibet* (Var. 30) leads to a restatement of the opening Aria, the first eight measures of which are quoted in Ex. 19-9.[11]

---

[11]An excellent analysis and chart of these inter-relationships may be found in Robert Cogan and Pozzi Escot, *Sonic Design: The Nature of Sound and Music* (Englewood Cliffs, N.J.: Prentice-Hall, Inc., 1976), pp. 264–76.

EXAMPLE 19-9

J. S. Bach: Aria (*Goldberg* Variations), meas. 1-8

ASSIGNMENT

Retaining the phraseology and melodic/harmonic framework of the "theme" in Ex. 19-10, compose at least four separate variations.

EXAMPLE 19-10

20

Further studies
in fugue

This chapter will concentrate on the four-voice fugue. Two fugues in four parts will be examined in more detail, one from *WTC* II and one from Bach's longer organ works. The basic characteristics of double and triple fugues will be presented, with a passing allusion to five- and six-voice pieces.

THE FOUR-VOICE FUGUE

Four voice fugues are the textural norm during this era. Although they are definitely in the minority in the *WTC* (18 out of 48), they account for nearly all such pieces in the organ and choral media. The basic aspects of fugal procedure remain largely unchanged, but several further points do require our attention.

A brief word on the topic of "chromatic" fugue subjects and their answers. Marpurg's remarks (in his *Abhandlung von der Fuge*) are particularly appropriate here, since he touches on two crucial areas. The first is the tonal answer which exchanges scale degrees Î and $\hat{5}$ or their reverse. In Ex. 20-1 a movement to the dominant is implied, which is answered by a motion back to tonic; Marpurg illustrates their diatonic bases. He also states that in general the chromatic segment(s) of the subject must be retained in its answer. In his example based on a theme of Fux (see Ex. 20-2), Marpurg rejects the first solution on the grounds that the chromaticism is incompletely stated (an e♭¹ would be incompatible with a return to D minor). This is rectified in the final version, even though an additional e♮¹ is required.

EXAMPLE 20-1 Marpurg's tonal answer of a chromatic subject

EXAMPLE 20-2 Marpurg's quotation of a chromatic subject and answer by Fux

In the typical exposition the final fourth entry is an answer in the dominant, producing a pairing of Subject/Answer (I—V), possible episode, and then Subject/Answer again (I—V). The "exposition episode", should it be utilized, retains its position between the second and third entries, effecting a modulation back to tonic. The use of a *bona fide* countersubject is fairly common. Indeed, two of the counterparts may be retained in subsequent subject entries, producing the quasi-triple counterpoint observed in the C minor Fugue, *WTC* I (Chapter 17). There is always the possibility of a redundant entry in the exposition. It may occur either in tonic or dominant and is sometimes preceded by a second episodic passage. If the fugue contains a counter-exposition, it is not unusual to find only three statements present, although still at I or V.

The order of voice entries is quite varied. Prout's comment that the final entry in three-voice fugues tends to be an outer part holds true for four voices as well. In later occurrences of the subject (such as those in closely related keys) the new statement will usually enter after a rest, thereby increasing the texture by one voice. The linking episodes, on the other hand, normally feature a reduced number of parts.[1]

---

[1]This again suggests Edward Cone's idea of a *ripieno/concertino* alternation, mentioned in Chapter 17.

In general there are no new technical problems here that have not been discussed in the introduction of four-voice polyphony. In the performance of four-part fugues on a single keyboard manual the soprano-alto and tenor-bass are often assigned to the right and left hands respectively. Be careful to keep the original subject within a restricted range, since themes greater than an octave can produce textural difficulties in composition and performance.

Discounting the use of the genre in choral movements,[2] there are many modestly proportioned, four-voice fugues in the Baroque keyboard literature. In addition to *WTC*,[3] one might cite the *Eight Little Preludes and Fugues* for organ (attributed to Bach), the opening pieces in his *Die Kunst der Fuge,* Johann Fischer's *Ariadne musica*, various harpsichord fugues by Handel, and numerous shorter works for organ by such masters as Pachelbel, Muffat, Buxtehude, and Walther.

The composition chosen for analytical comment here is the Fugue in E major (*WTC* II). The *ricercar*-like subject, cited in Ex. 20-3A, is probably based on an identical subject in a fugue of Fischer's *Ariadne musica;* its cantus-like profile resurfaces later in the Finale of Mozart's "Jupiter" Symphony.[4] The brevity and simplicity of the theme presented a potential problem to the composer. Having exhausted its imitative possibilities in various stretti early in the piece, Bach could either choose to invent *new* secondary counterpoints to set against the original idea, or to *vary* the subject itself through rhythmic transformation. He opted for the latter course—two different elaborated forms are developed in conjunction with the more remote tonal areas. The synchronized return of the original theme with the recurrence of the tonic key has almost the effect of a "recapitulation." You may want to examine the entire fugue in *WTC* II. To further appreciate the following discussion, you may wish to study Fischer's earlier piece.

The E major Fugue opens with a straightforward exposition (measures 1–6), with the subject rising from the bass to the soprano; the initial pitches are e b e^1 b^1. There is no episode between the second and third entries to interrupt the upward momentum. The four ascending quarter-notes of the counterpoint (see measure 3 of Ex. 20-3A) will reappear later in various guises. A brief transition (measures 7–8), culminating over a dominant pedal, introduces a counter-exposition in stretto (measures 9–12) with the tonal order now reversed: b e B e^1 (see Ex. 20-3B). The first full-fledged episode (measures 12½–16) employs the rising quarter-note

[2]See the discussion on choral fugue movements in Chapter 21.

[3]See Herman Keller, *The Well-Tempered Clavier by Johann Sebastian Bach,* trans. Leigh Gerdine (London: George Allen & Unwin, Ltd., 1976). Unfortunately, the most detailed examination of this work is as yet unavailable in English: Ludwig Czaczkes, *Analyse des Wohltemperierten Klavier,* Vols. I and II (Vienna: 1965).

[4]See Theme One in Ex. 23-5.

figure on the way to a cadence in the submediant (measure 16). A two-voice stretto in the alto-soprano (e¹ b¹) is echoed in the lower parts with the pitch classes raised a fifth (B f♯); see measures 16–21. A cadential preparation in measure 22 ushers in the supertonic key with another pair of two-voice stretti. Although the subject is now rhythmically modified and elaborated (see Ex. 20-3C), the progression of upward fifths continues: f♯¹ c♯¹ = soprano-alto and G♯ d♯ = bass-tenor. As the tonal motion moves toward the more familiar realms of dominant and tonic, a second rhythmic modification of the theme introduces another pair of two-voice stretti directed from soprano to bass (see measures 26–29 and Ex. 20-3D). This section concludes with a brief combination of this diminished version of the theme and the original subject (measure 30). An extended episode based in part on the quarter-note figure arrives in the mediant key at measure 35. This is immediately forsaken for tonic, which now controls the remainder of the fugue. A restatement of the Counter-exposition appears with additional counterpoints (measures 35–37). The last soprano entry (on e²) is delayed and then extended by a series of descending minims (measures 36–37). This is answered by the bass subject (on B), which is likewise expanded to the conclusion of the piece. The student is encouraged to make a structural diagram of this fugue.

EXAMPLE 20-3 Important subject entries in Bach's Fugue in E (*WTC* II)

A. Exposition

B. Counter-exposition (in stretto)

(continued)

EXAMPLE 20-3 (cont'd)

C. First rhythmic modification of Subject

D. Second rhythmic modofocation of Subject

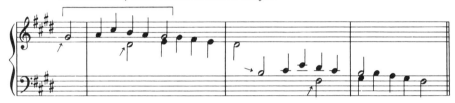

ASSIGNMENTS

1. Construct a structural diagram of the G minor Fugue in *WTC* I. Be sure to include measure numbers, subject and answer entries, episodes, and the basic tonal scheme. Figures 17-1 and 17-2 might serve as models. Douglass Green has suggested that the components of this composition are arranged in "arch-like" fashion around its third episode.[5] Does your diagram agree with this? Some other four-voice fugues for analysis are listed below:

  a. Bach: G♯ minor Fugue (*WTC* I)—more varied texture than most
  b. Bach: B♭ minor Fugue (WTC II)—longer complex fugue with stretti
  c. Handel: Fugue (Suite No. IV in E minor)—rather "open-voiced" with several unusual modulations
  d. Buxtehude: Prelude and Fugue No. 9 in E minor for organ (measures 47–100)—interesting "chromatic fugue"

2. Compose a four-voice exposition using either one of the subjects supplied in Ex. 20-4 or one of your own choice. Insert an episode between the second and third entries.

EXAMPLE 20-4

A. (after Frescobaldi)

[5]Green, *Form in Tonal Music,* p. 275.

B. (after Fischer)

THE LARGER ORGAN FUGUES

Most of the fugues examined thus far have been from harpsichord/clavichord collections, such as *WTC*. Although some of these, such as the A minor Fugue in *WTC* I, use extended "Italian-type" subjects which tend to expand their length, most are of fairly small dimensions. In comparison, many of the organ fugues of the period, especially those of Bach, seem gargantuan. The subject of one such piece is quoted in Ex. 20-5.[6] With themes of this magnitude, the exposition alone is raised to major proportions. On the organ the upper two voices are normally relegated to the top manual, the tenor to the middle manual, and the bass to the pedals.

EXAMPLE 20-5

Fugue subject of Bach's Toccata, Adagio, and Fugue in C BWV 564

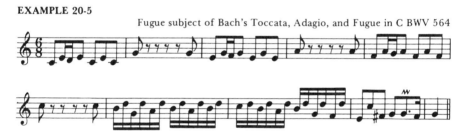

Most of these works are preceded by one or more movements—usually a prelude, fantasia, or toccata. It is unfortunate that the larger organ fugues are almost totally neglected in most counterpoint manuals, since, in the case of Bach, they represent some of the grandest examples of fugue in the entire literature.[7] One might cite the familiar "Little" G minor Fugue BWV 578 (see Ex. 15-7), the rollicking Italian character of the Prelude and Fugue in D major BWV 532, the diverging chromaticism of the E minor Prelude and Fugue ("Wedge") BWV 548 (Ex. 13-8D), and the triple fugues that conclude the Passacaglia in C minor and the *Klavierübung* Part III. Most of the more "open-type" organ fugues with their livelier extended subjects are less "device-prone". Although one may find examples of stretto (a lengthy illustration occurs in the Prelude and Fugue in G major BWV

---

[6]The themes from Bach's organ Preludes and Fugues in D major (BWV 532) and A minor (BWV 543) are of similar length. Handel is also fond of extended subjects, which occur in his Concerti Grossi and Organ Concerti.

[7]A good overview of Bach's organ fugues may be found in Volume 1 of Peter Williams, *The Organ Music of J. S. Bach* (Cambridge: Cambridge University Press, 1980).

541), instances of inversion or augmentation are less common. The "Dorian" Toccata and Fugue BWV 538 is an interesting case; here the subject is stated later in canon with itself. The first pedal entry in the Prelude and Fugue in C major BWV 547 features thematic augmentation with stretto and inversion (refer to Ex. 16-10).

Figure 20-1 diagrams the basic structural features of one such work, the last movement of Bach's "Great" Fantasia and Fugue in G minor BWV 542. The subject of this piece (supposedly derived from a Dutch folk song) and its counterpoints, two of which are usually held in triple counterpoint, are given in Ex. 20-6. Observe the Counter-exposition, the double set of related keys (Bb Dm F and Gm Cm Eb), the controlled variations in texture, and the recurrence of certain episodes.

EXAMPLE 20-6 Fugue subject and accompanying countersubjects in Bach's Fantasia and Fugue in g ("Great") BWV 542

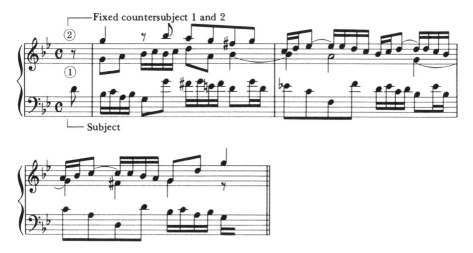

THE DOUBLE FUGUE

Although the fugue is usually monothematic (based on a single *primary* subject) sometimes one or more *other* themes may have equal prominence with the original subject. During the course of such a piece this *secondary* subject(s) must be presented several times in conjunction with the primary idea. Hence the use of invertible counterpoint (either at the octave and/or tenth or twelfth) becomes mandatory. Marpurg in his definitive treatise of fugue refers to such pieces as "double fugues", employing two *or* more subjects.[8] For our purposes they will be termed *multiple fugues,* either *double* (with two subjects) or *triple* (with three subjects).

[8]See Mann *The Study of Fugue,* pp. 191–199.

FIGURE 20-1 Structural diagram of Bach's "Great" Organ Fugue in g BWV 542

Circled numbers = measure numbers   Boxed Roman numerals = tonicized areas   Vertical arrows within boxes = cadences
Ep. = episode   ⌇⌇⌇⌇ = countersubject 1   - - - - - = countersubject 2
⦁⦁⦁⦁⦁ = countersubject 3   ──── = subject
                                    Voice part denoted by S, A, T, or B

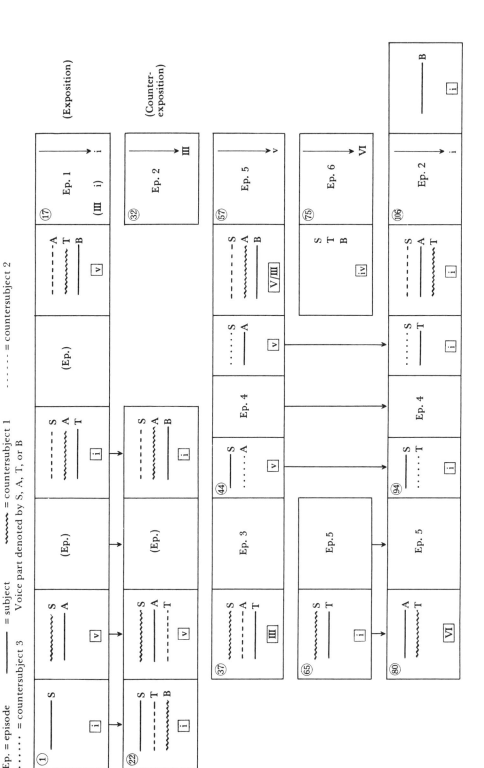

267

Marpurg lists two basic types of double fugues:

1. Both subjects appear at the outset of the piece, either simultaneously (Ex. 20-7) or in a slightly staggered fashion (Ex. 20-8). Despite their apparent equal status, one tends to subordinate the other. In subsequent restatements the two themes will always occur together, although each may be developed independently in episodic passages. This procedure is not to be confused with a free "accompanying" voice to the opening subject (as sometimes found in Bach's Inventions), since there the subordinate part is dropped and not developed further.

EXAMPLE 20-7 Double-fugue exposition from Bach's Toccata No. 5 in e BWV 915

EXAMPLE 20-8 Double-fugue exposition from Handel's
    Counterpoint Lessons for Princess Anne

By previous definition, *countersubject* has meant the initial counterpart to the answer that *recurs* with each subject entry. If this practice is consistent throughout the composition, one is compelled to call it a double fugue. Indeed Marpurg does so himself, citing the two-voice E minor Fugue in *WTC* I as an example. Both subject *and* countersubject may undergo separate motivic development during episodic passages. Example 20-9 quotes a familiar instance of this category of double fugue.

EXAMPLE 20-9 Fixed countersubject in Handel's "And with his stripes we are healed"
(*Messiah*)

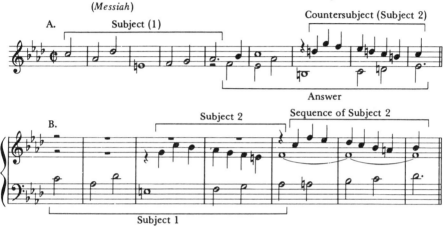

2. In the second double fugue classification the primary subject is given an exposition and normal "development." Following a definite cadence, the secondary subject is presented in a similar way. Only then are both subjects combined for the remainder of the fugue. Contrapunctus X in Bach's *Die Kunst der Fuge* is a model example of this procedure. Example 20-10 cites the opening of each exposition. The first (Ex. 20-10A) uses inversion,[9] while the second exposition (Ex. 20-10B) is based on the original theme of the entire cycle. Each exposition is in the tonic of D minor (measures 1–22 and 23–43). Example 20-10C records the first of the thematic combinations (measures 44–47), while Fig. 20-2 graphs all their appearances. In addition to the regular alternation of tonic with related keys, observe how Bach varies each double statement through invertible counterpoint at the tenth.

---

[9]For those so inclined, the initial six pitch classes of this subject and their relation to the remaining entries in the exposition make a fascinating study in set theory.

EXAMPLE 20-10 **Subjects 1 and 2 and their combination in Bach's Contrapunctus X** (*Die Kunst der Fuge*)

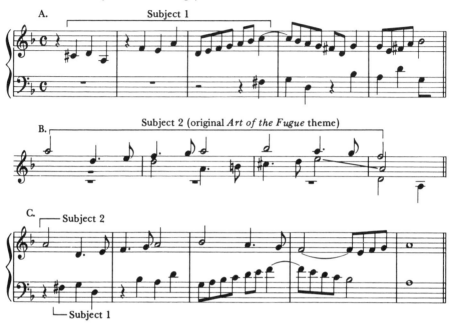

FIGURE 20-2 **Combinations of Subjects 1+2 in Bach's Contrapunctus X**

Subject	2 1	1 2	1 2	2 1	1 2	2 1	1 2
Type of Dbl. Cpt.	Orig.	at 10th	at 10th	at 10th + 8va (in 6ths)	at 8va	at 10th + 8va (in 3rds)	at 10th + 8va (in 3rds)
Keys	d	a	d	F	d	B♭	d
Meas. No.	44	52	66	75	85	103	115

Contrapunctus IX from the same work is slightly different. After a lengthy opening exposition on the first subject (measures 1–29), the second subject, an augmentation of the original *Kunst der Fuge* theme, is combined directly with the first, but *without* recourse to an exposition of its own (see Ex. 20-11). Again seven simultaneous restatements occur, this time utilizing double counterpoint at the twelfth. How are they similar to those of the previous Contrapunctus X (compare Fig. 20-3 with Fig. 20-2)?

EXAMPLE 20-11 Initial combination of Subjects 1 and 2 in Bach's Contrapunctus IX (*Die Kunst der Fuge*)

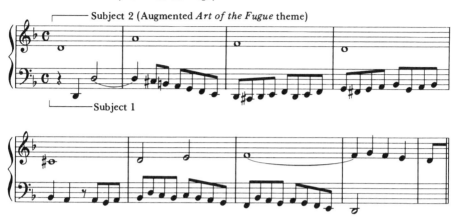

FIGURE 20-3 Combinations of Subjects 1+2 in Bach's Contrapunctus IX

Subject	2 1	1 2	2 1	1 2	1 2	1 2	2 1
Type of Dbl. Cpt.	Orig.	at 12th	Orig.	at 12th	at 12th	at 12th	Orig.
Keys	d	F	d	a	d	g	d
Meas. Nos.	35	45	59	73	89	99	119

Bach's Prelude and Fugue in C minor (for organ) BWV 537 might well be entitled "The Case of the Missing Double Fugue". Following an extensive exposition and working out of the initial subject, he turns to a completely new thematic idea based on an ascending chromatic tetrachord. The listener expects both themes to combine as usual during the final section of the piece. Instead, Bach returns to more restatements of the original subject and then quickly concludes the composition, so that the anticipated dual presentations never materialize. Scrutiny of both melodic ideas reveals that they will not "combine" anyway—thus this was never Bach's intention.

THE TRIPLE FUGUE

The *triple fugue* incorporates basically the same principles outlined above. Since all three subjects must now appear in conjunction, triple counterpoint is used.

The A major Prelude of *WTC* I is generally included in this genre of fugue. It belongs to the first category, in that all three subjects are presented in close proximity near the opening of the piece; the initial measures were quoted in Ex. 15-17. Three triple statements occur in the exposition at the usual tonic–dominant–tonic levels (measures 1–11). Two episodes frame the single occurrence of the subjects in the submediant key (measures 11–17), before their two final presentations in tonic (measures 17–24).

On the other hand the F♯ minor Fugue of *WTC* II is a good example of the last category. Consult the excerpts of Ex. 20-12. Subject 1 is stated with the usual exposition and several re-entries (measures 1–20; see Ex. 20-12A). Subject 2, which appears in dual form (Ex. 20-12B), is imitated in quasi-stretto during measures 20–28 and is then combined several times with the initial subject in measures 28–36 (see Ex. 20-12C). These are then dropped in favor of Subject 3, which is isolated in measures 36–51 before being counterpointed against the second theme (see Exs. 20-12D and 12E). The final section (measures 66–69) consists of two statements of all three subjects in triple counterpoint (Ex. 20-12F); themes 1 and 3 are never combined. The eventual melodic coalescence illustrated in the last example is typical of many triple fugues—the subjects are not of equal duration, but enter in a staggered fashion to reach a cadence with all three parts. These triple fugues tend to be rather expansive, due to the separate expositions and subsequent thematic combinations.

EXAMPLE 20-12 Subjects 1, 2, and their combinations in Bach's Fugue in f♯ (*WTC* II)

No discussion of this genre would be complete without a reference to the "St. Anne" Fugue in E♭ major which concludes Bach's *Klavierübung* Part III.[10] Here there are well-defined expositions of Subjects 1, 2, and 3. Although Subjects 1 + 2 and 1 + 3 occur together, all three themes never appear in combination. Some scholars rationalize this "omission" on theological grounds.[11] The proportions of this fugue, graphed in Fig. 20-4,

[10]This title is derived from the similarity of the opening subject to the melody *St. Anne,* used to set the well-known hymn of Charles Wesley, *O God, Our Help in Ages Past* (the opening of the tune is quoted in Ex. 12-8B). Bach, however, was not acquainted with this melody.

[11]This collection seems to be based on the number three—three flats in the framing movements, 3 × 7 chorale preludes, and the concluding fugue with three subjects—which possibly recalls the Medieval association with the Trinity. If one equates the three successive themes with Father, Son, and Holy Spirit, perhaps Bach is suggesting that the latter two spring from the fountainhead of the former. Also see David Humphreys, *The Esoteric Structure of Bach's Clavierübung* III (Cardiff: University of Cardiff Press, 1983).

are extremely interesting. Despite the three changes of meter, the half-note tactus remains constant throughout (C $\tactus = \frac{6}{4}\tactus = \frac{12}{8}\tactus$), so that it may be used as the basic unit of measure. Thus tactus 117, at the end of the Subject 2 exposition, divides the fugue exactly. Each of these sections is divided at the Golden Mean of .618 (71:117 = .616:1).[12]

FIGURE 20-4 Use of the Golden Mean in formal sections of Bach's "St. Anne" Fugue in E♭ (*Klavierübung* Part III)- using tactus as measure unit

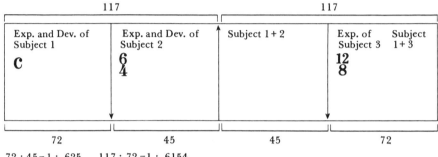

FIVE- AND SIX-VOICE FUGUES

Fugues of *more* than four voices are comparably rare in keyboard works of the period, so that one is forced to seek examples of five- or six-part fugues in the choral or ensemble/orchestral literature. Only two such pieces occur in the *WTC*—the C♯ minor and B♭ minor Fugues in Volume 1, both of which employ five voices. The former is a triple fugue which is analogous to Contrapunctus IX in format (consult Ex. 15-16 for a quotation of its three subjects). As each new theme appears, it is immediately allied with the previous one(s), creating a cumulative effect. This procedure allows more time to explore the combinations of the subjects in triple counterpoint. As a result they occur here ten times in conjunction (not counting the final double stretto).

We will close our study with brief mention of a work which may be the pinnacle of Bach's fugal output—the monumental six-part Ricercar which represents the climax of his *Musikalische Opfer*. It is not possible to do justice to this masterpiece within the space of a few paragraphs. The reader is

---

[12]There seems sufficient evidence that Bach was interested in symmetrical and dynamic proportion, and in the use of symbolic numerology. It is not accidental that the famous Haussmann portrait of Bach (1746) shows exactly 14 buttons and 14 notes in the upper voices of the canon he is holding in his hand. In the old Medieval code where A = 1, B = 2, C = 3, etc. (I/J = 9), B A C H = 14 and J S B A C H = 41, its inverse.

urged to consult the excellent commentary/analysis of Hans David in his book *J. S. Bach's Musical Offering,* pages 134–152.

ASSIGNMENTS

1. Compose the exposition of an original double fugue (four voices), in which the two subjects are presented in close proximity at the opening. Following the initial statement of the two themes in tonic, the pair of remaining voices should appear at the dominant level; review Ex. 20-7.

2. Do a structural diagram of Bach's Three-Part Invention in F minor, which is actually a triple fugue. Observe how the subjects occur in pairs; the use of triple counterpoint in the episodes was discussed in Chapter 15. The transposition of material by lower fifths should play an important role in the way your graph is laid out.

3. Make a comparison of the pair of triple fugues in Bach's *Kunst der Fuge*—Contrapuncti VIII and XI. The subjects of the latter are rough inversions of the former, but are presented in a different order.

21

✖✖✖✖✖✖✖✖✖✖✖✖✖✖✖✖✖✖✖✖✖✖✖✖✖✖✖✖✖✖✖✖✖✖✖✖✖✖✖

Choral writing

Up to this point, counterpoint has been treated as a textural attribute of absolute music. Although some excerpts were drawn from vocal literature, most originated in the instrumental writing of the period. This chapter will attempt to rectify this imbalance. The scope of the present text does not allow a detailed examination of all the vocal genre of the Baroque. There-fore consideration of the solo or duet literature will be excluded, and emphasis will be placed on the treatment of counterpoint and the structure of typical movements in the *choral idiom*.

WORDS AND MUSIC

The wedding of words to music harks back to the primal roots of the art of tone setting. This problem has been approached in many ways, favoring either words or music. The somewhat impersonal settings of the mass in the late Renaissance gave way to the pseudo-Greek declamation of the early recitative during the time of the Florentine Camerata (around 1600). Mon-teverdi rationalized his use of unprepared dissonance on the basis of the text. Although the emergence of a basically polyphonic style in the late Baroque (coupled with a strong instrumental influence) tended to effect idiomatic vocal writing for chorus, the composers tried to underpin their words with appropriate musical settings. Examples of *textpainting* in smaller and larger dimensions abound in this period.

A good illustration of this is the congregational singing of chorales in the Lutheran church. Since the hymnbooks contained only words, those in attendance sang the tune of the chorale in *unison,* usually after an organ chorale prelude. This allowed the organist to *vary* his harmonizations in accordance with the different literary content of each verse. Although these accompaniments were not recorded for posterity,[1] we can get a glimpse of this technique by comparing choral settings of different verses of the same hymn. The harmonizations of *O Haupt voll Blut und Wunden* which appear in Bach's *St. Matthew Passion* make a fascinating study. Even the harmonic contrasts from phrase to phrase of the *same* verse of a chorale are revealing. *Es ist Genug* offers one illustration. This hymn is somewhat unusual in that several melodic phrases are restated immediately. One phrase repetition is quoted in Ex. 21-1. *Without* the text provided, the shift from Bach's placid diatonic setting of the first phrase to the intensely chromatic language of the second is puzzling, to say the least. With the addition of the words, all comment becomes unnecessary. Although it is somewhat dated, the opening chapters of Volume 2 of Albert Schweitzer's *J. S. Bach* (1911) are important in pointing out Bach's aesthetic approach to words and music. Schweitzer was one of the first to observe that even in his purely instrumental settings of the chorale (like chorale preludes and fantasias), the accompanying counterpoint is influenced by the text. Thus in *Durch Adam's Fall* from the *Orgelbüchlein* the "falling" diminished sevenths in the bass are set off against the "serpent-like" figures in the inner voices.[2]

EXAMPLE 21-1 Bach's harmonization of phrases seven and eight of *Es ist genug*

(I safely journey on in peace)

(continued)

---

[1]Bach apparently made a collection of varied harmonizations for eighty-eight familiar chorale tunes, but they have unfortunately been lost.

[2]See Albert Schweitzer, *J. S. Bach,* Vol. 2, trans. Ernest Newman (New York: Dover Publications, Inc., 1966), pp. 1–122.

EXAMPLE 21-1 (cont'd)

(My wretched misery left behind)

A similar instance occurs in the chorus "For we like sheep" from Handel's *Messiah*. This text, taken from one of the Suffering Servant poems in Isaiah, Chapter 40, is divided into four short phrases, each of which is supplied with a delightfully appropriate musical setting. Referring to Exs. 21-2A through 2C, the opening *"For we like sheep"* is stated by the chorus, repeated by the orchestra, and again restated immediately by the chorus, suggesting the "following" tendency of herds of sheep. The diverging lines of "have all gone astray" is especially vivid. "We have turned" is set to a typical "turn" figure of the period, while the repeated C's picture the obstinant character of "everyone to his own way."

EXAMPLE 21-2 Thematic textpainting in Handel's "All we like sheep" (*Messiah*)

C.

we have turn -   ed ev - 'ry one to

his   own   way

THROUGHCOMPOSED POLYPHONIC SETTINGS

In regard to polyphonic setting of text for chorus, it is necessary to review briefly some of the precedents in previous periods. During the late Renaissance, an era of intensive contrapuntal procedure, the words from a typical motet or mass movement were divided into short cogent phrases of usually not more than twelve syllables. Each phrase was then assigned an appropriate musical theme or subject. Following an opening point of imitation during which the different voices entered, free counterpoint was employed, with the theme (coupled to its original text) restated in various parts. A cadential formula usually brought the section to a close. The same basic procedure was then repeated for the next phrase of text, and so on until the words were eventually exhausted. The rhythmic flow frequently continued through the cadential points, creating a seamless polyphonic texture. This technique has often been described as *sectional throughcomposition,* or *motet form.*

Although the tonal system and the rhythmic treatment of the late Baroque differed vastly from the Renaissance, certain similarities existed. The Handel chorus examined below is not strictly chordal or fugal, but represents an amalgam of textures. This example is not intended to serve as any "stereotype" of choral writing, since the eventual structure of each piece depends largely upon the text. Nevertheless, some general conclusions may be drawn from its analysis.

The source for the initial chorus of the *Messiah* ("And the glory of the Lord") is taken from Isaiah 11:5. Handel divides it into four short phrases, assigning each a theme or motive; these are labelled ① ② ③ ④ for the sake of reference and are quoted in Exs. 21-3 and 21-4. A structural diagram for the entire chorus appears in Fig. 21-1.

In the opening section (measures 1–42) the first two themes are presented successively (orchestra, chorus) and then combined simultaneously in double counterpoint (see Exs. 21-3A through C). The conclusion of this part of the piece features a restatement of ① and ② (chorus, orchestra). Note that ① is presented either by a single voice or *tutti* choir (denoted as T), while ② is more motivic, being tossed about between the various parts.

FIGURE 21-1 Structural diagram of Handel's "And the glory of the Lord" (*Messiah*)

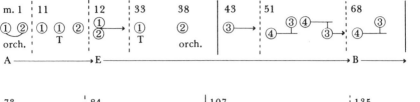

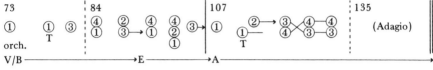

EXAMPLE 21-3

G. F. Handel: "And the glory of the Lord" (*Messiah*), measures 11-28

The next section (measures 43–72) introduces the final two phrases. Following the entries of ③ in the alto and tenor, the sustained ④ is placed in juxtaposition against ③; see Exs. 21-4A and 4B. Both are then inverted texturally.

EXAMPLE 21-4

G. F. Handel: "And the glory of the Lord" (*Messiah*), measures 43-57

Section three (measures 73–105) develops all four ideas in various combinations. This leads to a restatement of ① at the opening of the final section (measures 106–138). The themes now return in successive order, leading to a short concluding Adagio. The superimposition of the tonal scheme of the movement over the formal design described above is rather interesting (refer back to Fig. 21-1). The tonality shifts from the initial A major to the dominant key at the combination of ① and ② (measures 27ff). It continues until near the end of section two, where it moves a fifth higher to the supertonic relation of B *major*—a rather unusual procedure for this period. Section three begins on the V of B major and works its way back through the dominant key to the beginning of the final part, where the return of ① is synchronized with the restatement of tonic. The piece then remains in A major to the end.

This work contains several typical features of Handel's non-imitative treatment for chorus. Observe not only the thematic contrast but also the way the textural settings distinguish each idea. This is especially evident in the chordal *tuttis* and the reduced two-voice writing of ① and ② respectively. The only prolonged textural buildup occurs during the development of all four themes in section three (measures 91–102). At no time is the contrapuntal writing thick or turgid. Although we may shudder at the idea of performing this music with a choir of two thousand (such concerts actually did take place), the results are not as terrible as one might imagine, since the texture is full of "windows" which allow the lines to clearly emerge. Finally, observe Handel's favorite device of thematic combination, usually with double counterpoint, following the initial presentation of ideas.

In vivid contrast to Handel's more "open" contrapuntal writing, Bach's choral polyphony tends to be rather dense. For example in the opening chorus of his Christmas Oratorio there are only nine measures in which one or more vocal parts are resting out. This suggests that a more modest chorus would be appropriate, so the lines are distinct. Remember, Bach's own choir at Leipzig contained only about eighteen singers.

Some practical guidelines for the composition of choral movements in Baroque style are listed below:

1. Always write in full score, with each voice part assigned its own text below the separate staves. In using the "displaced" treble clef for the tenor voice, be sure that your pitches are in the correct octave.
2. Carefully work out the rhythmic setting of the text in relation to your thematic ideas. In general, English and German tend to place accented syllables on stronger metric positions. The syllable used for melismatic passages is also normally accented.
3. Watch that the tessitura of each voice part does not lie too high (be especially careful with the tenor). Although it may seem that the upper register of the choir is emphasized in many Baroque choruses (for instance, those more festive ones in D major where trumpets are often used), remember that the pitch level at that time was about a whole-tone lower.
4. For "softer" passages the lower ranges are effective, but do not "spread out" the voices in louder *tutti* sections. Here the basses should be kept rather high.
5. Regardless of the overall textural or structural plan of the movement, it is probably better at first to work with shorter, more concise thematic material. Don't be afraid to repeat your ideas, but vary the tonal environment and textural placement (through double counterpoint).
6. Compose a separate thoroughbass part. In less dense passages it provides the *true lowest* part, allowing the choral bass voice to take part in various contrapuntal activities; in *tuttis* the vocal bass will then double the thoroughbass. Go back and consult Exs. 21-3 and 21-4 in this respect.
7. Vary the density of the texture. Even in strict fugal movements one voice is often resting out prior to a subject entry.
8. Finally, remember that the individual parts are to be *sung*, not *played*. Strive for singable melodies. Sometimes an occasional voice-crossing can be helpful in achieving a better contour.

FUGAL MOVEMENTS

The use of strict fugal procedure in choral movements is common in this period. However, do not assume that because a piece opens with a *fugato* passage (or point of imitation), that it will continue that way. Actually, of all the choral movements in Handel's *Messiah,* only a handful are true "vocal fugues"—for instance, "And with His stripes we are healed" and "He trusted in God that He would deliver Him." In these cases the text is usually short, amounting often to a single phrase which can be stated within the initial fugal subject. Sometimes a second phrase of text is set to the countersubject, provided that it reappears consistently throughout the piece (refer back to Ex. 20-9 and also see Ex. 23-6).

Several of Bach's innovations in this field are noteworthy. One has been dubbed a *Permutationfuge,* in which the entries of the subject and countersubjects appear in the manner of a *rondellus* or *round;* see below where S = subject, A = answer, and CS = countersubject, and refer to Fig. 20-1.

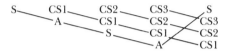

Bach also uses imitation or fugue to provide a contrasting section within an overall "ritornello-like" structure. The opening movement of his Christmas Oratorio may be graphed as follows:

				(fine)	
A	B	A	B	C	DaCapo
free/chordal	fugal	free/chordal	fugal	fugal/chordal	
m. 1–50	50–81	81–106	106–137	138–201	

THE CHORALE IN CHORAL WORKS

The emphasis placed by the North German composers on the Lutheran chorale can be observed in settings of cantatas, oratorios, and passions. The earlier innovations of Franz Tunder and his son-in-law Buxtehude culminated in the monumental works of J. S. Bach. Many of his sacred cantatas may be classified as *chorale cantatas.* These feature movements which incorporate both the text and melody of the hymn tune on which they are based, and normally employ various "chorale prelude" techniques. Recitatives and arias (for solo voice or duets) are usually based on original texts, which serve as commentary on the words of the hymn. Such works usually conclude with a harmonization of the chorale melody.[3]

In Bach's Cantata No. 4, *Christ lag in Todesbanden,* each of its seven choral movements incorporates *both* the hymn tune and the texts to its various verses. This Dorian chorale finds the origins of its text and hints of its melody in the ancient Gregorian Easter sequence *Victimae paschali laudes.* In addition to the first two phrases of this chant (Ex. 21-5A), a sixteenth-century version of the hymn (Ex. 21-5B) and its form during Bach's time (Ex. 21-5C) are quoted below. The change of the g♮ to g♯ forces the open-

---

[3]See Robert L. Marshall, "How J. S. Bach Composed Four-Part Chorales," *Musical Quarterly,* Vol. 56/2 (April 1970), pp. 198–220.

ing phrase into A minor, although the initial chord of D minor is retained for the first note to help define the mode. In the Bach cantata the chorale is transposed up a step to E Dorian (with a signature of one sharp).

EXAMPLE 21-5

A.   *Victimae paschali laudes*

B.   *Christ lag in Todesbanden* (1524)

C.   *Christ lag in Todesbanden* (early 1700s)

Bach takes this opening half-step and employs it as a recurring "melodic cell" throughout the cantata. This is evident in the orchestral Sinfonia which begins the work. A summary of the succeeding verses follows:

Verse I—Modified *Vorimitation* chorale prelude for full chorus, with soprano cantus (in ♩.). Extended derived coda on the word *Hallelujah*.

Verse II—Soprano/alto duet in free paraphrasing of the chorale tune over an eighth-note walking bass.

Verse III—Simple tenor setting of the separated phrases of the chorale (in ♩) over continuing polyphony in the strings (♫ vs. ♬); a textbook example of mixed second and third species.

Verse IV—Modified *Vorimitation* chorale prelude for chorus with alto cantus (in ♩).

Verse V—The only movement in 3/4 meter, the basses state each phrase of the melody, which is immediately repeated by the orchestra, under which the basses then invent new counterpoints.

Verse VI—Soprano/tenor duet, each statement of a chorale phrase is followed by free extensions in triplets.

Verse VII—A final harmonization of the hymn tune for full chorus.

Study this work, using the above comments as a guide. Notice the lack of recitative and aria, normally found in chorale cantatas. On the other hand the choral forces are distributed such that each voice part is given prominence. Gerhard Herz, in his perceptive analysis of this composition,[4] points out the arched framing of the movements around the central chorus of Verse IV:

[4]See his edition of this cantata in the *Norton Critical Scores* series (New York: W. W. Norton and Co., In., 1967).

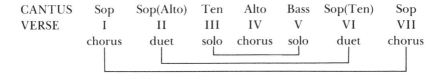

CANTUS	Sop	Sop(Alto)	Ten	Alto	Bass	Sop(Ten)	Sop
VERSE	I	II	III	IV	V	VI	VII
	chorus	duet	solo	chorus	solo	duet	chorus

This symmetry, typical of Bach's other works, may have its origins in theological symbolism related to the cross of Christ. This certainly seems to be the case in the final version of the *Credo* for his B minor Mass, where the various sections are grouped around the central *Crucifixus*.

Several other movements reveal Bach's imagination in adopting chorale prelude technique to the choral idiom. The tenor chorus from his Cantata No. 140, *Wachet auf, ruft uns die Stimme*, was quoted in Chapter 12 in an organ arrangement; it is an excellent example of *ritornello* technique. *Er ist auf Er den kommen arm* (No. 7) in the first part of the Christmas Oratorio features a simple soprano setting of the hymn *Gelobet seist du, Jesu Christ*, which is periodically interrupted by a bass recitative commenting on each chorale phrase. The triumphant opening chorus of Cantata No. 80, *Ein' feste Burg ist unser Gott*, employs *Vorimitation* technique with a canon on the cantus between the trumpet and orchestral basses. The initial chorus of Cantata No. 78, *Jesu, der du meine Seele*, combines a chorale prelude over a recurring chaconne bass of a chromatic tetrachord. Finally, the monumental movement that opens the *St. Matthew Passion* utilizes two choirs, the second of which interjects single-chord interrogations of "Who? How? When?". This intricate polyphony becomes the contrapuntal accompaniment to a unison soprano choir, which intones the chorale *O Lamm Gottes*.

The above discussion has touched on a few common procedures of choral polyphony. It is hoped that you will further pursue investigation of this fascinating topic.

ASSIGNMENTS

1. A chorale melody and a translation of one verse of its text are given in Ex. 21-6. Make a harmonization in four voices, attempting to conform your musical setting to the changing mood of each phrase.

EXAMPLE 21-6

Herr Gott, dich loben alle wir (Old Hundred)

Thou Son of God, through Thy dear Blood Here I es-

cape from Hell's dark flood; Tis Thou has paid the

(continued)

EXAMPLE 21-6 (cont'd)

price de - creed, And of God's wrath my soul re - lieved.

(translation by Charles Sanford Terry)

   2. If you feel more ambitious, compose a short choral movement (SATB) on the following text:

> *For behold, the darkness shall cover the earth,*
> *and gross darkness the people;*
> *but the Lord shall arise upon thee,*
> *and his glory shall be seen upon thee.*

Isaiah 60:2

22

✳✳

The pedagogical foundations
of counterpoint
in the
classical period

Until now we have discussed polyphony in the late Baroque (approximately 1700–1750). After the death of Bach, the Rococo period prepared the way for the Classical masters Haydn, Mozart, and Beethoven. The emphasis on homophony plus the expansion of the two-reprise form into the full-blown sonata lessened the popularity of counterpoint. Although its study was significant in the training of Classical composers, polyphony became subservient to the trend of melody/accompaniment. The final two chapters will examine the role of counterpoint in works written between about 1760–1827 (the death of Beethoven).

BACKGROUND

Chapter 3 established that most polyphonic instruction for the major composers of the late Baroque stressed linear movement, with the harmonic emphasis of thoroughbass. By 1775 a number of significant treatises by Mattheson, Marpurg, Rameau, and Kirnberger (listed in the Bibliography) were already in print. However, they tended to summarize the contrapuntal practices of the Baroque. One of these, Johann Fux's *Gradus ad Parnassum* (1725) looked even further back into the past, demonstrating a renewed interest in the techniques of the late Renaissance, and of Palestrina in particular. Although some of the Baroque composers were aware of Fux's work,[1] it probably did not influence their writing to any great extent, since their polyphonic instruction was of an earlier generation. But Fux's impact on the *new* generation was another matter. Perhaps because his system was so rigorous, the Classical composers seized upon it to codify the foundations of counterpoint in general.

This treatise became the fountainhead of all subsequent polyphonic instruction during this period. Fux's influence is well documented. Haydn himself prepared an abstract of *Gradus* (*Elementarbuch der verschiedenen Gattungen des Kontrapunkts* (1789).[2] Mozart employed it in his composition lessons to the English composer Thomas Attwood,[3] while the young Beethoven apprenticed under both Haydn and Albrechtsberger, whose treatise *Gründliche Anweisung zur Komposition* (1790) was based largely on the methods found in *Gradus*.[4]

FUX AND THE FIVE SPECIES

Fux handled dissonance and rhythm systematically. It is based on the use of a given *cantus firmus* in whole notes (usually written by Fux), to which counterpoints were added at increasingly more complex levels. The characteristics of the resultant five *species* are summarized below.

	RHYTHM AGAINST CANTUS	USE OF DISSONANCE
First Species	One-against-one (o vs. o)	Consonance only.
Second Species	Two-against-one (♩♩ vs. o)	Passing tones allowed on 3rd beat (4/4 meter).
Third Species	Four-against-one (♪♪♪♪ vs. o)	Unaccented passing tones, Cambiatas allowed on beats two and four. Accented passing tones allowed on beat three.
Fourth Species	Tied two-against one (♩♩♩♩ vs. o)	Suspensions allowed on beat one (ornamented suspensions)

---

[1]Spitta reports that Mizler's German translation of *Gradus* was made under the "very eyes" of J. S. Bach.

[2]A translation of this incomplete manual may be found in Alfred Mann's article "Haydn's *Elementarbuch:* A document of Classic Counterpoint Instruction", *Music Forum*, Vol. 3 (1973), pp. 197–237. Also see Denis Arnold, "Haydn's Counterpoint and Fux's *Gradus*," *Monthly Musical Record*, Vol. 87 (1957), pp. 52–58.

[3]These studies are included in Serie X:30 of the Mozart *Neue Ausgabe Sämtlicher Werke* (Kassel: Bärenreiter, 1965).

[4]See Gustav Nottebohm, *Beethoven's Studien, Erster Band* (Leipzig and Winterthur: J. Reiter-Biedermann, 1873).

| Fifth Species | Free rhythm-against one | All of the above, including eighth notes, anticipations (portamentos). No discussion of dissonant neighbors or appoggiaturas. |

The student was taken progressively through two, three, and finally four voices. Sometimes different species were combined in three or more parts.

It is difficult to ascertain whether Fux believed that his approach was original. Although we are not certain of his knowledge of earlier contrapuntal treatises, it does appear that he was acquainted with those of Angelo Berardi (1681 and 1689).[5] Banchieri, in his *Cartella musicale* (1614), suggests a similarity to Fux without, however, resorting to the term *species*.[6] In most of these treatises, this form of instruction was limited to two voices. Fux continues his *Gradus* with an introduction to imitation, followed by sections on fugue in two to four voices. The usual types of double counterpoint are also treated extensively. In this latter part of the treatise some of the musical examples begin to resemble the stylistic traits of the Baroque.

Although some scholars, such as Knud Jeppesen, have continued to apply Fux's methodology to the study of sixteenth-century polyphony (see his *Counterpoint* 1939), others have used the basic principles to discover underlying contrapuntal voice-leading in general. Schenker advocated the acquisition of skills in harmony, thoroughbass, and *species counterpoint* as prerequisites to his method of reductive analysis. Aside from his own *Kontrapunkt*,[7] one may cite Arnold Schönberg, *Preliminary Exercises in Counterpoint* (1963), Felix Salzer and Carl Schachter, *Counterpoint in Composition* (1969) and Peter Westergaard, *Introduction to Tonal Theory* (1975).

THE APPLICATION OF SPECIES TO CLASSICAL COUNTERPOINT

It is not difficult to see the influence of the species approach in the counterpoint of the Classical period. In the following illustrations, quotations from Fux's own manual and compositions from the period are given side by side. All five species in two voices are represented; refer to the previous chart to distinguish their basic characteristics.

---

[5]This is discussed in Alfred Mann's introduction to Fux's *Gradus ad Parnassum*, found in *Johann Joseph Fux Sämtliche Werke* Serie VII, Band 1, pp. xiv–xix.

[6]An excerpt of Banchieri's "species" is quoted in Robert Gauldin, *A Practical Approach to Sixteenth-Century Counterpoint* (Englewood Cliffs: Prentice-Hall, Inc., 1985), pp. 285–86.

[7]See Volume II of his *Neue musikalische Theorien und Phantasien* 1906–35, translated by John Rothgeb and Jurgen Thym in a forthcoming edition by G. Schirmer.

First Species

As might well be expected, instances of two-part, note-against-note style is rare. A passage in four voices is cited in Ex. 22-2, with the eighth-note figuration in two measures omitted.

EXAMPLE 22-1

Johann Fux: *Gradus ad Parnassum*

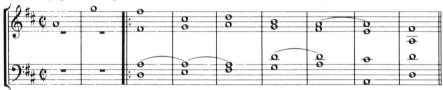

voices cross

EXAMPLE 22-2

Beethoven: String Quartet in D Op. 18 No. 3, I

(eighth-note figuration of Vln. I in meas. 3, 5, and 8 reduced)

Second Species

Example 22-4 is from a violin method where Cherubini set the major and minor scales with quasi-species accompaniments, to be performed by the teacher. In his illustration of two-against-one the use of passing tones is somewhat neglected. What is curious about measure two?

EXAMPLE 22-3

Johann Fux: *Gradus ad Parnassum*

EXAMPLE 22-4

Luigi Cherubini: *Méthode de Violon par Baillot, Rode, et Kreutzer*

Third Species

In Examples 22-6 through 22-8, various rhythmic settings are encountered: three-against-one, four-against-one, and even six-against-one.

EXAMPLE 22-5

Johann Fux: *Gradus ad Parnassum*

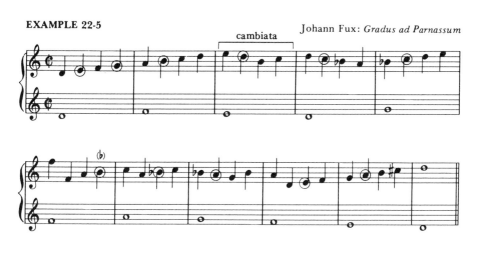

EXAMPLE 22-6

Beethoven: String Quartet in E♭ Op. 74, III

(continued)

EXAMPLE 22-6 (cont'd)

EXAMPLE 22-7

Haydn: Piano Sonata in D H. XVI No. 19, III

EXAMPLE 22-8

Beethoven: Symphony No. 3 in E♭, IV

Fourth Species

In the Mozart quotation (Ex. 22-10) the underlying fourth species is revealed upon reduction.

EXAMPLE 22-9

Johann Fux: *Gradus ad Parnassum*

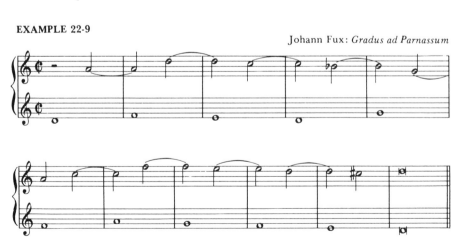

EXAMPLE 22-10

Mozart: String Quartet in G K. 387, IV

Fifth Species

Example 22-12 is an amusing setting of a hexachord on G. It begins in third species and then shifts into fourth.

EXAMPLE 22-11

Johann Fux: *Gradus ad Parnassum*

EXAMPLE 22-12

Johann Albrechtsberger: String Quartet in G (without opus)

The middle section of the final *Rondo* to Beethoven's Piano Sonata in C minor Op. 13 (beginning in ms. 79) is often cited in this regard, since the composer developed the sequence of falling fifths through rhythmic characteristics of the various species. The manuscript of Mozart's String Quartet in G major K. 387 contains two interesting sketches, showing how the composer evolved a short section from the last movement through species counterpoint. The passage appears to be modelled on a simple instance of fourth species in Ex. 22-13, creating a pattern of 4–3 suspensions through ascending fifth motion; enharmonic notation in flats is avoided. In the initial sketch (Ex. 22-14), Mozart rearranges the parts to create a quasi-canonic relation between the upper two voices; the bass is missing but is obviously implied. In the final version (Ex. 22-15), which appears in the Quartet proper, Mozart realizes that four parts are unnecessary; the bass is elaborated chromatically.

EXAMPLE 22-13 Underlying fourth-species model for Mozart sketches

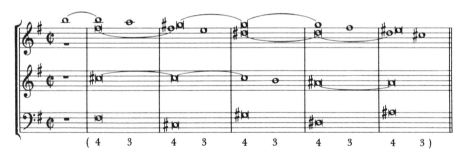

EXAMPLE 22-14

Mozart: Initial sketch for opening of development (String Quartet in G K. 387, IV)

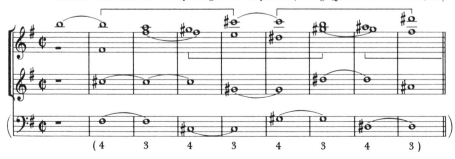

EXAMPLE 22-15

Mozart: Finished version of opening of development (String Quartet in G K. 387, IV)

ASSIGNMENT

No illustrations of species counterpoint involving three or more voices have been quoted from Fux's *Gradus*. Employing the cantus cited in Ex. 22-3, compose several examples of *combined species* in three parts (2nd + 3rd, 2nd + 4th, or 3rd + 4th), or even a four-voice piece using all three.

23

※※※※※※※※※※※※※※※※※※※※※※※※※※※※※※※※※※※※※※

Examples of counterpoint in the classical period

The scope of this text does not permit a detailed examination of the role of polyphony in the Classical literature. This chapter will summarize how counterpoint was used in this period.

The principles derived from the species approach underlie much of the voice-leading of this music. Felix Salzer and Carl Schachter cite numerous examples in their *Counterpoint in Composition* (1969) which support this premise. The passage in Ex. 23-1, although hardly a typical instance of "contrapuntal" writing, demonstrates through reduction a clear relation to the passing-tone technique of second species. Other examples in this chapter show passages or movements using procedures more commonly associ-

EXAMPLE 23-1   Beethoven: Piano Sonata in f Op. 2, No. 1, III

ated with polyphony. This survey is basically limited to the works of Haydn, Mozart, and Beethoven.[1]

INCIDENTAL PASSAGES OF POLYPHONY
WITHIN HOMOPHONIC MOVEMENTS

There are many instances of contrapuntal writing within the framework of larger homophonic forms: two-reprise (minuet and scherzo), rondo, variations, ternary, and sonata-form. These shorter passages provide textural variety to the prevailing melody/accompaniment. They sometimes employ diminutive examples of imitation (see Ex. 23-2). For longer illustrations consult Mozart's Symphony No. 38 in D major ("Prague") first movement (measures 143–81), and his Symphony No. 40 in G minor fourth movement (measures 161–75).

EXAMPLE 23-2   Mozart: Symphony No. 41 in C ("Jupiter"), III

More interesting are extended imitative sections which suggest the opening exposition of a fugue. These are often called *fugato* passages. Their placement at the opening of a movement may lead the listener to expect a complete fugue to follow; however, this rarely occurs, since the contrapuntal texture will normally cease after the initial point of imitation. Consult the beginning sections of Mozart's Overture to *The Magic Flute* (measures 16–38), Beethoven's Symphony No. 1 in C major second movement (measures 1–19), the Finale of his Piano Sonata in F major Op. 10,

[1]The best treatment of counterpoint in the Classical period is Warren Kirkendale's book on this subject; see the appropriate entry under History of the Fugue in the Bibliography. Other references of interest include John Cockshoot, *The Fugue in Beethoven's Piano Music* (London: Routledge and K. Paul, 1959); A. Hyatt King, "Mozart's Counterpoint; its Growth and Spirit," *Music and Letters*, Vol. 26 (1945), pp. 12–20; Alfred Einstein, "Mozart and Counterpoint," *Mozart: His Character, His Works*, trans. Arthur Mendel and Nathan Broder. (New York: Oxford University Press, 1945), pp. 144–156.

No. 2 (measures 1–12), and the Scherzo to the Symphony No. 9 in D minor (measures 9–28).

Fugato passages are usually found within quasi-developmental sections of larger movements. Here they show how polyphony can be used in *thematic development.* Other examples include Haydn's String Quartet in A major Op. 55, No. 1, where the theme in the middle section of the last movement is treated as a fugue subject (measures 61–99); and the delightful passage in the final Rondo of his Symphony No. 101 in D major ("Clock"), in which the second return of the original refrain is now set in a point of imitation (measures 189–218).

Many extended fugato sections appear in Beethoven's orchestral works. These include the Symphony No. 3 in E♭ major ("Eroica"), second movement (measures 115–45), and fourth movement (measures 117–63 and 277–314); the Trio to the Scherzo of his Symphony No. 5 in C minor; Symphony No. 7 in A major, second movement (measures 183–210); measures 101–95 of the *Alla Marcia* section from the Finale of the Symphony No. 9 in D minor ("Choral")—a double fugue; and the Rondo from his Piano Concerto No. 3 in C minor (measures 230–49). The pair of fugatos from the last movement of the *Eroica* are interesting since they occur within quasi-developmental sections of variation form and thus employ the same subject—the opening notes of the bass line from Beethoven's famous "Contradance" theme.[2] The initial measures of the latter are quoted in Ex. 23-3. It employs a fixed countersubject, suggesting double-fugue technique. The answer is at the subdominant.

EXAMPLE 23-3   Beethoven: Symphony No. 3 in E♭ ("Eroica"), IV

[2]See Ludwig Misch, "Fugue and Fugato in Beethoven's Variation Form," *Musical Quarterly*, 42/1 (Jan. 1956), pp. 14–27.

HYBRID FORMS

There are movements which seem to lie between the incidental use of counterpoint and the strict application of polyphony. Such "hybrid" pieces often take on a half-fugue/half-sonata structure, freely alternating between contrapuntal and homophonic textures.

   The Finale to Mozart's String Quartet in G major K. 387 opens with a fugato passage (see Ex. 23-4A), which gives way to the sonata-form. The secondary theme (in the dominant area) is presented first in imitation (Ex. 23-4B) and then combined in double counterpoint with the opening material (Ex. 23-4C). Chromaticism is stressed during the development. Note the stretto of the first theme during the coda. The basic melodic elements in the last movement of Mozart's Symphony No. 41 in C major ("Jupiter") consist of five distinctive motivic ideas, which are subjected to a variety of contrapuntal and homophonic settings. In the coda, the composer combines all five in *quintuple* counterpoint. Of the 120 possible permutations Mozart employs but five; one is cited in Ex. 23-5. It is interesting that both of these movements open with a quasi-cantus theme in whole-notes. The Finale to Beethoven's last "Rasumofsky" String Quartet in C major Op. 59, No. 3 is a curious sonata-form. Its begins with an extended fugato exposition, which returns at the recapitulation coupled with a half-note countersubject that is reminiscent of a section in the coda of the *Egmont* Overture (measures 307–11).

EXAMPLE 23-4

A. Theme 1 Fugato

Mozart: String Quartet in G K. 387, IV

(continued)

EXAMPLE 23-4 (cont'd)

B. Theme 2 Fugato

C. Theme 1 + 2

EXAMPLE 23-5   Mozart: Symphony No. 41 in C ("Jupiter"), IV

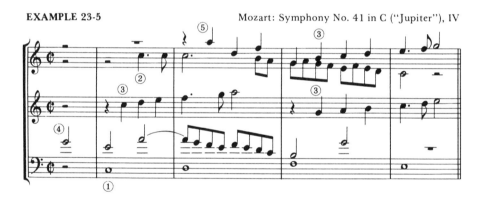

THE FUGAL MOVEMENT

The use of strict fugal technique as the basis for an *entire* movement is more frequent in the sacred choral works of the period. The conclusion of Haydn's *The Creation* ("Sing to the Lord, Ye Voices All") is an extended double fugue with continual use of invertible counterpoint. A pair of subjects is likewise present at the opening of the *Kyrie eleison* section of Mozart's Requiem in D minor. The composer ingeniously assigns the brief *Kyrie* and *Christe* texts to the two different themes, thereby eliminating the need for a separate *Christe* section (see Ex. 23-6). This fugue is strikingly Baroque in style, although several modulations to foreign keys may be noted.[3] Betho-

---

[3]Completing this work posthumously, Mozart's pupil Franz Süssmayr recapitulates this entire fugue for the concluding *Dona nobis pacem.*

ven concludes the "In gloria Dei patris, amen" section of the *Gloria* from his *Missa Solemnis* Op. 123 with a massive fugue for chorus and solo quartet. The original countersubject is maintained for about half of the movement and then dropped. Several remarkable stretti passages can be observed.

EXAMPLE 23-6   Mozart: *Kyrie eleison* (Requiem Mass in d)

Consistent fugal procedure is less common in instrumental compositions. String quartets Nos. 2, 5, and 6 from Haydn's Op. 20 set (the "Sun" Quartets) feature fugal finales. They represent one method Haydn used to equalize the roles of the four instruments, thereby freeing the texture from the tyranny of the accompanied Violin I. All are multiple fugues with secondary subjects presented at the outstart. The last movement of the F minor (No. 5) is a double fugue based on the familiar diminished-seventh leap. Compare its countersubject with those employed by Handel and Mozart for essentially the same theme (see Ex. 23-7 and relate to Ex. 23-6 and Ex. 20-9). This fugue abounds with stretti, mirror, and even features an embedded two-voice canon of thirteen measures. Number 6 in A major employs three subjects. The episodes, based on thematic fragments, are especially interesting. The writing of the last twenty measures is unusually dense. Number 2 in C major is a *quadruple* fugue; by the time the last entry is made in the exposition, all four subjects are present. However, most of the movement develops only the first two ideas.

EXAMPLE 23-7

                                          Haydn: String Quartet in f Op. 20, No. 5, IV

Mozart's *Stück* in F minor K. 608 (for mechanical clock) contains a four-voice fugue, following a thirteen measure introduction. A clever pairing of *inversus* and *rectus* forms of the subject in stretto appears in measures

48–53. The final movement of his *Phantasie Nr. 1 mit Fuge* K. 394 utilizes a number of stretto passages, one with simultaneous augmentation of the subject. Finales of cyclic sonatas which feature strict fugal technique are somewhat rare with Mozart. Two instances are the last movement of the String Quartet in D minor K. 173, whose subject is based on a descending chromatic tetrachord; and the Finale to the String Quartet in F major K. 168, which incorporates a more diatonic theme. Both exhibit extensive stretto.

The fugal finale becomes increasingly important during Beethoven's last period, as illustrated by the Finale of his Cello Sonata in D major Op. 102, No. 2, entitled *Allegro fugato*. The registral role which the cello performs in relation to the overall texture is noteworthy. The fugal last movement of the Piano Sonata in B♭ major Op. 106 ("Hammerklavier") features a scalar subject eight measures long. In the later Neapolitan section (B minor), Beethoven presents this theme three times in strict retrograde motion! The 6/8 fugue which concludes the Piano Sonata in A♭ major Op. 110 is interrupted about halfway through with a return of the Adagio Arioso. The subject is then mirrored (*L'inversione della Fuga*).

You may want to examine the double fugue that closes Beethoven's *Diabelli* Variations Op. 120. The two subjects are derived from motivic fragments of the original waltz theme. The last two fugues cited below make an interesting comparative study, since both are based on the same four-note motive that opens the String Quartet in A minor Op. 132: G♯ A f e. In the gigantic *Grosse Fuge* Op. 133, originally intended to serve as the final movement of the String Quartet in B♭ major Op. 130, this idea is expanded to B♭ B♮ a♭ g, B♮ C a b♭ (note the final retrograde of Bach's name). This work actually consists of three separate fugues (in B♭, G♭, and A♭), each of which constitutes a different treatment of the same subject.[4]

Most instrumental fugues during this period were either individual pieces or the *final* movement of a cyclic sonata. Beethoven takes exception to this by opening his String Quartet in C♯ minor Op. 131 with a prolonged *ricercar*-like fugue. The initial notes of the subject (g♯¹ b♯¹ c♯² a¹) relate back to the motive of Op. 132, with the last note now in the initial position. Its recapitulation features several interesting stretti, one with augmentation. Both the exposition and the final tonic section employ real answers at the subdominant.

CANONIC TECHNIQUE

Classical composers delighted in writing miniature vocal canons or *rounds* (usually at the unison) on various texts. Some of these even found their way into larger instrumental works. For instance, the amusing little round of

---

[4]See William Kirkendale, "The *Great Fugue* Op. 133: Beethoven's *Art of the Fugue*," *Acta Musicologica*, Vol. 35 (1963), pp. 14–24.

Beethoven on Maelzel's metronome emerged as the theme (without the canonic imitation) in the second movement of his Symphony No. 8 in F major.

Brief canonic passages, usually employing only two voices, may be encountered within various genre of this period. The second theme of the initial movement of Beethoven's Symphony No. 4 in B♭ major (measures 141–48) is a short self-contained canon for clarinet and bassoon, while in Mozart's Piano Sonata in D major K. 576 the opening melody is subjected to canonic treatment (see measures 17–24, 52–64, and 96–108, noting the different temporal distances). In the initial movement of Beethoven's Piano Sonata in B♭ major Op. 106 ("Hammerklavier") the development section employs this device; see the series of canons in measures 136–75. An ingenious canon for four voices at the octave occurs at the opening of the slow movement of Mozart's String Quartet in F major K. 168 (measures 1–11).

Entire movements in strict canonic technique are rare. It is usually limited to the more modest dimensions of the minuet. In Haydn's String Quartet in D minor Op. 76, No. 2 ("Quinten") the minuet section of the third movement is a two-part canon doubled at the octave, while in Mozart's Wind Serenade in C minor K. 388 both the Minuet and Trio employ this device. The first two-reprise of the Minuet features strict imitation between the soprano and bass, although the canon is broken at the beginning of the second reprise. However, the Trio is a double canon in inversion between a pair of oboes and bassoons. The way Mozart confines this procedure within the tonal scheme of a typical rounded-binary form repays careful study; the first reprise of this Trio is quoted in Ex. 23-8.

EXAMPLE 23-8   Mozart: *Trio in canone al roverscio* (Serenade for Wind Octet in c K. 388)

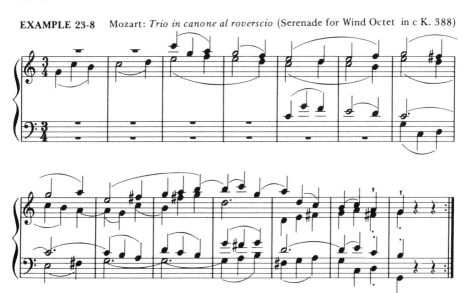

VARIOUS OTHER CONTRAPUNTAL DEVICES

Some other polyphonic procedures of the Classical period will be briefly noted. Haydn was particularly fond of double counterpoint at the octave; consult the opening of the Minuet from his String Quartet in F major Op. 55, No. 2, and the concluding Allegro from the initial movement of his String Quartet in E♭ Op. 76, No. 6. Instances of invertible counterpoint at the tenth or twelfth are rare, although occasionally a composer will resort to triple counterpoint. It plays an important role in the opening fugato section of the second movement of Beethoven's String Quartet in C minor Op. 18, No. 4 (see Ex. 23-9).

EXAMPLE 23-9

Beethoven: String Quartet in c Op. 18, No. 4, II

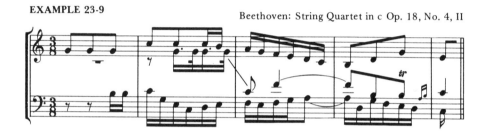

The Minuet from Haydn's Piano Sonata in A major Hob. XVI 26 is a charming instance of crab motion. The second-reprise sections of both the Minuet and its Trio restate their respective first reprises in exact retrograde motion; see Ex. 23-10.

EXAMPLE 23-10

Haydn: *Minuetto al Rovescio* (Piano Sonata in A Hob. XVI 26)

The Fugue in C minor K. 426 (for two pianos) by Mozart, with its opening diminished-seventh leap and "sighing" chromatic figures, represents a virtual lexicon of stretto technique.[5] Following the opening exposition and first episode, there are five separate stretto sections, featuring both *rectus* and *inversus* forms of the subject. Although all employ the intervallic distance of either an octave or fifth, the temporal distances vary from six to two beats, including one simultaneous presentation of both upright and mirrored forms.

Continuous variation is rare during the Classical era, giving way to the usual Theme and Variations with its typical two-reprise theme. One strange exception is Beethoven's Thirty-two Variations on an Original Theme, WoO 80. It is based on the familiar descending chromatic tetrachord of the Baroque with a short extension. The succeeding variations, however, do not overlap rhythmically, nor are they generally contrapuntal in nature. A more interesting case is the *Maggiore* Trio to the Allegretto from Beethoven's String Quartet in E minor Op. 59, No. 2. It combines imitative technique with a "fixed" melody (the celebrated *Theme russe*, a folk song employed later by Moussorgsky in *Boris Godounoff*). The latter occurs sixteen times, always at the tonic or dominant levels, thus suggesting a melding of fugue with quasi-passacaglia procedure. The phrase periodicity of the six-measure theme is interrupted but three times (twice in remarkable stretti), before the final transition to the Da Capo. Two countersubjects are employed (see measures 1–28 and 29–53); both utilize extensive invertible counterpoint.

Since the geographical area around Vienna was largely Catholic, the use of the Lutheran chorale prelude fell into relative obscurity during this

---

[5]The subject of this fugue, which is quoted in Ex. 23-12, bears a curious resemblance to the "Royal Theme" of Bach's *Das Musikalische Opfer;* refer to Ex. 13-1.

period. One remarkable example occurs in *The Armed Men* section from Mozart's *Magic Flute* (see Ex. 23-11).[6] The final portion of the Molto Adagio from Beethoven's String Quartet in A minor Op. 132 suggests a "figured" chorale prelude, although the half-note cantus is itself imitated in various voices. The movement bears the title *Heiliger Dankgesang* (Hymn of Thanksgiving) in the Lydian mode.

EXAMPLE 23-11

Mozart: "The Armed Men" (*The Magic Flute*)

Indeed we may wish to raise our own hymn of thanksgiving that this chapter brings to a close the survey of eighteenth century counterpoint. Polyphony continued to play a significant role in the following centuries of

[6]The chorale employed by Mozart is *Ach Gott, vom Himmel sieh' darein.*

music history. Such a work as Wagner's *Meistersinger* draws heavily on the contrapuntal vocabulary of the late Baroque: thematic combination, double counterpoint, chorale prelude, and fugue. The freer polyphonic techniques of Richard Strauss and Mahler were absorbed into the atonal practices of the second Viennese school. In particular the neo-Baroque tendencies of Busoni, Stravinsky, and Hindemith resurrected many of the procedures of that earlier era.[7] But that is another story. . . . . .

ASSIGNMENTS

1. Example 23-12 quotes the subject of Mozart's Fugue in C minor K. 426. Employing only imitation at the octave or fifth (either *rectus* or *inversus*), see how many ways you can use stretto with this theme. Compare your results with Mozart's.

EXAMPLE 23-12

Mozart: Subject of Fugue in c K. 426

2. As a final project take the example of triple counterpoint in Ex. 23-13 and use it as the basis for composing a Finale for a string trio. Each of the three themes will appear as the subject for separate fugal sections (in the order ① ② and ③). You might wish to transpose the middle fugue based on ② to the dominant key for tonal contrast. At the conclusion of the movement combine all three ideas several times, as in the coda of the Finale in Mozart's Symphony No. 41 in C major ("Jupiter"). Incorporate as many contrapuntal devices as you think appropriate with the different subjects.

EXAMPLE 23-13

---

[7]For instance, see Busoni's *Fantasia contrappuntistica*, Stravinsky's Octet for Wind Instruments and Piano Concerto, and Hindemith's *Ludus Tonalis*.

✖✖

Appendix:
characteristics
of dance movements

This appendix lists the stylized dance movements usually associated with the Baroque suite, including their typical tempi, meters, density and layout of texture, and rhythmic characteristics. References are made either to musical examples in this text or works of J. S. Bach.[1]

Many suites of the period open with an *Allemande,* the first dance of the normal *Allemande-Courante-Sarabande-Gigue* sequence. All the French Suites of Bach employ this format. However, the use of an introductory movement is frequent. It is not usually in the two-reprise structure, typical of the other movements. Several possibilities are listed below:

Prelude (Preludium, Preambulum)—Meter varied; tempo usually moderately fast to fast. The music is in a continuous non-sectional design, often employing figuration-prelude technique. Some are of considerable length. All of Bach's keyboard English and Unaccompanied Cello Suites utilize a prelude.

Overture—Slow ($\frac{4}{4}$) followed by fast ($\frac{3}{4}$ or $\frac{3}{8}$). This is the standard French overture, with its dotted rhythms in the initial chordal section and its lively fugal writing in the second. See Bach's Partita in D major BWV 828.

[1]See Louis Horst, *Pre-Classic Dance Forms* (New York: The Dance Observer, 1937).

Sinfonia—Usually multisectional. Bach's Partita in C minor BWV 826 opens with a slow chordal introduction, followed by an elaborate "arioso" and fast fugue, both in two-voice texture.

Toccata—The Partita in E minor BWV 830 of Bach begins with a free section which leads into a strict fugue.

Fantasia—This movement, which initiates Bach's A minor Partita BWV 827, seems to resemble a typical prelude. The use of the toccata and fantasia as the first movement of a suite should not be confused with the use of these terms as separate genre. The more imposing organ pieces, for instance, tend to alternate between free "recitative-like" sections (sometimes featuring foreign modulations) and strict contrapuntal or even fugal passages.

The most frequently encountered dance types will be considered first: *Allemande, Courante* (or *Corrente*), *Saraband(e)*, and *Gigue* (or *Giga*). These will be followed by the usual optional movements.

Allemande—$\frac{4}{4}$ or C; moderate to moderately fast. Usually opens with a short upbeat. The density may vary but tends to be on the "busy" side, with short running figures passed between the various voices. See Ex. 14-6A.

Courante (French)—$\frac{3}{2}$ or $\frac{6}{4}$; moderately slow to moderate. Normally featuring a brief upbeat, this sedate and refined dance typically employs a somewhat denser texture than the preceding *Allemande*. Hemiola (♩♩♩ vs. ♩. ♩.) is sometimes used. See Ex. 14-6B.

Corrente (Italian)—$\frac{3}{4}$ or $\frac{3}{8}$; moderately fast to fast. Running figures in a kind of "melody/accompaniment" format are common. The texture is thinner than the *Courante,* with no use of hemiola. Most editors of music do not abide by Bach's distinctions between the two. In his Partita in G major BWV 829 the third movement is properly a *Corrente.*[2]

Saraband(e)—$\frac{3}{4}$ or $\frac{3}{2}$; slow. Beginning on the downbeat, this stately dance tends to stress the second beat (♩♩ or ♩ ♩. ♪). The texture may vary from two to four voices. See Exs. 7-6 and 14-6C.

Gigue (French)—Compound meter ($\frac{6}{8}$ $\frac{9}{8}$ $\frac{12}{8}$); fast. This usual closing movement begins with an upbeat and often employs various dotted figures (♩. ♫ or ♪. ♫). Imitation is frequent at the opening of both the first and second reprise. Thematic mirroring can also be noted. The melodic style is frequently disjunct in nature. See Exs. 14-6D and 16-1C.

Giga (Italian)—Usually in compound meter, but the tempo is faster than the *Gigue*. It is non-imitative, sharing a textural similarity to the *Corrente*. The final movement of Bach's A minor Partita BWV 807 is modelled after the *Giga*. One may also occasionally encounter the English *Gig* or *Jig* (see some of Handel's works).

[2]Even the Bach thematic index (Schmieder's *Thematisch-systematisches Verzeichnis der Werke Johann Sebastian Bach*) is negligent in this respect.

The following "optional" dances are often found between the *Sarabande* and *Gigue*.

Minuet—$\frac{3}{4}$; moderately slow to moderately fast. The rhythmic figuration in the graceful dance tends to be rather simple, with greater adherence to phrase regularity and periodicity. The texture is normally two or three voices. The occurrence of a second Minuet or even Trio is possible. This is the only suite movement that survived into the Classical period. See Exs. 7-4, 7-5, and 14-10.

Gavotte—$\frac{4}{4}$ or C ; moderate to moderately fast. A "hopping" dance characterized by a half-measure upbeat which is maintained throughout. The texture is usually somewhat thin. See Ex. 1-18C.

Bourree—$\frac{2}{4}$ or C ; rather fast. A lively movement with an upbeat, and a similar texture to the *Corrente*. They are often in pairs: Bourree I and II. See Bach's English Suite in A minor BWV 807.

Listed below are the less common of the optional dances.

Air—See Bach's French Suite in E♭ major BWV 815. Handel was fond of writing variations on this movement.

Badinerie—Bach's Overture in B minor for Flute and Strings BWV 1067.

Burlesca—Bach's Partita in A minor BWV 827.

Cappriccio—Bach's Partita in C minor BWV 826 (in place of the Gigue).

Forlane—Bach's Overture for Orchestra in C major BWV 1066.

Passepied—Bach's English Suite in E minor BWV 810.

Polonaise—Bach's French Suite in E major BWV 817.

Rondeau—Bach's Partita in C minor BWV 826.

Scherzo—Bach's Partita in A minor BWV 827.

One may occasionally find a variation or *Double* immediately following a dance movement; see the Courante II in Bach's English Suite in A major BWV 806. In other cases it may be called *Les agréments* or ornamented; see the Sarabande in Bach's English Suite in G minor BWV 808. It should be noted that many of the suites or *ordres* by French composers feature extremely fanciful titles.

Bibliography

The bibliography is divided into three sections. An annotated list of tonal counterpoint texts is followed by a selection of historical treatises ranging from the seventeenth to the present century. These conclude with two surveys on the history of the fugue. Only the Fux, Gedalge, Prout, Horsley, and Mann are annotated. The concluding category consists of a cross-section of related books, articles, and analyses in English.

TEXTBOOKS

These counterpoint texts, ranging from 1902–1984, provide instruction for the simulation of eighteenth-century polyphony. While most focus on the practices of the late Baroque period, some include examples from composers in the Classical and even Romantic eras. None utilize figured bass, and only the Parks and Proctor illustrate voice-leading through reductive methods.

GOETSCHIUS, PERCY. *Counterpoint Applied.* New York: G. Schirmer, 1902.

While this older text contains useful information, in some ways it is amusingly dated—see the comments on Wagner ("uncomfortable sensation of harmonic bewilderment") and the harmonic analyses of Chopin and Brahms. Most of the Baroque quotations are drawn from Bach and Handel, but the literature cited stretches well into the nineteenth century. The examples are labelled by composer only, so it is difficult to identify the pieces. However, the additional references to other works are useful. The opening presentation of two-voice polyphony begins with basic contrapuntal principles and proceeds into imitation and invention. At this point the three- and four-voice inventions are considered. The following section on Chorale Figuration contains a valuable compendium of chorale-prelude types. The study of fugue is limited to four or more parts, including multiple fugues. The last section is devoted exclusively to the study of canon in various textures. Goetschius includes little analysis of selections, either structurally or tonally. However, there are numerous student exercises.

KENNAN, KENT. *Counterpoint (Based on Eighteenth-Century Practice)*, 2nd edition. Englewood Cliffs, N.J.: Prentice-Hall, Inc., 1972.

The basic characteristics of two-voice polyphony are presented through a quasi-species approach, which leads to a consideration of short pieces employing free counterpoint (suite movements and preludes). A chapter on canon and invertible counterpoint provides the background for a discussion of the invention. Following a study of pieces in three-voice texture (species is now omitted), Kennan continues with the three-voice invention and fugue. The section on fugue is expanded to include four- and five-part works. The final chapters feature an excellent survey of chorale prelude and a perfunctory presentation of variation.

One of the text's most valuable assets is the scope, number, and varied length of the musical examples. Some complete pieces are included, and the reader is often referred to additional compositions for analysis. The majority of the music is drawn from Bach, Handel, and K. P. E. Bach, but isolated illustrations from Corelli, Muffat, Purcell, Buxtehude, Pachelbel, Vivaldi, Walther, Albrechtsberger. and even Mozart and Brahms may be noted. Some of these are analyzed in terms of contrapuntal procedures, but there is generally little concern for tonal schemes. The pedagogical tools necessary to develop strong writing skills are neglected in favor of studying techniques through the musical examples. Student assignments are at the end of each chapter.

Krenek, Ernst. *Tonal Counterpoint in the Style of the Eighteenth-Century.* London: Boosey & Hawkes, Inc., 1958.

All of the musical examples in this brief outline (a companion to the composer's other manuals on sixteenth- and twentieth-century counterpoint) are original, with the longest about twenty measures. Following an introduction to melodic writing, the material focuses on the handling of dissonance in two-voice texture. Although there are short sections on invertible counterpoint and canon, the discussion of imitation is limited, with such devices as stretto missing altogether. The final four pages are devoted to three-voice writing. Eight "model" inventions are included, but fugue is omitted. The text lacks both student exercises and an index.

Lieberman, Maurice. *Creative Counterpoint.* Boston: Allyn and Bacon, Inc., 1966.

This study of Baroque polyphony is based on the compositions of J. S. Bach. However, examples are rarely longer than four measures, and only two complete works are included in an appendix (the D major Three-Part Invention is analyzed according to contrapuntal procedures). No reductive technique is employed, although some use of Roman numerals may be noted. The first six chapters introduce two-part texture as derived from the outer voices of SATB chorale settings. After non-harmonic tones and modulation are added, imitation and canon are presented. The latter topic is quite extensive, with an excellent section on canonic sequences. Following a discussion of the two-part invention, the standard contrapuntal devices are introduced, which lead logically into a treatment of the three-voice fugue. There are numerous, but similar, exercises at the end of each chapter.

Mason, Neale. *Essentials of Eighteenth-Century Counterpoint.* Dubuque, Iowa: Wm. C. Brown Co., 1968.

This manual seems more in the nature of an expanded outline. All of the musical examples, drawn exclusively from Bach's keyboard works, are fragmentary, with the exception of one complete piece (the C major Two-Part Invention). After an introduction to melody, two-voice writing is presented in terms of a rhythmic "species" approach. Little attempt is made, however, to demonstrate the systematic handling of dissonance or underlying voice-leading frameworks. After discussing canon, sequence, and double counterpoint, the text explores the two-part invention, which is categorized into stereotyped "models". An introduction to three-voice texture leads to an examination of the three-part invention and fugue. The final section deals with four-voice writing. Aside from the occasional use of functional harmonic analysis via Roman numerals, there is little discussion of structural or tonal schemes for entire movements. "Artificial" and triple counterpoint, in addition to multiple fugues, are included in an appendix, as is an interesting comparison of non-harmonic tone terminology in various harmony texts. The student exercises are grouped into either study questions or writing problems, some of which are well contrived.

PARKS, RICHARD. *Eighteenth-Century Counterpoint and Tonal Structure.* Englewood Cliffs, N.J.: Prentice-Hall, Inc., 1984.

This author is more concerned than most with the tonal process in Baroque polyphony. The first half of the text is devoted to a rigorous species presentation, treating both two- and three-voice settings within each species; only occasional application is made to actual musical literature. The approach here has been modified from strict Fuxian principles so that the first species examples resemble a kind of Schenkerian middleground. No references to species technique from historical treatises of the period are included in this section, although allusions to some manuals may be found later in the text. Basic voice-leading principles via species are applied to various genre in the second part of the book. The order of presentation is: grounds, binary pieces, imitative compositions (inventions), fugue, and chorale prelude. There are many useful structural graphs and tonal reductions. Indeed, this is the only text which consistently employs reductive procedures. The musical excerpts are from a limited selection of J. S. Bach's keyboard works; the sole exception is Dido's *Lament* from Purcell's opera. Most of the examples are short, but Appendix IV features Schenkerian voice-leading reductions of nine pieces, graphed at various hierarchical levels. Unfortunately, seven of these are binary dance movements, with only one imitative piece (the C major Two-Part Invention). Other appendices include characteristics of stylized dance movements, tunings, and non-harmonic tones. The brief bibliography contains several curious entries (Berry and Schoenberg). Plentiful student assignments are grouped according to analysis, short technical problems, and larger writing projects.

PISTON, WALTER. *Counterpoint.* New York: W. W. Norton & Co., Inc., 1947.

An apparent companion to his well-known volumes on *Harmony* and *Orchestration,* Piston seems to view counterpoint as an alternative option to homophonic texture. Any discussion of polyphonic genre, such as invention, chorale prelude, or even fugue, is avoided. The illustrations from music literature range from the late Baroque to Franck; few are longer than ten measures with no complete pieces cited. The four introductory chapters deal with melodic "curve" and rhythm; with the addition of a harmonic basis, non-harmonic tones and harmonic rhythm are then discussed. The technical features of two-part polyphony consist mainly of brief comments on the musical examples. There is no attempt to propose any systematic didactic approach (such as species). After a chapter on motive interplay and a short paragraph on sequence, three-voice texture is introduced, with attention paid to the underlying harmonies and spacing of the parts. Imitation is briefly mentioned, but the distinction between real vs. tonal answers is omitted. The final two sections are devoted to invertible counterpoint and canon, including the usual devices. Each chapter concludes with several exercises.

PORTER, QUINCY. *A Study of Fugue Writing.* Boston: Loomis & Co., 1951.

This tiny manual is based exclusively on Bach's *WTC*. Although it assumes previous polyphonic instruction, a useful list of general principles of contrapuntal writing and common errors appears at its conclusion. The basic topics covered include the Subject, Answer, and the Structure of Fugue, with a diagram of the C minor Fugue from *WTC* I. Although the list of "hints" on fugue writing is perceptive, the system of modulation and functional harmonic analysis is overly fussy and old-fashioned.

PROCTOR, LELAND. *Tonal Counterpoint.* Dubuque, Iowa: Wm. C. Brown Co., 1952.

This interesting text sets as its goal the stylistic simulation of the chorale prelude and keyboard prelude (*WTC*), based on models of J. S. Bach. Assuming the student's skill in four-voice chorale harmonization, it begins with three-part note-against-note settings, gradually adding rhythmic and linear considerations. The sections on dissonance are particularly perceptive and exhaustive, with numerous short examples of "good and bad" procedure (for instance, see the chapter on the changing-tone figure). Two-voice polyphony is then introduced with concurrent material on motivic development. Consideration of the Embellished Chorale leads to "free counterpoint" and quasi-prelude technique. Some instances of voice-leading reduction may be noted, as in the useful chapter on sequence. With four exceptions, all of the musical quotations come from Bach; however, no examples from actual literature appear before page 83. The appendix consists of various chorale-prelude excerpts. There is no index or bibliography. The lack of reference to invertible counterpoint is somewhat strange. A "summary" and student assignments appear at the conclusion of each chapter.

TREATISES

Important theoretical treatises dealing with Baroque and Classical polyphonic practice are cited below. The number of entries prohibits individual annotations on each. It will be noted that most as yet remain in their original languages; only English translations are given. The various treatises have been grouped according to their basic content and listed chronologically.

I. Seventeenth-Century Treatises

The following works continue stylistic Renaissance idioms and the didactic approach to polyphony laid down by Gioseffo Zarlino in his *Le Istitutione harmoniche* Part 3 (1558). Translated by Guy Marco and Claude Palisca. New York: W. W. Norton and Co., Inc., 1976.

MORLEY, THOMAS. *A Plaine and Easie Introduction to Practicall Musicke* (1597). New edition by R. Alec Harman. New York: W. W. Norton and Co., Inc., 1952.
DIRUTA, GIROLAMO. *Il Transilvano* Part 2 (1609), trans. Edward Soehnleins. Ann Arbor: University Microfilms, Inc., 1975.
CERONE, PIETRO. *El melopeo y maestro* Books 9–24. Naples, 1613.
BANCHIERI, ADRIANO. *Cartella musicale*. Venice, 1614.
ZACCONI, LODOVICO. *Prattica di musica* Part 2. Naples, 1622.

Certain characteristics of Baroque style (in particular, allusions to free figurations, major-minor tonality, and tonal answers) may be found in the following works. The basic contributions of these theorists to the art of counterpoint is discussed on pages 19–49 of Alfred Mann's *The Study of Fugue.*

BERNHARD, CHRISTOPH. *Tractatus compositionis augmentatus* (c. 1650), trans. Walter Hilse. *The Music Forum* 3, pp. 1–196.
NIVERS, GUILLAUME GABRIEL. *Traité de la composition musicale* (1667), trans. Albert Cohen. Brooklyn: Institute of Medieval Music, 1961.
BONONCINI, GIOVANNI MARIA. *Il Musico prattico*. Bologna, 1673.
BERARDI, ANGELO. *Documenti armonici*. Bologna, 1681.
———. *Miscellanea musicale*. Bologna, 1689.
PURCELL, HENRY. "Of Fuge, or Pointing." *An Introduction to the Skill of Musick*, John Playford, 12th ed. London, 1694.

II. Eighteenth-Century Treatises

These are five of the more important writings on figured bass.

NIEDT, FRIEDRICH ERHARDT. *Musikalische Handleitung* (Part I). Hamburg, 1707–17. (English translation by Pamela Poulin is forthcoming by Oxford University Press.)
HEINICHEN, JOHANN DAVID. *Der Generalbass in der Komposition*. Dresden, 1728. (Also see George J. Buelow. *Thorough-Bass Accompaniment According to Johann David Heinichen.* Berkeley: University of California Press, 1966.)
MATTHESON, JOHANN. *Grosse Generalbass-Schule*. Hamburg, 1731.
BACH, KARL PHILIPP EMANUEL. *Versuch über die wahre Art das Klavier zu spielen*, Berlin, 1753, 1762, trans. William Mitchell. New York: W. W. Norton and Co., Inc., 1949.
KIRNBERGER, JOHANN PHILIPP, *Grundsätze des Generalbasses, als erste Linien zur Komposition.* Berlin, 1781.

Due to its subsequent influence, the work of Fux merits additional comment.

Fux, Johann Joseph. *Gradus ad Parnassum (Pars Activa)*. Vienna, 1725.

The first portion has been translated by Alfred Mann as *The Study of Counterpoint.* New York: W. W. Norton and Co., Inc., 1965. Selections from the latter part are contained in Mann's *The Study of Fugue*, pp. 75–138.

The two listings above represent the extent of material from Fux's treatise currently available in English translation from the original Latin. Mann draws his two excerpts from the second volume of Fux's text, entitled *Pars Activa,* the first dealing with the use of cantus firmus, and the second devoted to the study of fugue and double counterpoint.

This treatise is in the form of a dialogue between master and pupil. Fux never states that he intends to base his study of counterpoint on the practice of the late Renaissance; he does, however, identify the master Aloysius with Palestrina. The sections on fugue and double counterpoint assume a more Baroque flavor.

Although the treatises below relate to the contrapuntal and fugal practice of the late Baroque period, Fux, Marpurg, Albrechtsberger, and Martini were significant in the instruction of the Classical masters. (See pages 49–61 in Mann's *The Study of Fugue.*)

RAMEAU, JEAN PHILIPPE. *Traité de l'harmonie* (1722), trans. Philip Gossett. New York: Dover Publications, 1971.
MATTHESON, JOHANN. *Der vollkommene Kapellmeister*, Part 3 (1739), trans. Ernest Harris. Ann Arbor: University Microfilms, Inc., 1977.
MARPURG, FRIEDRICH WILHELM. *Abhandlung von der Fuge*, Berlin, 1753–54. (Portions appear in Mann's *The Study of Fugue*, pp. 142–212.)
KIRNBERGER, JOHANN PHILIPP. *Die Kunst des reinen Satzes in der Musik* (1771–79), trans. David Beach and Jurgen Thym. New Haven and London: Yale University Press, 1982.
KIRNBERGER, JOHANN PHILIPP. *Gedanken über die verschiedenen Lehrarten als Vorbereitung zur Fugenkenntniss* (1782), trans. Richard Nelson and Donald Boomgaarden. *Journal for Music Theory*, Vol. 30/1 (Spring 1986), pp. 71–94.
MARTINI, GIAMBATTISTA. *Esemplare o sia saggia fondamentale prattico di contrappunto*. Bologna, 1774–76. (Selections appear on pages 269–314 of Mann's *The Study of Fugue*.)
ALBRECHTSBERGER, JOHANN GEORG. *Gründliche Anweising zur Komposition*, trans. Sabilla Novello. London: Novello, Ewer, and Co., n.d. (Selections appear on pages 221–62 of Mann's *The Study of Fugue*.)

III. Nineteenth - and Twentieth-Century Treatises

These later treatises gradually abandoned the actual compositions of the Baroque masters as fugal models in favor of the more theoretically pedantic "academic fugue" (or *fuge d'ecole*). They are grouped according to three "nationalistic" schools: French, German, and English. The Gedalge and Prout texts contain annotations. (Also see pages 63–77 of Mann's *The Study of Fugue.*)

1. French

REICHA, ANTON. *Traité de haute composition musicale.* Paris, 1824–26.
CHERUBINI, LUIGI. *Traité de la fugue* (1837), trans. Cowden Clark. London: Novello, Ewer, and Co., 1854.
FÉTIS, JOSEPH FRANÇOIS. *Traité du contrepoint et de la fugue.* Paris, 1846.
GEDALGE, ANDRÉ. *Traité de la fugue* (1901), trans. Ferdinand Davis. Norman, OK: University of Oklahoma Press, 1965.

Gedalge restricts his consideration to the scholastic fugue (*fugue d'ecole*), "so called because it is a modification for teaching purposes of the fugues created by the masters of contrapuntal writing". His justification is the practical *application* of fugal construction in musical composition, *not* to write fugues. Previous contrapuntal training is assumed; there is practically nothing on canon, invertible counterpoint, or sequences in episodes. Most of the treatise consists of a series of inflexible restrictions, many of which are difficult to rationalize in the light of existing literature, such as "coda" of the subject, counterexpositions which include only two entries (answer, then subject), or a strict order of modulation.

Also included are extensive rules on the use of tonal answers, charts on the layout of the exposition, and a detailed section on the "stretto section of the fugue". The last chapter lists check points for fugue writing. Although there are liberal examples from Bach in the beginning, as later topics are introduced, the literature seems curiously limited to French composers of the nineteenth century. Following an appendix on multiple fugues, the last section is devoted to the quotation of nine scholastic fugues from students at the Conservatoire during this period. Brief student exercises conclude each chapter.

2. German

ANDRÉ, JOHANN ANTON. *Lehrbuch der Tonsetzkunst* II. Offenbach, 1932–42.
MARX, ADOLF BERNHARD. *Die Lehre von den musikalischen Komposition* (1837–47), trans. Hermann Savoni. New York: F. J. Huntington, 1852.
RICHTER, ERNST FRIEDRICH. *Lehrbuch der Fuge* (1859), trans. Arthur Foote. Boston: O. Ditson and Co., 1878.
RIEMANN, HUGO. *Grosse Kompositionslehre*, Vol. 2. Berlin and Stuttgart: W. Spemann, 1903.

3. English

HIGGS, JAMES. *Fugue.* London: Novello, Ewer, and Co., 1878.
PROUT, EBENEZER. *Fugue.* London: Augener, Ltd., 1891.

According to the author, this volume analyzes over one thousand fugues spanning the Baroque to Brahms, and including *all* of Bach's works in this genre. Previous experience in polyphonic writing is taken for granted, since some topics such as double counterpoint are glossed over. Following a survey of the characteristics of the subject, an extensive section is devoted to real and tonal answers, based on numerous quotations from the literature. After a discussion of the countersubject is a study of the exposition and subsequent episodes, stressing modulation and sequence in the latter. There is a useful section on how to write a stretto. Prout states that "every fugue . . . . . . is in its main outline constructed in the same general form . . . three part form": chief subject-tonic key/episodes-related keys/chief subject-tonic key. This hypothesis is followed by four analyses from Bach's *WTC* (no organ fugues are included) and several "models" to follow. The book concludes with considerations of the fughetta and fugato, multiple fugue, fugal technique in chorale preludes, and the "accompanied fugue". Student exercises are mainly restricted to writing answers to given subjects.

KITSON, CHARLES HERBERT. *Studies in Fugue.* Oxford: Clarendon Press, 1909.
OLDROYD, GEORGE. *The Technique and Spirit of Fugue.* London: Oxford University Press, 1948.

IV. History of the Fugue

HORSLEY, IMOGENE. *Fugue: History and Practice.* New York: The Free Press, 1966.

The author states that the purpose of this text is "to provide the material for a course that combines the historical study of fugue with exercises in writing fugue." The chapters on historical and practical approaches alternate. The former trace the evolution of the fugue from the Renaissance through the nineteenth century by examples and references to theoretical treatises: (1) Canon; (4) Subject and Answer; (6) Exposition, Counterexposition, and later Statements of the Subject; (7) Fugue and Form; (9) Multiple Fugues; and (10) Fugue in the Development of Western Music. These sections are well documented and contain numerous, interesting examples from literature. The remaining chapters are devoted to the practical application to fugal writing; prior contrapuntal training is assumed. This part of the book seems somewhat weaker; it suffers from a focused pedagogical approach and lack of sufficient examples. Suggested analyses and exercises are provided, however. The three excellent appendices contain supplemental analysis material and extensive bibliographical entries on treatises and the history of the fugue.

MANN, ALFRED. *The Study of Fugue,* New York: W. W. Norton and Co., Inc., 1965.

This valuable historical study is in two main sections. The first is an excellent survey of the evolution of terminology and concepts related to polyphony in general and the fugue specifically, ranging from the late

Renaissance through the nineteenth century. Attention is given to the treatises of Vicentino, Zarlino, Praetorius, Bernhard, Reinken, Rameau, Fux, Marpurg, Albrechtsberger, and Martini, with particular emphasis on Fux and his influence. The second portion of Mann's study includes a cross-section of translations, most for the first time, of selections of works by Fux, Marpurg, Albrechtsberger, and Martini, each preceded with an informative preface. (The page numbers may be found under the bibliographical entries of the theorists above.)

The following studies give a good account of polyphony from the early Classical through the Romantic periods. Unfortunately, the last is not available in translation.

KIRKENDALE, WARREN. *Fugure and Fugato in Rococo and Classical Chamber Music*, 2nd ed. Trans. Margaret Bent and author. Durham, NC: Duke University Press, 1979.

TRAPP, KLAUS. *Die Fuge in der deutschen Romantik von Schubert bis Reger*. Frankfort: Hessen, 1958.

OTHER REFERENCE SOURCES

I. Books

ALDWELL, EDWARD, AND CARL SCHACHTER. *Harmony and Voice-Leading*, Vols. I and II. New York: Harcourt, Brace, and Jonanovich, Inc., 1978.

BARBOUR, MURRAY J. *Tuning and Temperament: A Historical Survey*. East Lansing: Michigan State College Press, 1953.

BERRY, WALLACE, AND EDWARD CHUDACOFF. *Eighteenth-Century Imitative Counterpoint*. New York: Appleton-Century-Crofts, 1969.

BUKOFZER, MANFRED. *Music in the Baroque Era*. New York: W. W. Norton and Co., Inc., 1947.

COCKSHOOT, JOHN V. *The Fugue in Beethoven's Piano Music*. London: Routledge and K. Paul, 1959.

DAVID, HANS T. *J. S. Bach's 'Musical Offering': History, Interpretation, and Analysis*. New York: G. Schirmer, Inc., 1945.

DAVID, HANS, and ARTHUR MENDEL. *The Bach Reader*. New York: W. W. Norton and Co., Inc., 1945.

DICKINSON, ALAN. *Bach's Fugal Works*. Wesport, CT: Greenwood Press, Inc., 1979.

DONINGTON, ROBERT. *A Performer's Guide to Baroque Music*. London: Faber and Faber, 1973.

EINSTEIN, ALFRED. *Mozart: His Character, His Works*, trans. Arthur Mendel and Nathan Broder. New York: Oxford University Press, 1945. See "Mozart and Counterpoint" on pp. 144–56.

EMERY, WALTER. *Bach's Ornaments*. London: Novello, 1953.

GREEN, DOUGLASS. *Form in Tonal Music*, 2nd edition. New York: Holt, Rinehart, and Winston, 1979.

HUMPHREYS, DAVID. *The Esoteric Structure of Bach's Clavierübung* III. Cardiff: University of Cardiff Press, 1983.

JOHNSON, THEODORE. *An Analytical Survey of the Fifteen Two-Part Inventions by J. S. Bach*. New York: University Press of America, 1982.

KELLER, HERMAN. *The Well-Tempered Clavier by Johann Sebastian Bach*, trans. Leigh Gerdine. London: George Allen & Unwin, Ltd., 1976. (also see Czaczkes, Ludwig. *Analyse des Wohltemperierten Klaviers* (Vienna: 1965.)

LANG, PAUL HENRY. *George Frideric Handel*. New York: W. W. Norton and Co., Inc., 1966. See pp. 603–12 on Handel's counterpoint and fugue.

NALDIN, CHARLES. *Fugal Answer.* London: Oxford University Press, 1969.
NELSON, ROBERT. *The Technique of Variation.* Berkeley: University of California Press, 1962.
NEUMANN, FREDERICH. *Ornamentation in Baroque and Post-Baroque Music.* Princeton: Princeton University Press, 1978.
PALISCA, CLAUDE. *Baroque Music.* Englewood Cliffs: Prentice-Hall, Inc., 1968.
SALZER, FELIX, AND SCHACHTER, CARL. *Counterpoint in Composition.* New York: McGraw-Hill Book Co., 1969.
SCHWEITZER, ALBERT. *J. S. Bach,* trans. Ernest Newman. New York: Dover Publications, Inc., 1966.
SPITTA, PHILIPP. *Johann Sebastian Bach,* Vols. I, II, III, trans. C. Bell and J. A. Fuller-Maitland. New York: Dover Publications, Inc., 1951.
STAUFFER, GEORGE. *The Organ Preludes of Johann Sebastian Bach.* Ann Arbor: UMI Research Press, 1980.
TOBIN, JOHN. *Handel at Work.* London: Cassell & Co., Ltd., 1964.
TUSLER, ROBERT L. *The Style of J. S. Bach's Chorale Preludes.* New York: Da Capo Press, 1968.
TOVEY, DONALD FRANCIS. *A Companion to 'The Art of the Fugue'.* London: Oxford University Press, 1931.
WILLIAMS, PETER. *The Organ Music of J. S. Bach,* Vols. I, II, III. Cambridge: Cambridge University Press, 1980 and 1984.
WHITTAKER, WILLIAM J. *The Cantatas of Johann Sebastian Bach: Sacred and Secular.* London: Oxford University Press, 1959 and 1964.

II. Articles

ARNOLD, DENIS. "Haydn's Counterpoint and Fux's *Gradus.*" *Monthly Musical Record,* Vol. 87 (1957), pp. 52–58.
BLUME, FRIEDRICH. "J. S. Bach's Youth." *Musical Quarterly,* Vol. 54/1, Jan. 1968, pp. 1–30.
BRINKMAN, ALEXANDER. "The Melodic Process in Johann Sebastian Bach's *Orgelbüchlein.*" *Music Theory Spectrum,* Vol. 2 (1980), pp. 46–73.
BUTLER, GREGORY. "Ordering Problems in J. S. Bach's *Art of the Fugue* Resolved." *Musical Quarterly,* Vol. 69/1, (Winter 1983), pp. 44–61.
DERR, ELLWOOD. "The Two-Part Inventions: Bach's Composer's Vademecum." *Music Theory Spectrum,* Vol. 3 (1981), pp. 26–48.
GEIRINGER, KARL. "Symbolism in the Music of Bach." *Lectures on the History and Art of Music.* New York: Da Capo Press, 1968. pp. 121–38.
GRAVE, FLOYD. "Abbé Vogler and the Study of Fugue." *Music Theory Spectrum,* Vol. 1 (1979), pp. 43–66.
KING, A. HYATT. "Mozart's Counterpoint; its Growth and Spirit." *Music and Letters,* Vol. 26 (1945), pp. 12–20.
KIRKENDALE, WILLIAM. "The *Great Fugue* Op. 133: Beethoven's *Art of the Fugue.*" *Acta Musicologica,* Vol. 35 (1963), pp. 14–24.
MANN, ALFRED. "Beethoven's Contrapuntal Studies with Haydn." *Musical Quarterly,* Vol. 56/4 (Oct. 1970), pp. 711–26.
———. "Haydn as Student and Critic of Fux." *Studies in Eighteenth-Century Music.* Ed. by H. C. Robbins Landon. London: George Allen and Unwin, Ltd., 1970, pp. 323–32.
———. "Haydn's *Elementarbuch;* A Document of Classic Counterpoint Instruction." *Music Forum,* Vol. 3 (1973), pp. 197–237.
MARSHALL, ROBERT L., "How J. S. Bach Composed Four-Part Chorales." *Musical Quarterly* Vol. 56/2 (April 1970), pp. 198–220.
MISCH, LUDWIG, "Fugue and Fugato in Beethoven's Variation Form." *Musical Quarterly,* Vol. 42/1 (Jan. 1956), pp. 14–27.
SERWER, HOWARD J. "Marpurg vs. Kirnberger: Theories of Fugal Composition." *Journal of Music Theory,* Vol. 14/2, (Winter 1970), pp. 209–36.
SNYDER, KERALA J. "Dietrich Buxtehude's Studies in Learned Counterpoint." *Journal of American Musicological Society,* Vol. 33/3 (Fall 1980), pp. 544–64.
WALKER, THOMAS. "Ciaccona and Passacaglia: Remarks on their Origins and Early History." *Journal of American Musicological Society,* Vol. 21/3 (Fall 1968), pp. 300–20.

III. Analyses

BERRY, WALLACE. "J. S. Bach's Fugue in D♯ minor (*WTC* I, No. 8): A naive approach to linear analysis." *In Theory Only*, Vol. 2/10 (Jan. 1977), pp. 4–7.

CINNAMON, HOWARD, "Durational Reduction and Bach's C Major Invention." *In Theory Only*, Vol. 7/4 (Nov. 1983), pp. 25–36.

COGAN, ROBERT, AND POZZI ESCOT. *Sonic Design: The Nature of Sound and Music.* Englewood Cliffs: Prentice-Hall, Inc., 1976. (See the analysis of Bach's *Goldberg* Variations on pp. 264–76.

HINDEMITH, PAUL. *The Craft of Musical Composition*, Book I, trans. Arthur Mendel. London: Schott & Co., Ltd., 1942. (See the analysis of Bach's Three-Part Invention in F minor, measures 1–12, on pp. 207–09).

LARSON, STEVE. "J. S. Bach's Two-Part Invention in C Major." *In Theory Only*, Vol. 7/1 (May 1983), pp. 31–45.

MARCOZZI, RUDY. "Deep-Level Structures in J. S. Bach's D minor Chaconne." *Indiana Theory Review*, Vol. 6/1 and 2 (1983), pp. 5–16.

McIRVINE, EDWARD C. "Form and Tonality in J. S. Bach's Settings of *Jesu, der du meine Seele.*" *Indiana Theory Review*, Vol. 5/1 (Fall 1981), pp. 1–22.

NEUMEYER, DAVID. "The Two Versions of J. S. Bach's A-minor Invention [BWV 784]." *Indiana Theory Review*, Vol. 4/2 (1981), pp. 69–99.

SCHACHTER, CARL. "Bach's Fugue in B♭ Major, *Well-Tempered Clavier* Book I, No. XXI." *Music Forum*, Vol. 3 (1973), pp. 239–67.

SCHENKER, HEINRICH. *Five Graphic Analyses* New York: Dover Publications, Inc., 1969. (See the analysis of Bach's C major Prelude, *WTC* I, on pp. 36–37).

———. "The Largo of J. S. Bach's Sonata No. 3 for Unaccompanied Violin [BWV 1005]," trans. John Rothgeb. *Music Forum*, Vol. 4 (1976).

———. "The Organic Aspect of the Fugue," trans. Sylan Kalib in *Thirteen Essays from the yearbooks 'Das Meisterwerk in der Musik'.* Ann Arbor: University Microfilms, Inc., 1973. (For an analysis of the Prelude and Fugue in C minor, *WTC* I, see pp. 246–321 of Vol. 2).

———. "The Sarabande of J. S. Bach's Suite No. 3 for Unaccompanied Violoncello [1009]," trans. Hedi Siegel. *Music Forum*, Vol. 2 (1970), pp. 274–82.

TRAVIS, ROY. "J. S. Bach, Invention No. 1 in C Major: Reduction and Graph." *In Theory Only*, Vol. 2/7 (Oct. 1976), pp. 3–7.

———. "J. S. Bach, Invention No. 13 in A Minor: Reduction and Graph." *In Theory Only*, Vol. 2/8 (Nov. 1976), pp. 29–33.

In addition to the separate analyses above, there are voice-leading reductions of nine pieces at three different levels which may be found on pages 305–324 of Richard Parks, *Eighteenth-Century Counterpoint and Tonal Structure* (see under Textbooks). Numerous framework reductions of excerpts from pieces in the Baroque period may also be found in the following:

SALZER, FELIX. *Structural Hearing: Tonal Coherence in Music* (Vol. 2), New York: Dover Publications, Inc., 1962.

SALZER, FELIX, AND CARL SCHACHTER. *Counterpoint in Composition*, New York: McGraw-Hill Book Company, 1969.

SCHENKER, HEINRICH. *Free Composition* (Vol. 2), trans., ed. Ernst Oster. New York: Longman, 1979.

Index of names
and works

This index lists composers, authors, and their works as cited in the text, footnotes, and musical examples; the bibliography is not included. More extensive references in the text are denoted by bold-face type. The bold-face type in musical examples indicates complete compositions. In the case of authors, only historical treatises have been included. The numerous less significant allusions to major figures of the period, such as J. S. Bach, have been omitted.

Index of terms